THE CHINA BUSINESS MODEL

Elsevier
Asian Studies Series

Series Editor: Professor Chris Rowley,
Cass Business School, City University, London, UK;
Institute of Hallyu Convergence Research, Korea University, Korea
Griffith Business School, Griffith University, Australia;
(email: c.rowley@city.ac.uk)

Elsevier is pleased to publish this major Series of books entitled Asian Studies: Contemporary Issues and Trends. The Series Editor is Professor Chris Rowley of Cass Business School, City University, London, UK and Department of International Business and Asian Studies, Griffith University, Australia.

Asia has clearly undergone some major transformations in recent years and books in the Series examine this transformation from a number of perspectives: economic, management, social, political and cultural. We seek authors from a broad range of areas and disciplinary interests covering, for example, business/management, political science, social science, history, sociology, gender studies, ethnography, economics and international relations, etc.

Importantly, the Series examines both current developments and possible future trends. The Series is aimed at an international market of academics and professionals working in the area. The books have been specially commissioned from leading authors. The objective is to provide the reader with an authoritative view of current thinking.

New authors: we would be delighted to hear from you if you have an idea for a book. We are interested in both shorter, practically orientated publications (45,000+ words) and longer, theoretical monographs (75,000–100,000 words). Our books can be single, joint or multi-author volumes. If you have an idea for a book, please contact the publishers or Professor Chris Rowley, the Series Editor.

Dr Glyn Jones
Email: g.jones.2@elsevier.com;

Professor Chris Rowley
Email: c.rowley@city.ac.uk

THE CHINA BUSINESS MODEL

Originality and Limits

Edited by

ELISABETH PAULET

CHRIS ROWLEY

ELSEVIER

CP
CHANDOS
PUBLISHING

An imprint of Elsevier • elsevier.com

Chandos Publishing is an imprint of Elsevier
50 Hampshire Street, 5th Floor, Cambridge, MA 02139, United States
The Boulevard, Langford Lane, Kidlington, OX5 1GB, United Kingdom

British Library Cataloguing-in-Publication Data
A catalogue record for this book is available from the British Library

Library of Congress Cataloging-in-Publication Data
A catalog record for this book is available from the Library of Congress

ISBN: 978-0-08-100750-1 (print)
ISBN: 978-0-08-100757-0 (online)

For information on all Chandos Publishing publications visit our website at https://www.elsevier.com

Publisher: Glyn Jones
Acquisition Editor: Glyn Jones
Editorial Project Manager: Harriet Clayton
Production Project Manager: Debasish Ghosh
Cover Designer: Maria Inês Cruz

Typeset by MPS Limited, Chennai, India

CONTENTS

LIST OF CONTRIBUTORS

Ivana Beveridge
Université Panthéon-Assas Paris 2-Sorbonne Universités, LARGEPA, Paris, France

Harish C. Chandan
Argosy University, Atlanta, GA, United States

Kirk Chang
HC HRM Consultancy Ltd, Manchester, United Kingdom; University of Salford, Manchester, United Kingdom

Kuo-Tai Cheng
National Hsinchu University of Education, Hsinchu City, Taiwan

Zhang Chi
KEDGE Business School, Talence, France

Riturpana Das
Adamas University, Kolkata, West Bengal, India

Sam Dzever
Telecom Ecole de Management, Evry, France

Zhao Guoqin
Central University of Finance and Economics, Beijing, China

Javed G. Hussain
University of Birmingham, Birmingham, United Kingdom

Johannes Kadura
Peking University, Beijing, China

Jun Li
University of Essex, Colchester, United Kingdom

Nirjhar Nigam
ICN Business School, Metz, France

Elisabeth Paulet
ICN Business School, CEREFIGE, Pole Lorrain de Gestion, Nancy, France

Tang Renwu
Beijing Normal University, Beijing, China; Zhejiang Normal University, Zhejiang, China

Chris Rowley
Professor Emeritus, Cass Business School, City, University of London, London, United Kingdom; Professorial Fellow, Institute of Hallyu Convergence Research, Korea University, Seoul, Korea; Adjunct Professor, Griffith Business School and Griffith Asia Institute, Griffith University, Brisbane, QLD, Australia; Visiting Fellow, Institute of Asia and Pacific Studies, Nottingham University, Nottingham, United Kingdom

Jonathan M. Scott
Teesside University, Middlesbrough, United Kingdom

Travis Selmier II
Indiana University, Bloomington, IN, United States

Hong Seock-Jin
KEDGE Business School, Talence, France

Andreas Stratemeyer
California State University, Fresno, CA, United States

Julie Taylor
University of Cumbria, Carlisle, United Kingdom

Duane Windsor
Rice University, Houston, TX, United States

EDITORS' BIOGRAPHY

Elisabeth Paulet is Professor of Finance at ICN Business School in Nancy and member of the research center CEREFIGE, University of Lorraine. Following her PhD at the European University Institute of Florence, she holds a Jean Monnet Chair. Her main interests are in banking structures and financial policy of firms, on a historical and contemporary level. She has published several articles and books in this field.

Chris Rowley is Professor Emeritus at Cass Business School, City, University of London, United Kingdom; Professorial Fellow, Institute of Hallyu Convergence Research, Korea University, Seoul, Korea; Adjunct Professor, Griffith Business School and Griffith Asia Institute, Griffith University, Australia; and Visiting Fellow, Institute of Asia and Pacific Studies, Nottingham University, United Kingdom. He has researched widely on Asian business and human resource management with over 600 academic and practitioner publications of various sorts. He is Editor of the leading journal, *Asia Pacific Business Review* and *Journal of Chinese Human Resource Management*. He has been a visitor to many universities in Asia and has given practitioner talks, seminars, and workshops and regularly appears in a range of international media, including TV, radio, and newspapers.

AUTHORS' BIOGRAPHY

Ivana Beveridge is a PhD candidate at the Université Paris 2–Sorbonne Universités (LARGEPA). She is a partner at Sunrise International Education, a branding consultant, and a lecturer at the Université Sorbonne Nouvelle (Paris 3). She holds an MBA from the University of Warwick and has extensive industry experience with leading marketing communications and branding agencies in Asia, the Middle East, the United States, and Europe.

Dr. Harish C. Chandan is Professor of Business at Argosy University, Atlanta. He was interim chair of the business program in 2011. He received President's award for excellence in teaching in 2007, 2008, and 2009. His teaching philosophy is grounded in the learner needs, learning styles, collaborative, experiential, and life-long learning. His research interests include change management, innovation, leadership, marketing, and organizational behavior. He has published 20 peer-reviewed articles in business journals and 15 book chapters in business reference books published by IGI Global, Routledge and Elsevier. Dr. Chandan is Coeditor of an upcoming Business reference book and has presented conference papers at Academy of Management, International Academy of Business and Management, Southeast Association of Information Systems, and Academy of International Business.

Kirk Chang is an HR consultant and legal mediator. He is also professor and research convenor for the Salford Business School, University of Salford, Manchester, United Kingdom. His research interests lie in the areas of employee behavior, organizational dynamics, and people management. His recent research output appear in: *International Journal of Human Resource Management*, *Journal of Managerial Psychology*, *Journal of Strategy and Management*, *Industrial Relations*, and other management journals.

Kuo-Tai Cheng is an Associate Professor of Public Policy and Management and he works for the Department of Environmental and Cultural Resources, National Hsinchu University of Education, Hsinchu, Taiwan. His research is in the field of organizational behavior, public policy, and management. His recent research output appears in: *International Journal of Management and Innovation*, *Advances In Management*, *Utilities Policy*, and other related journals.

Dr. Rituparna Das is Professor of Economics at Adamas University. He taught at University of Petroleum and Energy Studies (UPES). Prior to that he was heading the Centre for Studies in Banking and Finance, set up by the corpus of the Reserve Bank of India at National Law University Jodhpur. His prior academic associations include National Institute of Bank Management, National University of Juridical Sciences and Indian Institute of Social Welfare and Business Management, and is certified by the University Grant Commission and College Service Commission. He has postgraduate qualifications in Economics and Management and a PhD in Econometric Modelling. He is recognized by the biographers like Marquis Whos Who and International Biographical Centre, and visiting guest lecturer at City University of Hong Kong.

Sam Dzever is Professor of Management at Télécom Ecole de Management, France. His research in the fields of marketing, supply chain management, industrial organization, and Asia-Pacific business has appeared in noted international academic journals, including *Industrial Marketing Management, Journal of Business and Industrial Marketing, Journal of Marketing and Communication, European Journal of Purchasing and Supply Management, Supply Chain Management: An International Journal, Journal of the Asia Pacific Economy, Asian Business and Management, Indian Journal of Science and Technology*, among others. He has also authored 12 books, research monographs, and edited collections, including *The Economic Relations Between Asia and Europe: Organisations Trade and Investment* (coedited with Bernadette Andreosso-O'Callaghan, Jean-Pascal Bassino, Jacques Jaussaud, Chandos Publishing, Oxford, 2007); *Evolving Corporate Structures and Cultures in Asia: The Impact of Globalization* (coedited with Jacques Jaussaud and Bernadette Andreosso-O'Callaghan, ISTE and Wiley, London and New Jersey, 2008).

Seock-Jin Hong is assistant professor at University of North Texas (UNT), USA and Professor at the Kedge Business School in Bordeaux, France. Prior to joining UNT and Kedge, Prof. Hong was an Associate Professor and Director at the Graduate School of Logistics at the University of Incheon. Dr. Hong was a Research Associate at the Air Transport Department of the Korea Transport Institute (KOTI) and an Assistant General Manager in Korean Airlines Seoul from 1988. Dr. Hong has a PhD from the University of Toulouse 1 of France, in addition to a Master of Transport Economics from Ecole National des Ponts et Chaussées in Paris, France.

Javed Ghulam Hussain holds a BA (Hons) in Economics, M. Soc. Sci in Money Banking and Finance, and a PhD from the University of

Birmingham. He has spent most of his career in the university sector in his main area of specialization: entrepreneurial finance. Previously he worked for 5 years for Birmingham City Council (1986–88) then Forward Trust (now a subsidiary of HSBC) (1988–90) as a finance officer and financial analyst respectively. He joined Birmingham City University (then University of Central England) as a Senior Lecturer in 1990, was promoted to Reader, and to Professor in 2010. In addition to teaching Corporate Finance, he was Director of the MBA and PhD programmes, and has served as Research Co-ordinator for the Department of Accounting and Finance. His research interests are entrepreneurial finance, microfinance and ethnic enterprise. He has served on the editorial board of journals and has published extensively in international journals and contributed towards book chapters.

Dr. Johannes Kadura is founding partner and Managing Director of Think Asia Group, and the founding partner and business coach at China Entrepreneur.net. He has served as Associate Fellow at the German Council on Foreign Relations, and as an Adjunct Professor at Peking University. He holds a PhD from the University of Cambridge.

Jun Li is a Senior Lecturer (Associated Professor) in Entrepreneurship and Innovation at Essex Business School, University of Essex, UK. He previously held a post at Chinese Academy of Sciences and was the President of Chinese Economic Association (UK/Europe) in 2012–13, and currently serves as Editor of *Journal of Entrepreneurship in Emerging Economies*. He teaches and researches in the areas of entrepreneurship and policies, innovation management, and Chinese entrepreneurship. Among his previous publications are *China's Economic Dynamics: A Beijing Consensus in the Making?* (2014, Routledge) and *Incentives for Innovation in China* (2015, Routledge).

Dr. Nirjhar Nigam is an Associate Professor working with the Finance department at ICN Business School, and affiliated to CEREFIGE and LARGE research laboratories. She teaches Corporate Finance, Financial Analysis, Financial Strategy, and Governance at various levels (Bachelors, Masters, and Executive Education). She earned her Doctorate in Finance and Management from the University of Luxembourg and University of Strasbourg. Dr. Nigam's contributions to the field of Finance have been recognized and published with leading academic journals in Finance such as *Journal of Banking and Finance*. She has collaborated on several successful research projects with the Fonds National de la Recherche (FNR),

Luxembourg, Standards and Poor's, Strasbourg University and Agence Nationale De La Recherche (ANR), France.

Jonathan M. Scott is a Reader in Entrepreneurship and Head of the Centre for Strategy & Leadership at Teesside University Business School where he teaches strategic management, entrepreneurship, and doctoral research methods. He is a Visiting Research Fellow at the Entrepreneurship Unit, University of Turku, Finland, and at Waikato Management School, New Zealand. He has extensively published in international Journals and coauthored a number of books: Thompson et al.'s textbook *Strategic Management Awareness and Change*,7th ed. (Cengage, 2014), and coeditor of Hussain and Scott's *Research Handbook on Entrepreneurial Finance* (Edward Elgar, 2015). His research interests are access to entrepreneurial finance, business support and policy, and international comparative differences.

W. Travis Selmier II, PhD Travis worked in international investments for 17 years during which he researched, and traveled to, 60 countries. Named in Barrons Top 100 Portfolio Managers list in 1998, he was one of the first foreigners to sit for the Chartered Market Analyst Exam—in Japanese—in 1992. He taught Finance at IU's Kelley School of Business from 2008 to 2011 and completed his PhD in Political Economy. He presently researches language economics, international financial markets governance, property rights of financial goods, East Asian banking, and mining CSR. He reads six languages and publishes in business, international economics, policy and international political economy, including *Boao Review, Business Horizons, International Review of Economics & Finance, Journal of International Business Studies, Review of International Political Economy, World Economy*, and various book chapters.

Andreas W. Stratemeyer is an Associate Professor of Marketing at California State University, Fresno. He earned a BS in Advertising from the University of Texas at Austin, and an MBA and PhD in Marketing from New Mexico State University. Dr. Stratemeyer has published numerous articles in such journals as *Journal for Advancement of Marketing Education, Journal of Travel and Tourism Marketing, Journal of Consumer Marketing, Academy of Marketing Science Review, Services Marketing Quarterly*, and others.

Tang Renwu is Professor of Public Administration, Dean of the Academy of Government, Beijing Normal University, and Professor and Dean of the

School of Economics and Management, Zhejiang Normal University, P.R. China. Prof. Tang has published widely in both national and international academic journals and contributed to numerous books, research monographs, and edited collections in the field.

Julie Taylor is principal lecturer of Lifelong and Interprofessional Learning. She is also programme leader of MSc Legal and Criminological Psychology and works for the College of Law and Social Science, University of Cumbria, Carlisle, United Kingdom. Her research focuses on organizational issues, workplace stress, citizenship, and job satisfaction. Her recent research output appears in: *Applied Psychology Research*, *Forensic Update*, *Forensic Update Compendium*, *Industrial Relations*, and other cognate journals.

Duane Windsor (PhD, Harvard University) is the Lynette S. Autrey Professor of Management in Rice University's Jesse H. Jones Graduate School of Business. His research emphasizes corporate social responsibility, stakeholder management, and anticorruption reforms. His research has appeared in various journals and chapters in various collections.

Zhang Chi has been a research assistant at Kedge Business School in Bordeaux since June 2014 and is a PhD candidate of Ecricome Business School. His research focus is on *guanxi*'s impact on supply chain collaboration for Chinese overseas companies. Zhang has attended several international conferences concerning air transportation and supply chain management and teaches several classes in Kedge Business School including: air transportation, supply chain strategy in Asia pacific, lean management.

Zhao Guoqin is a researcher at the Institute of Finance and Economics, Central University of Finance and Economics, Beijing, China. His research interests include regional governance, international trade, and public management. He has published a large number of articles in domestic mainstream journals, and has undertaken several research projects under the auspices of the National Social Science Fund and the Beijing Social Science Fund.

ACKNOWLEDGMENT

Professor Chris Rowley would like to thank the Korea Foundation for its generous fellowship toward field research and acknowledge their valuable support.

CHAPTER 1

Introduction: The China Business Model in Context—Setting the Scene

Elisabeth Paulet[1] and Chris Rowley[2,3,4,5]
[1]ICN Business School, CEREFIGE, Pole Lorrain de Gestion, Nancy, France
[2]Professor Emeritus, Cass Business School, City, University of London, London, United Kingdom
[3]Professorial Fellow, Institute of Hallyu Convergence Research, Korea University, Seoul, Korea
[4]Adjunct Professor, Griffith Business School and Griffith Asia Institute, Griffith University, Brisbane, QLD, Australia
[5]Visiting Fellow, Institute of Asia and Pacific Studies, Nottingham University, Nottingham, United Kingdom

1.1 INTRODUCTION

Since the 1980s, China has moved from a closed, centrally planned system to a more market-oriented one. Several reforms led to this situation in domains such as agriculture, fiscal decentralization, state-owned enterprises (SOE) autonomy (Li, 2011), growth of the private sector and small- and medium-sized enterprises (SMEs), creation of a diversified banking system, development of stock markets and opening up to trade and foreign direct investment (FDI). The commensurate shifts in management, marketing, accounting, as well as mergers and acquisitions, SOEs and SMEs have been noted (see Rowley & Cooke, 2010), as have those regarding labor and management, human resource management (HRM), business relations and trust, corporate social responsibility (CSR) (Dyllick and Hockerts, 2002), and bank–corporate relationships (Warner & Rowley, 2011) and financial services, impression management, institutional isomorphic pressure on internationalization, international HRM, competitive strategy choices, and innovative performance of start-ups (Warner & Rowley, 2014).

The reforms and changes were undertaken gradually in order to make the transition toward a form of market capitalism. This development can also be placed in the context of different types of capitalism (see Rowley & Oh, 2016a, 2016b; Rowley & Yukongdi, 2016) and business relations. Indeed, it is commonly noted that Chinese firms are characterized by the inclination to incorporate personal relationships in decision making among which personal control, *guanxi* (Warner & Rowley, 2011, 2014, 2016) and interpersonal trust or *xhinyong* are the most well-known.

The China Business Model. DOI: http://dx.doi.org/10.1016/B978-0-08-100750-1.00001-2

In terms of business organization, China has renewed its support for SOEs in sectors it considers important to "economic security"—explicitly looking to foster globally competitive national champions. There were reforms of SOEs from late-1990s onwards, with the worst closed or privatized and their employment halving from 70 million in 1997 to 37 million by 2005 (Wildau, 2016). This, however, ended with the government's stimulus responding to the 2008 Global Financial Crisis through massive lending by government fiat to SOEs acting in the national interest. This consequently fueled the construction boom for factories, housing, and infrastructure, which in turn increased demand for output from SOEs. Now reform is in the air again, this time by mergers—with 6 SOEs having merged in 2015 and 1.8 million coal and steel jobs to be cut, although the government remains wary of job losses with the fear of social, unrest (Wildau, 2016).

In terms of the finance area, after keeping its currency tightly linked to the US dollar for many years, in 2005 China revalued it by 2.1% against the US dollar. From then until late 2008 the cumulative appreciation of the renminbi against the US dollar was more than 20%, but the exchange rate remained virtually pegged to the dollar from the onset of the 2008 Global Financial Crisis until mid-2010. The government's financial intervention produced economic growth, although the rate of increase has been declining. This calls into question the veracity of the once-vaunted China business model, requiring an examination of its underpinnings and elements. Chinese firms are characterized by specific characteristics in their business model.

Our introductory chapter will present the current situation and subsequent changes, underlining the originality and limits of the China business model. The different compositional factors of business management and organization, culture, and finance and investment will be taken into account to help make the reader more aware of the ongoing transformations of the China business model.

1.2 SETTING THE SCENE

Since 2012, China's gross domestic product (GDP) growth has been slowing down: 10.5% in 2010, 9.3% in 2011 and decreased to 7% by mid-2015 (see Fig. 1.1). After the 2008 Global Financial Crisis, the government reinforced its efforts to reduce reliance on trade and investment (*The Times*, January 20, 2014; Wildau & Weinland, 2016). Unexpectedly reduced global demand for Chinese goods has recently reduced output and increased unemployment—reaching 4.1% of the active population by 2016. Concerns about the debts owed by local governments that have borrowed

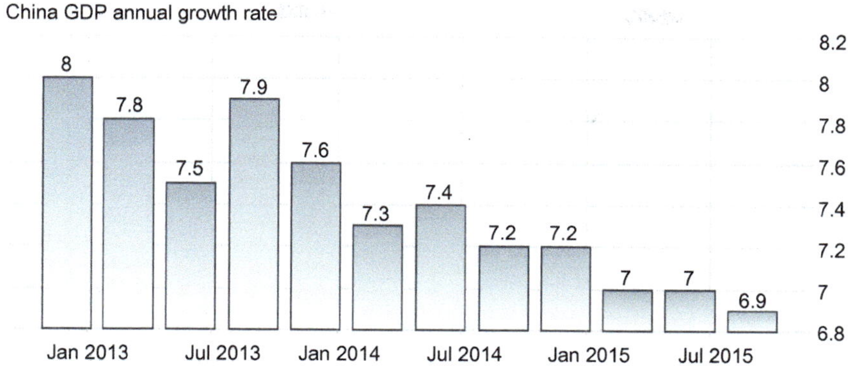

Figure 1.1 Annual growth rate in China. www.tradingeconomics.com | *National Bureau of Statistics of China.*

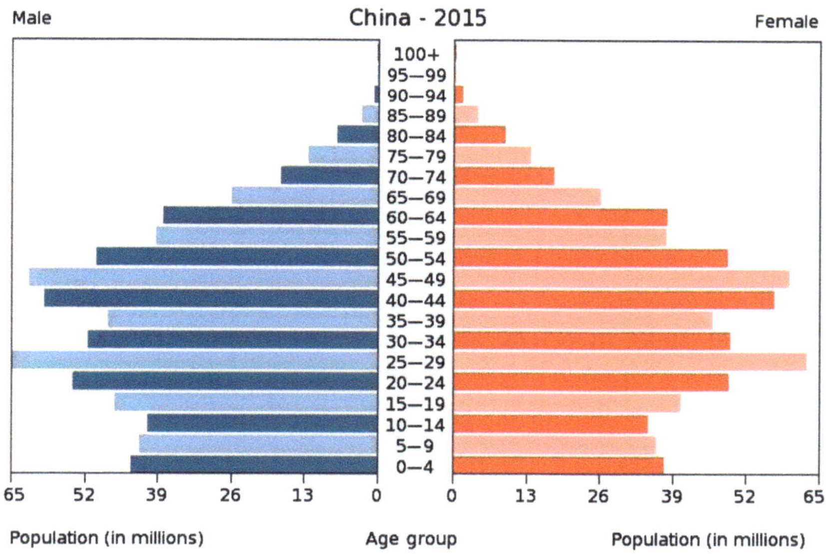

Figure 1.2 Population age distribution. *CIA Factbook.*

heavily is contributing to a deterioration in the situation, *The Financial Times* issue "What China Wants" (2016) notes that local governments ran up debts of 10.7 trillion yuan (US$1.6 trillion) over the decade 2000–10— equal to about one-quarter of China's annual economic output. The ending of the "migration miracle" (Clover, 2015; Waldmeir, 2015) as the fuel for the Chinese economic miracle—the vast rural labor force—dries up and the "demographic time bomb" of a growing aging population and shrinking workforce ticks ever louder (see Fig. 1.2), in the context of limited social security provisions.

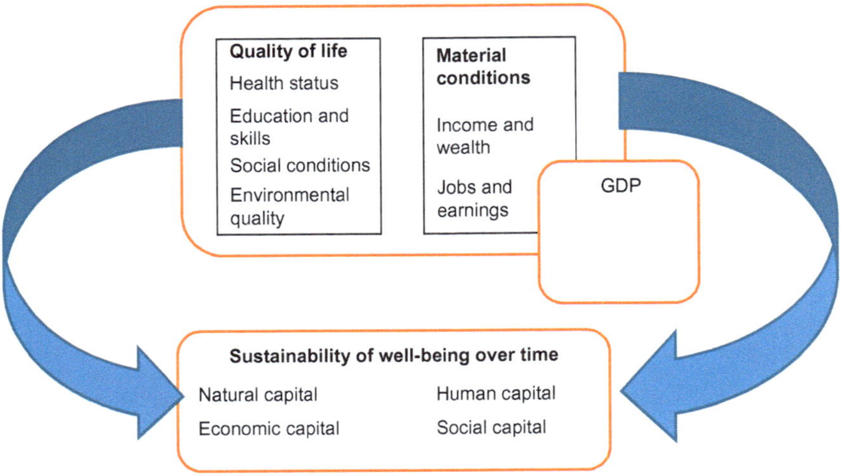

Figure 1.3 Factors explaining well-being of Chinese population.

These economic developments and social conditions have affected the well-being of the population and social progress in the country (see Fig. 1.3). In 2013, 13.6% of the population was below the poverty line. This situation is partly explained by a distortion of distribution between capital and labor. According to the Gini Index, China had a distribution of family income ranking of 47.4 (2013) due to wage disparities between workers belonging to private and public companies, or people leading their activities in rural zones or industrial cities. Reduced social benefits have contributed to increasing inequalities among workers throughout the country (World Bank Indicators, 2014).

Despite these negative developments, China exhibits some potential to move in the right direction; China and Australia recently sealed a landmark Free Trade Agreement, significantly expanding ties between the world's second largest economy and one of Washington's closest allies in Asia. As reported by the Australian department of Foreign Affairs and Trade, the deal will open up Chinese markets to Australian farm exporters and the service sector, while easing restrictions on Chinese investment into Australia. Despite China already being Australia's top trading partner, these commercial agreements will reinforce its position. The two countries also agreed to work jointly to combat climate change by sharing technology aimed at improving coal use efficiency.

Economic transition has produced a high degree of institutional uncertainty in China (Nee, 1992) and transaction costs remain high for firms to secure necessary inputs and legitimacy. As the uncertainty increases, firms more eagerly turn to *guanxi* networks to lower external dependence for key resources and to improve their validity. A *guanxi* network helps firms overcome the lack of resources to accommodate growth while alleviating substantial bureaucratic costs from internalizing operations, aiding smooth business transactions.

As in many Western countries, Chinese firms are commonly SMEs (Cunningham & Rowley, 2010, 2011). The advantages associated with SMEs are those of entrepreneurial dynamism, internal flexibility and responsiveness to changing circumstances The SME Promotion Law in 2002 emphasized SMEs' scientific and technological innovations and upgrading. In 2004 the constitution was amended to grant non-SOEs a legal status (Chen & Tjosvold, 2006; Zhu & Sanderson, 2009). Since most SMEs are non-state-owned, such a legislative move shows broad acknowledgment of the importance of the private sector, which in turn is more conducive to the further development of these firms.

Credit allocation has been characterized by government intervention and has been biased toward SOEs (Cull, Xu, & Zhu, 2009; Li, Zhao, Tan, & Liu, 2008). The 2008 Global Financial Crisis tightened credit constraints for SMEs around the world, and particularly in emerging economies. Additionally, there are imperfections in capital markets which create a "wedge" between the cost of internal and external finance (debt and new share issues). The principal source of the "wedge" may be due to asymmetric information between firms and potential suppliers of external finance. Information problems can lead to adverse selection and moral hazard problems in markets for external finance. Moreover, the extensive use of debt finance is not appropriate for many firms, especially those whose projects have little collateral value because of asset specificity. As most Chinese firms are family enterprises (Lim & Gosling, 1983), these arguments are even more pertinent.

FDI in China grew at its strongest pace in nearly 4 years in January 2012, surging 29.4% in 1 year and reaching US$13.9 billion with investors largely avoiding the troubled manufacturing sector and focusing more on services. The Chinese service sector accounted for 48.2% of China's economic output in 2014, leading the traditional manufacturing sector by 5.6% (KPMG, 2015), including a growth of ecommerce, with annual sales reaching US$354 billion, 11/4% of total retail sales, in August 2014–15 (Clover, 2015). This growth, however, relies on super cheap delivery (just US$1.5–2 for overnight packages), creating swatches of *kuaidi*: exploitative, insecure, long hour, low paid, and poor status courier jobs.

Capital market imperfections are very present in China. By law, the largest Chinese banks, predominantly state banks, were instructed not to lend to private firms until 1998. This instruction was embedded in the political notion that private firms do not rank high in terms of political status. This political "pecking order" in the allocation of credit, where private firms were disadvantaged, should have been alleviated since 1998. Evidence suggests, however, that credit constraints for private firms are still present and these may impede the growth of the economy (Huang, 2012). In fact, central and local governments define mandatory rules with different priorities and commercial banks have to obey. The various, large, specialized banks are not institutions with independent management and are responsible for their own loss and profit. As a consequence, these banks are not as concerned about the operational efficiency of credit.

1.3 AIMS AND STRUCTURE

The aim of this book is to examine the development and transformation of the Chinese business model. The impact of the financial crisis on countries and China will help the reader to understand its evolution toward a form of market capitalism. We develop three main parts as a framework: The business model of companies and how it affects the performance and the management of firms; business culture and its influence of financing policy of enterprises; finance and investment and how the financial sector could help the development of companies.

The first issue considered is structural organization and management in China. Here we address the following questions: What are the main factors that explain the spatial and economic development of China? Does governance have an impact on the performance of companies? Since the 2008 Global Financial Crisis, corporate governance developed a new dimension regarding enterprise performance. In its broader sense, governance can be understood through the different forms of decisions and control that exist inside a firm. Implicitly, such concepts aim to define how power is distributed within a firm and the decision-making process then justifies the form of corporate governance. It must take into consideration the property rights specific to the institution, which could be public or private (Brickley, Smith, & Zimmerman, 1997). To enable shareholders to fulfill this role, their participation on the General Assembly Board is essential to guarantee their monitoring role concerning managerial decisions. Moreover, each member must have reliable information about the objectives of the company. Hence, asymmetric information problems should be solved. Only in this context will good management be possible in order to achieve higher performance.

The concept of CSR is diverse and applied in China (Warner & Rowley, 2011, 2014; Yeung, Ramasamy, & Rowley, 2016). In 2006 the most recent version of China's Company Law became effective.[1] This explains the conditions under which CSR should be applied to Chinese companies (Brohier-Meuter, 2011). This states that companies "shall comply with the laws and administrative regulations, social morality, and business morality" and "shall act in good faith, accept the supervision of the government and the general public, and bear social responsibilities" and codifies the obligation of businesses to observe the basic principles of CSR and provides a legal basis for CSR in China.[2]

CSR (*gongsi shehui zeren*) is correlated to corporate sustainable development (CSD) (Romero & Lamadrid, 2014). CSD is seen as a business strategy that attempts to meet the needs of organizational stakeholders without compromising the resources and interests of the local community. CSD has been the object of much work in recent decades and researchers have adopted varying perspectives.

Even if these values are now more integrated in business management, CSR's implementation is diverse among Chinese companies for several reasons. First, many major corporations are SOEs and controlled by the government. Nearly a quarter of corporate assets are state-owned (National Bureau of Statistics of China, 2009). Second, Chinese CSR implementation refers to a top-down planning process, which incorporates company law, with guidelines that do not have the status of law and environmental requirements for credit and listing on the stock exchange (Brohier-Meuter, 2011). Third, the integration of company's inherent social responsibilities has to cope with traditional Chinese business management (Lin, 2010). Fourth, SOEs are unaccustomed to authentic public accountability. Therefore, responsible corporate behavior does not develop naturally among Chinese companies, even as the economy moves toward a market model.

All these considerations help us to understand why corporate ownership in China is so concentrated (Claessens, Djankov, & Lang, 2000; Faccio &

[1] Company Law of the People's Republic of China (promulgated by the Standing Comm. Nat'l People's Cong., Oct. 27, 2005, effective January 1, 2006) (hereinafter Chinese Company Law), available at http://www.fdi.gov.cn/pub/FDI_EN/Laws/law_en_info.jsp?docid=50878.

[2] Chinese Company Law supra note 1 art. 5.

Lang, 2002). The institutional context discussed earlier, together with weak legal or regulatory protection for minority shareholders, exacerbate agency problems, interest conflicts, and make the Chinese stock market highly conducive to "tunneling" activities (e.g., Jiang, Lee, & Yue, 2010; Peng, Wei, & Yang, 2011), whereby majority shareholders use their personal position to make additional profits. As a result, the conflict of interest between controlling and minority shareholders, rather than the one between the delegated manager and diverse investors, becomes the central theme of agency problems in Chinese firms.

Given all of the above, Chinese management is different from what is expected in the Western context. Several issues have to be considered. The first issue concerns participative management and corporate governance. In reference to our preceding argument, public firms focus on distribution policy toward their workers. For private and foreign enterprises, interaction between managers and employees is a key issue in defining "good managerial practices" in a Chinese context. The latter refers to leadership and empowerment, which are crucial to Western managerial processes. The question is how to adapt such concepts to Asia (see Rowley & Ulrich, 2012a, 2012b). In this particular context, where conflict of interest often exists in companies, it is easy to understand why Chinese employees are not really willing to share responsibility with managers. Participative management questions the traditional model, but also appeals to the construction of a new paradigm to satisfy the Chinese environment for firms.

The second issue to consider is the financing policy and performance of Chinese firms. The financing of an investment project will induce a hierarchical choice regarding the financial structure of firms. In particular, small firms prefer internal financing (internal funds, bonds) and use banking loans as the last resort. Medium size companies also have some difficulties in accessing financial markets and will privilege bank loans. Large firms operate an optimum choice between banking credit, bonds, and financial assets. These facts should be adapted to the particular form of Chinese culture where *guanxi* plays a very important role in business culture. As a product of Chinese traditional culture, *guanxi* has a huge influence on Chinese society and business behavior (Wang & Rowley, 2016; Warner & Rowley, 2011, 2014) and in the way firms finance their investment projects.

The banking system is controlled by the government and used as a policy tool for addressing national and social priorities. Access to credit may be determined by political considerations as well as connections, rather than solely on a commercial basis. Many studies show that large firms and SOEs have priority in obtaining bank loans (Martin, 2012); while small and private firms have more restricted access. The market segmentations in China provide opportunities to observe how the shock in the bank loan supply affects the corporate capital structure of different firms.

A third issue is that monetary policy and bank loan supply can be frequently adopted to stimulate economic growth in countries. A recent phenomenon is the significant credit growth since 2008 in large emerging markets, such as China (Onaran in *Bloomberg Business Week*, 2013). In China, the supply of bank loans substantially increased in 2009 and 2010 following an expansionary monetary policy. However, disparities in investment policies exist among Chinese firms across the country. Hence, three industrial models coexist: the Suman Model, characterized by local, state-directed, township and village enterprises; the Pearl River Delta Model, corresponding to externally driven development and exo-urbanization; and the Wenzhou model, composed of family-owned small business. This unequal industrial development is not specific to China. For example, there are similar situations in Italy and Germany (Hadjimichalis, 2006; Schamp, 2005). Government policies during the Maoist era of state investment made Wenzhou's economy less oriented to SOEs and so unequal access to credit could explain the differences in Chinese industry. In particular, investment in fixed assets in rural firms came from bank loans (Peng, 1994), while Wenzhou enterprises were generally financed by extended families, social networks and "underground" financial institutions (Tsai, 2002). Some questions then follow. Could investment policy help industrial relocation to create wealth and development? And will size, ownership, and governance affect this relocation?

Despite the recent financial crisis, many enterprises have continued largely using banking credit to finance their projects. As China's economy slows further, companies are seeking lower rates of return on investments. The system is showing stress. Standard and Poor's noted in November 2014 (Standard and Poor's warns on China corporate risks) that China suffered its first corporate default when a solar firm failed to make a payment to bondholders. So far, central government initiatives to restrain credit growth have largely failed. Companies are even turning to unconventional financing options—increasing their debts in the process. The question is how to contain debt growth without damaging the economy.

And how does this difficulty in finding liquidity for investment projects affects the performance of firms?

Such questions naturally lead to consideration of the financial and banking system. China's banking sector is dominated by four state-owned banks (SOBs), which prefer to provide loans to SOEs—often very large firms. There are also 12 joint-stock banks, which, in terms of size, are in between SOBs and the third banking type: city commercial banks. Due to their relatively small size and local business orientation, most city commercial banks target local SMEs. Universal banks, private institutions, and SOEs play a central role in credit distribution, as pointed out earlier. Despite apparent strength, the stress tests conducted by central banks and regulatory institutions have indicated the fragility of the banking system. In particular the solvency II ratio of Basel III is far from being respected by private and public Chinese banks. The task is to evaluate the measures taken by the government to ensure the stability of the Chinese banking system.

Apart from banks, financial markets are mostly underdeveloped in China. Equity financing is a relative new development and remains trivial (Allen & Shen, 2012). Enterprises rarely use direct finance for their investment projects. Access to security markets is controlled by the state and constitutes a supplement of funds for large SOEs. It is highly volatile, as security prices do not appear to be efficiently set, so prices do not provide either a positive signaling function or a disciplinary factor for the management of firms. As a consequence, Chinese security markets do not provide adequate opportunities for the management of financial risks. Two questions then arise. Firstly, what are the main sources of financing for Chinese firms and how will they impact on their productive investments? Second, what are the factors that influence investment in Asian countries?

Given our structure above, our book will provide answers to our questions, which will allow a better understanding of the business world in China—explaining both the managerial and financial strategy of its firms. We now outline the content of our book that fulfills this aim.

1.4 CONTENT

Our book is divided into a trio of interrelated parts and a total of 11 chapters. These parts and the chapters are set out in Table 1.1. This gives readers a quick overview of the structure and content as well as the links between parts and chapters.

Table 1.1 Structure, Content, Themes and Coverage

Chapter	Part	Content and Themes	Sector Coverage
1		Setting the scene and aims, structure, and content	General
	I	Management and Culture	
2		*Guanxi* culture, characteristics, practices, and exchange mechanisms	General
		Role of public sector in implementation	
3		Motives and behaviors of business owners and managers	Private businesses
		Dimensions of business motives/behaviors: corruption, favoritism, reliability, responsibility	SOEs
4		CSR/CSD historical perspective, theoretical framework, government role, consumer responses	Textiles and apparel Telecommunications
		Benefits to performance	
	II	Financial Innovation and Application	
5		Equity gap and finance innovation	Technology-based
		Private and public venture and capital funds	SMEs
6		Supply chain management	Pharmaceuticals
		Medicine distribution and spatial distribution	
7		Managers and employees from different ethnic backgrounds—heterophily	US-owned
		Stress and psychological acceptance at work and management style	Pharmaceuticals, food, cosmetics
	III	Finance and Investment	
8		Informal finance, financial contracting, and folk lending	SMEs
		Banking system versus P2P lending	
9		FDI and internationalization	Services
		Transnational entrepreneurs and Transfer–Adapt–Scale framework	
10		Economic growth, competitiveness, and financial and environmental performance	Transnational corporations
		FDI, banking system and financial stability	
11		Implications and what we can learn	General

Part I is concerned with a discussion of the way business is conducted in China in terms of management and culture, and contains three chapters. Chapter 2, *Guanxi* Culture, explores *guanxi*, its nature and effects on business performance. After defining the *guanxi* culture of business companies, an emphasis is given to its impact on business performance. *Guanxi* can help explain business behaviors and many foreign managers regard it as key to doing business in China. The rules and codes integrated in the *guanxi* business model influences every aspect of the business domain, including relationship marketing, supply chain management, and market performance. It is also crucial in the arguments developed in Parts II and III of our book.

Chapter 3, Interpreting China's Model for Business: Roles of Corruption, Favoritism, Reliability, and Responsibility, positions a transition from a command economy toward a market economy within a theory of comparative political economies, and addresses an interpretation of the business model. This suggests that China remains a one-party regime, resisting transition to constitutional democracy, while managing marketization and privatization. The findings provide insights concerning the roles of four dimensions of the business model: corruption, favoritism (including *guanxi*), political reliability, and CSR.

Chapter 4, The Evolution of Corporate Social Responsibility (CSR) and Corporate Sustainability (CS) Practices in China, focuses on CSR. The policies and regulations of the Chinese State Environmental Protection Agency aim to improve the environmental performance of corporations. This chapter covers also the evolution of Corporate Sustainability (CS) and CSR and the role of the government in leading initiatives. The global CSD reporting initiative, GRI, based on the UN Global Compact, and reporting challenges facing Chinese firms, are discussed. Content analysis of reports published by Chinese companies is presented in comparison to those from firms in the United States.

This first part of our book constitutes the background of how Chinese firms apply management and governance to improve their performance in the global market. Part II contain three chapters concerned with the application of the Chinese business model to different sectors and financial innovation to tackle liquidity constraints.

Chapter 5, The Equity Gap Amongst Technology-Based Small Firms: Challenges for Government-Backed Venture Capital in China, explores financing for innovation and technology-based entrepreneurs. It examines the context of state intervention and the structural economic issues that embed it. The review captures the issues related to the equity gap for entrepreneurs and considers initiatives, responses and supply side state intervention strategies used to help to try to mitigate the finance gap. It examines what necessitates the state's intervention and its implications for creating market imperfections and how efficient the state is in narrowing the finance gap for technology-based SMEs.

The two following chapters illustrate the situation of two specific sectors of Chinese economic development. Chapter 6, Assessing the Impact of the New Medical Reform on China's Pharmaceutical Supply Chain: The Case of Essential Medicines Distribution in Yuping, Luochuan, and Minhang Regions, analyzes supply chain management as it becomes more prevalent in Asia. The new round of reform in China's medical system is said to be bringing about significant improvements in the pharmaceutical supply chain. This, in turn, has led to unprecedented opportunities and challenges for operators and consumers alike. The reform has also brought about an urgent need for rigorous analysis of the impact this may have on the country's pharmaceutical supply chain, especially as it relates to the rural areas.

As Asia constitutes an attractive market, foreign investors are attracted to businesses in this part of the world. Management can come from American or European countries. Chapter 7, Exploring MEH (Manager-Employee-Heterophily) in US-Owned and Managed Plants in Taiwan, explores the influence of managers coming from different ethnic and cultural backgrounds on local workers in Taiwanese firms. Sources of disharmony between employees and managers could cause stress that may be improved through HRM practices. Managers, expatriates from overseas parent companies, need to take into account different organizational cultures which will impact on HRM.

As a whole, this second part of our book gives insights into the interactions of Chinese business culture and management. Part III contains three chapters concerned with financial aspects of management. The comparative analysis presented in this part will help the reader to better understand the specificity of Chinese management.

Chapter 8, Monitoring Maturation in Chinese Financial Intermediation, examines shifts from folk-lending [民间借贷—*Mínjiān jièdài*] to peer-to-peer online lending platforms [P2P 平台—*ping tai*] by the maturation in Chinese financial contracting involving SMEs. Its analysis helps understand why peer-to-peer online lending has exploded in China since 2010 and why Wenzhou is one of the main centers for so-called P2Ps. As already mentioned in Part II of our book, SMEs have difficulties in finding the necessary liquidity to finance investment projects. The use of the P2P platform is a way to reduce or even avoid such liquidity constraints.

Suggesting that this change in financial context requires a paradigm shift, Chapter 9, Internationalization Strategy and Service Adaptation in China: Perspective of Transnational Entrepreneurship, proposes a new FDI model suited to services. This strategic Transfer–Adapt–Scale framework is specifically tailored toward transnational entrepreneurs (TEs). Many study multinational companies in China, but few focus on TEs. It suggests that TEs in China are in a unique position to utilize this unparalleled change of context as the Chinese service sector expands. The aim of this chapter is to give an emphasis to cultural values that TEs need to consider in order to successfully conduct their business. Applied to the service sector, this will give readers insights regarding the adaptation stage TEs must set up when doing business in China.

Chapter 10, China Versus India: Emerging Giants in the World Economy, provides knowledge about China, in comparison with India, in order to illuminate the factors needed to understand their investment climates, development, and the basic foundation required for investing in these countries or initiating business opportunities. As per the Global Competitiveness Report (2014–15), which covers 144 countries, India is ranked 71st and China 28th. They have achieved high rankings in key parameters like Market Size (3rd for India, 2nd for China), Innovation (49th for India, 32nd for China), and sound financial market development (51st for India, 54th for China). The purpose of this chapter is to give the reader an insight into financial factors that explain the economic development of these two countries.

All these considerations in Part III will help readers to better understand how financial structures are organized and how they can contribute to productive investment.

1.5 CONCLUSION

We have set out our aims and the commensurate logic, rationale, linkages, and structure for our book. We have provided a context and overview of the chapters. As the economy slows, China's business model is under strain and stress—and hence, reevaluation. The model is composed of many interlocking and self-reinforcing factors, which we grouped into a trio of: management and organization; culture and finance; finance and investment. We looked at these in detail and conclude that these issues will provide a better understanding of the business world in China by explaining both the managerial and financial strategy of firms in the new economic context, albeit in the traditional culture of *guanxi*. In addition, it will help the reader to clarify the strengths and weaknesses of firms.

REFERENCES

Allen, W.T., & Shen, H. (2012). In J. Fan & R. Morck (Eds.), *Assessing China's top down securities markets in capitalizing China*. Chicago: University Chicago Press.

Brickley, J. A., Smith, C. W., & Zimmerman, J. L. (1997). Management fads and organizational architecture. *Journal of Applied Corporate Finance, 10*(2), 24–39.

Brohier-Meuter, J. (2011). The rise of CSR Public Policy in Asia: The case of Southeast Asia and China: *Responsible management in Asia*. UK: Palgrave Macmillan, 65–86.

Chen, Y. F., & Tjosvold, D. (2006). Participative leadership by American and Chinese managers in China: The role of relationships. *Journal of Management Studies, 43*, 1727–1752.

Claessens, S., Djankov, S., & Lang, L. (2000). The separation of ownership and control in East Asian Corporations. *Journal of Financial Economics, 58*, 81–112.

Clover, C. (2015). Delivering the Jack Ma Economy. *Financial Times, 15 September*, 11.

Cull, R., Xu, L. C., & Zhu, T. (2009). Formal finance and trade credit during China's transition. *Journal of Financial Intermediation, 18*(2), 173–192.

Cunningham, X. L., & Rowley, C. (2010). The changing face of SME management in China. In C. Rowley & F. L. Cooke (Eds.), *The changing face of management in China*. London: Routledge.

Cunningham, X. L., & Rowley, C. (2011). SMEs in China: A literature review, HRM and suggestions for further research. In M. Warner & C. Rowley (Eds.), *Chinese management in the "harmonious society": Managers, markets and the globalised economy*. London: Routledge. pp. 47-67.

Dyllick, T., & Hockerts, K. (2002). Beyond the business case for corporate sustainability. *Business Strategy and the Environment, 11*(2), 130–141.

Faccio, M., & Lang, L. H. P. (2002). The ultimate ownership of Western European Corporations. *Journal of Financial Economics, 65*(3), 365–395.

Financial Times (2016). China debt load reaches record high as economy mounts. *April*.

Hadjimichalis, C. (2006). The end of third Italy as we knew it? *Antipode, 38*, 82–106.

Huang, Y. (2012). How did China take off? *The Journal of Economic Perspectives*, 147–170.

Janda, M. (2014) Standard and Poor's warns on China corporate risks. *Standard and Poor's* 17 November.

Jiang, G., Lee, C. M., & Yue, H. (2010). Tunneling through intercorporate loans: The China experience. *Journal of Financial Economics, 98*(1), 1–20.

KPMG, A. (2015). Switzerland in co-operation with the Institute of Management at the University of St. Gallen (nd). Performance through focus Seizing the global private banking opportunity, dostupno na http://www.kpmg.com/LU/en/IssuesAndInsights/Articlespublications/Documents/2012-Private-Banking-Study-Performancethrough-focus.pdf, poslednji put pregledano, 25.

Li, X. (2011). Sources of external technology, absorptive capacity, and innovation capability in Chinese state-owned high-tech enterprises. *World Development, 39*(7), 1240–1248.

Li, Y., Zhao, Y., Tan, J., & Liu, Y. (2008). Moderating effects of entrepreneurial orientation on market orientation-performance linkage: Evidence from Chinese small firms. *Journal of Small Business Management, 46*(1), 113–133.

Lim, L.Y., & Gosling, L.P. (Eds.), (1983). *The Chinese in Southeast Asia: Volume 1: Ethnicity and economic activity*. Singapore: Maruzen Asia.

Lin, L. W. (2010). Corporate social responsibility in China: Window dressing or structural change. *Berkeley Journal of International Law, 28*, 64.
Martin, M.F. (2012). China's banking system: Issues for congress. In *CRS report for congress*, February 20.
National Bureau of Statistics of China. (2009). *Communique on major data of the Second National Economic Census (N°1)*. <http://www.stats.gov.cn/english/newsandcomingevents/t20091225_402610168.htm>.
Nee, V. (1992). Organizational dynamics of market transition: Hybrid forms, property rights, and mixed economy in China. *Administrative Science Quarterly, 37*(1), 1–27.
Peng, W. Q., Wei, K. J., & Yang, Z. (2011). Tunneling or propping: Evidence from connected transactions in China. *Journal of Corporate Finance, 17*(2), 306–325.
Peng, Y. (1994). Capital formation in rural enterprises. In C. Findlay, A. Watson, & H. X. Wu (Eds.), *Rural enterprises in China* (pp. 93–116). New York, NY: St. Martin's Press.
Romero, K. C. C., & Lamadrid, R. L. (2014). Rethinking corporate social responsibility within the sustainability agenda. *Journal of Global Responsibility, 5*(2), 180–202.
Rowley, C., & Cooke, F. L. (Eds.), (2010). *The changing face of management in China*. London: Routledge.
Rowley, C., & Oh, I. (2016a). Business ethics & the role of context: Institutionalism, history & comparisons in the Asia Pacific region. *Asia Pacific Business Review, 22*(3), 353–365.
Rowley, C., & Oh, I. (2016b). Relinquishing business ethics from a theoretical deadlock: The requirement for local grounding & historical comparisons in the Asia Pacific region. *Asia Pacific Business Review, 22*(3), 516–521.
Rowley, C., & Ulrich, D. (2012a). Setting the scene for leadership in Asia. *Asia Pacific Business Review, 18*(4), 451–464.
Rowley, C., & Ulrich, D. (2012b). Lessons learned & insights derived from leadership in Asia. *Asia Pacific Business Review, 18*(4), 675–681.
Rowley, C., & Yukongdi, V. (2016). Business networks & varieties of capitalism in Thailand: Adding the context of history, political structures and social & cultural values. In J. Nolan, C. Rowley, & M. Warner (Eds.), *Asian Business Networks in East Asia*. Amsterdam: Elsevier.
Schamp, E. W. (2005). Decline of the district, renewal of firms. *Environment and Planning A, 37*, 617–634.
Tsai, K. S. (2002). *Back-alley banking*. Ithaca, NY: Cornell University Press.
Waldmeir, P. (2015). Children of the revolution. *Financial Times, 20 December*, 9.
Wang, B., & Rowley, C. (2016). Business networks and the emergence of *Guanxi* capitalism in China: The role of the invisible hand. In J. Nolan, C. Rowley, & M. Warner (Eds.), *Business Networks in East Asian Capitalisms*. Amsterdam: Elsevier.
Warner, M., & Rowley, C. (Eds.), (2011). *Chinese management in the "harmonious society": Managers, markets and the globalised economy*. London: Routledge.
Warner, M., & Rowley, C. (Eds.), (2014). *Demystifying Chinese management: Issues and challenges*. London: Routledge.
Wildau, G. (2016). The zombie economy. *Financial Times, 1 March*, 11.
Wildau, G., & Weinland, D. (2016). Rapid climb in China's debt raises concerns over the economy. *Financial Times, 25 April*, 7.
World Bank Group. (2014). *World Development Indicators 2014*. World Bank Publications.
Yeung, M., Ramasamy, B., & Rowley, C. (2016). Initial job choice in the greater China region: The role of corporate social responsibility. *Journal of General Management, 41*(3), 55–72.
Zhu, Y. M., & Sanderson, J. W. (2009). The key obstacles and countermeasure against development of innovative SMEs in China. *China Soft Science, 9*, 23–31.

PART I

Management and Culture

CHAPTER 2

Guanxi Culture: How it Affects the Business Model of Chinese Firms

Zhang Chi and Hong Seock-Jin
KEDGE Business School, Talence, France

2.1 INTRODUCTION

The Chinese term *guanxi* has been discussed in Western management publications since the 1980s when it first appeared as a concept for Western companies to consider when doing business in China. In order to succeeding in doing business in China, Western companies have spent many years trying to understand what *guanxi* is and how to practice *guanxi* in China. *Guanxi* has been special Chinese cultural factor and has played a very important role in Chinese social and economic systems. So, what is *guanxi* exactly?

According to the Chinese *Xinhua Dictionary*, the basic meaning of *guanxi* comes from combining two Chinese words: *guan* (关) and *xi* (系). *Guan* (关) means a "gate or barrier," and *xi* (系) means "connection or link." So *guanxi* literally means to "go through the gate and get a connection." The definition of *guanxi* given by the Chinese authority's dictionary is "certain properties of contacts or relations among people." So *guanxi* can be simply translated as "personal relationship" or "social connection." Because *guanxi* is deeply rooted in Chinese culture, it is more complex than a purely personal relationship as found in Western countries. So we leave this Chinese word untranslated, because there is no English word with a correspondent meaning.

In research before 1990, *guanxi* was defined in a vague way as a "special" relationship or "particular" ties to differentiate it from common personal relationships (Alston, 1989). With subsequent in-depth studies of *guanxi*, more and more Western scholars have a better understanding of the *guanxi* phenomenon. Subsequently, *guanxi* has been defined as relationships or social connections based on mutual interests and benefits, which is achieved by exchanging favors and giving social status between

The China Business Model. DOI: http://dx.doi.org/10.1016/B978-0-08-100750-1.00002-4

guanxi partners. So the *guanxi* interaction is not only commercial but also reflects a social act that binds exchange partners with reciprocal obligations (Yang, 1994). Generally, it's believed that *guanxi* is an interpersonal utilitarian relationship for reciprocal exchange, taking place only at individual levels (Davies, Leung, Luk, & Wong, 1995). Recent research, however, has proved that this kind of interpersonal *guanxi* can also be applied at the organizational level (Cai, Jun, & Yang, 2010; Gu, Hung, & Tse, 2008).

Using a business perspective, *guanxi* is not only a cultural factor but also an institutional force and governance structure. At the firm level, *guanxi* can be regarded as social capital and a cooperative resource to gain clear advantages in terms of financial performance, marketing channels, and so on (Cai et al., 2010; Cao, Baker, & Schniederjans, 2014; Gu et al., 2008). *Guanxi* study has been favored by more and more Western investors in recent years. They see *guanxi* as a "magic weapon" to access Chinese markets and gain competitive advantages. *Guanxi* study is also seen as relationship marketing in Chinese markets (Davies et al., 1995).

Different scholars define *guanxi* using different perspectives because the word *guanxi* can refer to different but related things: *guanxi* states, *guanxi* practices, and *guanxi* exchanges. In most cases, *guanxi* refers to *guanxi* states, i.e., the relationships or ties between people, firms, or even between individuals and the government. This kind of *guanxi* relationship is based on emotional attachment and utilitarian purposes (see Section 2.6). *Guanxi* states come from *guanxi* bases (see Section 2.3). However, *guanxi* sometime means *guanxi* practices or *guanxi* behaviors (see Section 2.4). *Guanxi* practices refer to the process when people expand their *guanxi* networks though a set of social behaviors such as wining and dining. *Guanxi* is not only static but also a dynamic process. It needs to "pull *guanxi*" actively to achieve more mutual benefits. For instance, *guanxi* begins when one party starts to look for favors from another party. If another party cannot always respond to this favor, he or she will ask others to fulfill this favor through his or her *guanxi* networks. This process will involve more and more actors and will conclude only when the problem is solved or abandoned (Fan, 2002). Because *guanxi* is a utilitarian relationship based on exchanging favors, it can be used for exchange as social capital under a code or a set of social norms (see Section 2.5).

This chapter is divided into eight sections. After this introduction, the background of *guanxi* culture (Section 2.2) is presented. Then, three *guanxi*-related concepts are introduced in the following parts: *guanxi* bases (Section 2.3), *guanxi* practices (Section 2.4), and *guanxi* exchange mechanisms (Section 2.5). Section 2.6 elaborates *guanxi*'s main characteristics, whilst Section 2.7 focuses on *guanxi*'s impact on business performance, with the conclusion in Section 2.8.

2.2 BACKGROUND

The deeply rooted *Guanxi* culture has profoundly influenced the way of doing business in China. It is therefore imperative to have a thorough understanding of why *guanxi* matters so much. The popularity of the *guanxi* phenomena in Chinese society can be explained from two aspects: traditional cultural values and modern social atmosphere.

2.2.1 Traditional Cultural Values

Guanxi is a product of a Confucian culture that rules social behaviors between people. Because *guanxi* culture is so closely linked with Confucianism, it's necessary to understand Confucianism and its influence on *guanxi* culture.

Confucianism is an ethical, religious, and philosophical system that has enjoyed a long-term dominant cultural influence in East Asia and Southeast Asia (including China, Korea, Japan, Vietnam, etc.). The philosophy was started by Confucius (551–479 BCE), one of the most influential philosophers and educators in China, during the "Spring and Autumn" period (approximately 771–476 BCE). Confucian ideas have been used as a ruling ideology since the Han dynasty (206 BCE–AD 220), influencing Chinese intellectuals and laboring people alike for thousands of years.

The core value of Confucianism is *Ren* which means "love others" and "treat others well." *Ren* codifies an ethical rule for personal relationships. It emphasizes that we should treat others with love and compassion to get along harmoniously and with friendship. It believes that through harmonious relationships, the whole society will become more tolerant and stable. Under this Confucian social theory, Chinese people pay particular attention to interpersonal relationships with others. In this way, Chinese society has become a relational society, and the *guanxi* (personal relationship or social connection) culture flourishes there.

Confucian theory also emphasizes that all relationships start from kinship and the clan system. It underlines that each individual person attaches to a whole family, and the worship of ancestors has priority over other relationships, giving emphasis to the family-value orientation of Chinese culture. Seen from this perspective, the Confucian culture can be interpreted as a clanship culture, with Chinese personal relationships and social order maintained by blood ties and emotion. Unlike the individualism found in Western countries, where each has a social division of labor, Chinese society consists of family units. Every Chinese is subordinate to his or her own family and is responsible to the family. In China, the family relationship always takes priority over other social relationships tied through contracts. So the *guanxi* phenomenon always starts from inside the family, then ventures to outside acquaintances. Because there is a lack of confidence in strangers, Chinese people choose to believe insiders (people with whom they share *guanxi*) rather than outsiders (people with whom they don't share *guanxi*).

Guanxi shares some similarities in other East Asian cultures that are highly influenced by Confucianism: *Kankei* in Japan and *kwankye* in Korea have similar meanings as *guanxi* in China and it corresponds to *blat* in Russian culture. This phenomenon also exists in other societies dominated by collectivist cultures, such as Italy, Israel, and South Korea, which regard kinship as a key social resource (Gu et al., 2008). Even though *guanxi* culture shares some similarities with other personal network cultures in the world, *guanxi* operates in a unique way that is not exactly the same as its counterparts in other cultures (Gu et al., 2008).

In summary, Chinese culture is deeply influence by Confucianism, which emphasizes interpersonal relationships, especially clanship. And *guanxi* phenomenon (people relying on social connections) is a product of Confucian values. China is a relational society, and Chinese people use *guanxi* as a basis for their important social resources.

2.2.2 Modern Social Atmosphere

The traditional cultural viewpoint of *guanxi* reveals how it is embedded in Chinese society and deeply influences Chinese people's daily life and social conducts. On the other hand, the Chinese modern social atmosphere, including contemporary and institutional Chinese environments, also promotes the development of *guanxi* culture. In this case *guanxi* means an "institutionally defined system" and is more related to institutional structure than cultural factors (Guthrie, 1998).

As mentioned, China is a relational society in which people rely more on personal relationships than rational laws. This can be partly attributed to the Cultural Revolution, which took place in China from 1966 to 1976. During that period, social orders, organization disciplines, and laws were destroyed by frequent parades, and people preferred to believe a person they knew rather than social orders (Yang, 1994). Even though this disaster is nearly 40 years past, and China has enjoyed high-speed economic development since the 1980s, Chinese business environments and legal systems have been criticized as unstable and of high uncertainty. Because of the absence of an adequate legal system and the lack of universal formal rules, people rely more on personal relationships than formal contracts to avoid possible business risks. This is true for private companies, which are more vulnerable to potential damages from an underdeveloped legal system. Therefore in such an uncertain business environment, people rely more on *guanxi* and its informal rules and unwritten codes than formal structures, which are disadvantageous for protection and risk avoidance (Xin & Pearce, 1996). *Guanxi* is also regarded as a crucial institutional force to counter outside high-risk environments (Cai et al., 2010). During this period of economic reform, because of the nontransparency of market information and unclear policies, some important factors, such as key information, rare resources, land, and business licenses, were controlled by a small group of people. These "bourgeois individualisms" chase their own interests and adversely affected the social atmosphere (Yang, 1994). At this time, people needed to try to build *guanxi* with self-interested persons to gain key resources. With the deepening of China's economic development, however, the Chinese government has begun to pay more attention to laws and regulations, and rebuild a rational-legal system. However, because more and more foreign investments are coming to China, market competition has become increasingly intense, which will weaken *guanxi*'s importance. In this view, people use *guanxi* to get rare resources though a "back door" (corruption), and political protection to counter the risks of an unstable legal system (Guthrie, 1998).

Apart from the uncertainty of the legal system, the inefficiency and ineffectiveness of business infrastructures and related institutions can be another main institutional reason causing *guanxi* culture formation in China (Gu et al., 2008). Chinese regulatory systems are criticized for their lack of efficiency and effectiveness because of underdeveloped infrastructure, length of negotiations, bureaucratic delays, and institutional ambivalence. People believe that through *guanxi* practices many unnecessary business processes are cut and lengthy reviews are dramatically shortened. Accordingly, the treatment of related business formalities is more efficient. Therefore as long as the regular Chinese system remains ineffective and inefficient, *guanxi* will play an important role for subsequent effectiveness in business (Ambler, Styles, & Xiucun, 1999).

2.3 *GUANXI* BASES

When we say that person A has *guanxi* with person B, it means that there's a type of link between person A and person B. This link can be a family tie, social tie, or other kinds of ties. This link between people is called a *guanxi base.* Although *guanxi* bases do not necessarily produce active *guanxi* connections that make things happen, *guanxi* bases are still regarded as a prerequisite of *guanxi* practice (Yang, 1994; Yi & Ellis, 2000).

There are a variety of *guanxi* base types. For example, a *guanxi* base generally can be divided into blood base and social base. The blood base is a familial tie, and a social base reflects a relationship gained through social activities. The nature of *guanxi* bases determines the quality of *guanxi* between persons. Some researchers classify *guanxi* into four categories, from the closest to the most distant: family and kinship, neighbors and native place ties, nonkin relationships of equivalent status, and nonkin superior-subordinate relations (Yang, 1994). Except for family and kinship, which is an inherent relationship, the three other sorts of bases can be categorized as sharing commonalities. These kinds of *guanxi* are based on commonalities shared by two persons, such as classmates (have studied at the same school), fellow villagers (coming from the same place), coworkers (working at the same company), and so on. In this chapter, *guanxi* bases are divided into two categories: kinship *guanxi* bases and commonality *guanxi* bases.

2.3.1 Kinship *Guanxi* Bases

This type of *guanxi* base refers to relationships by birth or blood. It includes natal and nuclear families, extended families, consanguine relationships, and more distant sets of relatives. As discussed, because China is a family-oriented society, and Chinese people are deeply influenced by a kinship culture, family and kinship *guanxi* bases are ranked as the closest and most stable *guanxi* base. Within this family *guanxi* base, immediate family is the closest relationship, then comes the extended family, and the last is the distant family. Family ties are relatively permanent and stable. Family *guanxi* is a pure emotional tie, every family member is obliged to make a contribution to the whole family without asking for anything in return. And the resource distribution inside the family is based on need, which is fair but not necessarily equal (Hwang, 1987). For instance, rich family members with worse economic situation will get more financial support from the whole family.

2.3.2 Commonality *Guanxi* Bases

Yi and Ellis (2000) believe the establishment of *guanxi* begins with finding commonalities. These commonalities can be birthplace, school, company, profession, and so on. Through these commonalities, people feel closeness and become tied together through these common points. This kind of *guanxi* base is also called "relationship by nature" (Fan, 2002).

2.3.2.1 Neighbors

There's an old Chinese saying that "close neighbors are better than distant relatives." In daily life, close neighbors can have more interactions with people than with distant relatives, resulting in more emotional attachment compared to a distant relative whom they have hardly seen in years.

2.3.2.2 Same Hometown

Sharing the same hometown is a native place tie, which the Chinese value greatly. Because China is such a large country with different regional cultures, people feel close to others who come from the same hometown. When people go to a new place far away, they will join an association composed of people from the same place to feel protected. This phenomenon is very popular not only in China but also worldwide. For example, in France, people from *Whenzhou* (a city in the Zhejiang province) will associate together to do business and gain common benefits.

2.3.2.3 Same School

This *guanxi* base includes classmates, alumni, teachers and students, and so on. Chinese people believe that the *guanxi* base of coming from the same school creates a valuable and long-term relationship. The *guanxi* established during campus life is emotional rather than utilitarian. There's no pecuniary interest in this relationship, and people feel less at risk than through *guanxi* established at the workplace (Yang, 1994).

2.3.2.4 Same Working Place

This *guanxi* base includes colleagues, masters and apprentices, superiors and subordinates, and so on. Compared to the same school *guanxi*, this kind of *guanxi* is more utilitarian. It is also less stable because of potential conflicts of interest in workplaces.

Certainly, in real life, *guanxi* bases are too varied to detail here. Even though a particular *guanxi* base could largely determine the quality of *guanxi* between individuals, no one *guanxi* base always maintains priority over the other bases. For example, we cannot say that classmate *guanxi* is better than colleague *guanxi*. The closeness of *guanxi* depends not only on the *guanxi* base but also another more important aspect: *guanxi* practice. Even though family *guanxi* has been regarded as the most stable and close *guanxi* base, it could also be weakened by distance and be less close than neighbor *guanxi*, for example. And the quality of the *guanxi* base will change as environments change: Neighbors' relationships were at a high level of *guanxi* base during the 1980s because most Chinese lived in dormitory style quarters with a kitchen and toilet shared with neighbors. At that time, Chinese people had more interactions with neighbors. However, since the 1990s, Chinese people have moved to modern apartments instead of collective dormitories, living more separately so neighbor *guanxi* is not as close as before.

2.4 *GUANXI* PRACTICES

Guanxi bases reflect the existing links between individuals, but they cannot guarantee producing an active *guanxi*. An active *guanxi* relationship means individual people can take advantage of a *guanxi* base to achieve his or her own goals. For example, when you ask a favor of your classmate, whom you haven't spoken to in 10 years, he may refuse your request because of the lapse in time. However, an active *guanxi* may also be established between two individuals (person A and person B) with no existing *guanxi* base. In this case, they need a mediator or introducer (person C) to establish *guanxi* between them. Even though a *guanxi* base between person A and person B does not yet exist, both have a *guanxi* base with the mediator person C. Through their social network, a *guanxi* relationship can be established. In fact, in modern society, with the increase in social networks, establishing *guanxi* in this way is getting more and more popular. Unlike previous *guanxi*, which are based on existing *guanxi* links, this method reflects an acquired relationship (Fan, 2002). In the business world, because acquired *guanxi* (*guanxi* established through social activities) is most popular, this article focuses on social-based *guanxi*. Simply, we need to use *guanxi* practice to find *guanxi* or to establish *guanxi* base, and these *guanxi* practices contain a set of activities that follow Chinese social norms. Generally there are two phases to go from stranger to close *guanxi* partners: *guanxi* initiation phase and *guanxi* cultivation and maintenance phase.

2.4.1 *Guanxi* Practice During the Initiation Phase

The *guanxi* initiation phase is a process during which an outsider becomes an insider of a particular *guanxi* circle. People with a *guanxi* base include groups of people sharing commonalities (kinship can also be regarded as a group of people sharing commonalities). Inside a *guanxi* group is a *guanxi* network, and these insiders are called in-group members or in-network members. Insiders of the *guanxi* circle are treated very differently from outsiders in that insiders are trusted more and receive more help.

Therefore outsiders need to go through the group barrier and become insiders to obtain useful information and resources. The key point of *guanxi* initiation is to find the commonality (link point) and establish the *guanxi* base. In a collective society such as China, people feel emotional attachments with others who share common characteristics (Zhuang et al., 2010). Perceived similarity is proved to be an ancestor to *guanxi* establishment (Lee, Pae, & Wong, 2001). These similarities can be created by nature, but they can also be acquired by social activities such as knowing a person in common and dining at the same place, and so on.

2.4.2 *Guanxi* Practice in the Cultivation and Maintenance Phase

Just because a *guanxi* base or link has been created doesn't mean that an active *guanxi* has been established. People need to cultivate *guanxi* and maintain *guanxi* through *guanxi* practice. These practices are used to develop the quality of *guanxi* between individuals through the exchange of gifts and favors. *Guanxi* practices are formalized as a series of social activities or social rituals such as gift-giving, exchanging of favors, banquets, and so on (Yang, 1994). The Chinese believe that through these *guanxi* interactive behaviors, their *guanxi* state will be improved (Zhuang, Xi, & Tsang, 2010).

2.5 *GUANXI* EXCHANGE MECHANISMS

Because *guanxi* is based on reciprocal obligations and exchange of favors, it can be explained by social exchange theory (Yang & Wang, 2011). With this perspective, there are two basic things that we need to establish: (1) what exactly is being exchanged in this relationship and (2) under what rules?

2.5.1 *Renqing* (Favor)

Guanxi is a process of exchanging favors, and this kind of favor is called *renqing* in Chinese (exchanging resource in *guanxi*). Unlike in Western contexts, where favors refer only to tangible or specific things such as money, goods, or services, *renqing* can also include some abstracts such as opportunity, affection, and so on. When someone does you a favor, you will own him or her *renqing*. And you need to pay this *renqing* at the appropriate time. *Renqing* is the exchange resource in *guanxi* relationships. Compared with other resources in social exchange, such as goods, information, lands, and so on, *renqing* is a resource of high particularism and middle concreteness (Hwang, 1987). *Renqing* is highly particular because it can be repaid only by a particular person in particular way. Unlike other resources such as money, *renqing* can be transferred through people. And *renqing* can hardly be measured. Second, *renqing* is considered to be middle concrete because it can be repaid by tangible goods and also intangible affections.

Table 2.1 summarizes the differences between *renqing* resources and other common social exchange resources, such as money, service, goods, information, and so on.

Table 2.1 delineates the differences between *renqing* and other exchange resources in the following six aspects: value, measurement, favor return circle, process, transferability, and boundary. Common social exchange resources such as goods or information have certain prices. Although *renqing* contains emotional and beneficial elements, it can never be calculated objectively, so the *renqing* exchange is an unequal exchange. Subsequently, in common social exchange, when a partner returns the favor, the exchange process is finished, and this reciprocal action will be returned in a short time. However, because *renqing* cannot be clearly measured, one cannot pay off all the *renqing* he or she owes, and so the *renqing* exchange is an endless process. In addition, Chinese culture is oriented long term (Hofstede, 2001). A *renqing* favor does not need to be repaid immediately; you can return the favor when the other partner needs it. Therefore *renqing* is a long-term action. And, because *renqing* is a resource of high particularism, *renqing* exchange can take place only between particular people, although goods, money, and services are transformable resources. Lastly, unlike Westerners, who separate business and private favors, Chinese people mix the two relationships and will do a business favor to repay a personal *renqing* (see Hwang, 1987; Wang, 2007).

Table 2.1 Difference Between *Renqing* Resources and Common Social Exchange Resources

	***Renqing* Resources**	**Common Social Exchange Resources**	**Sources**
Value	Unequal value	Equal value	Hwang (1987)
Measurement	Can't calculated objectively	Have a certain price	Hwang (1987)
Favor return circle	Long term	Short term	Wang (2007)
Process	Endless process	Clear start and end points	Hwang (1987)
Transferability	Nontransferable	Transferable	Hwang (1987)
Boundary	Mix business and personal favors	Business and social relationships are separated.	Cao et al. (2014)

2.5.2 *Renqing* Rule

Guanxi is a mixed tie that contains emotional and utilitarian purposes. In terms of exchange, *guanxi* exchange respects *renqing* rules (Hwang, 1987), which are the social norms and behavior rules that *guanxi* partners need to follow during their reciprocal exchanges. Similar to trust and relationship commitments, which play very important roles in relationship marketing, *renqing* is the underlying mechanism of *guanxi* (Wang, 2007).

Renqing rules can be interpreted through two parts: reciprocity rules and empathy rules (Wang, 2007). Reciprocity rules refer to when *guanxi* partners are obliged to return favors as necessary. *Guanxi* is based on mutual benefits and interests, so when you receive a favor from someone, you need to pay it back at a future time. Furthermore, in a *guanxi* network, you need to help the insiders who are in trouble even if they don't ask for specific requests. If you refuse to return a favor, you will lose face (your social reputation), which could cause your *guanxi* relationship to end (Hwang, 1987). Unlike common social exchange, the favor exchanged in *guanxi* is not equal. According to the reciprocity rule, the favor returned always has higher value than what was received. The reciprocity rule indicates the obligation to return the favor; however, when to return this favor and in what way is another thing. The way to return favors should respect the empathy rule.

Empathy means the ability to see a situation from another person's perspective, which involves understanding, consideration, forgiveness, and *ganqing* (affectional attachment) toward others (Wang, 2007). In a *guanxi* relationship, there are usually two parts: a *renqing* allocator and a *renqing* petitioner. Because *renqing* return is a long-term situation and cannot be measured precisely, an empathic petitioner shouldn't ask for an immediately returned favor or equal-valued return favor. As for the allocator, being empathetic means figuring out the exactly need of petitioners and doing them favors at the appropriate time. China is a high-context country, and people prefer to present their desires obscurely. Consequently, the *renqing* allocator needs to do corresponding favors according to a particular situation even without petitioners' directly asking. The empathy rule here is similar to "anticipatory communication" (Wang, 2007). If you fail to interpret a petitioner's need, or pretend to not understand, you will be criticized for not understanding *renqing*.

2.5.3 *Xinyong* (Trustworthy) and *Mianzi* (Face)

Xinyong can be translated as "trustworthy" or "credible" in English. If we say someone has *xinyong*, it means this person is trustworthy and reliable.

Whether a person can fulfill his or her reciprocal obligation depends on his or her *xinyong* credit. Different from systems of trust in the West at the organizational level, *xinyong* is an interpersonal trust (Leung, Lai, Chan, & Wong, 2005) and is not based on written contract but a person's oral commitment. *Xinyong* is based on one's past reputation of returning favors, which is highly related to one's business ethical integrity (Hwang, 1987; Leung et al., 2005). People prefer to do a *renqing* exchange with one who has high *xinyong* credit, because he or she has shown the ability to respect *renqing* rules. One who does not have *xinyong* will lose his or her future opportunities to exchange favors.

People who violate the *renqing* rule in a *guanxi* exchange will not only lose *xinyong* but also lose *mianzi* (face). *Mianzi* refers to one's reputation, social stature, and the power to influence others in *guanxi* relationships. The Chinese place a high value on their *mianzi*, hence "saving *mianzi* rather than losing it becomes a primary objective in Chinese society" (Hwang, 1987).

2.6 *GUANXI*'S MAIN CHARACTERISTICS

Previously we introduced three *guanxi*-related concepts: *guanxi* state, *guanxi* practice, and *guanxi* exchange. This part focuses on *guanxi*'s main characteristics in order to differentiate it from other confusing concepts, such as pure interpersonal relationships, relationship marketing, and so forth.

2.6.1 Utilitarian Aspect

As discussed, *guanxi* is based on mutual interests and benefits. Therefore people establish *guanxi* for certain purposes. The *guanxi* process is full of reciprocal exchanges, and *guanxi* parties are bound by obligation and indebtedness (Yang, 1994). Therefore the utilitarian aspect is a main characteristic of *guanxi* that differs from common interpersonal relationships.

There are at least three main differences between *guanxi* and a pure interpersonal relationship: first, the reciprocal process is not always equal. As an old Chinese says, "The favor of a drop of water has been rewarded with the gratitude of a fountain of water": when we receive a favor, we should repay this favor with value added. This concept is deeply rooted in Chinese society and results in a social norm of profound reciprocity. Second, *guanxi* practice needs to comply with some existing rituals, such as gift exchanging, wining and dining, and so on. Maintaining *guanxi* is more formal than the cultivation of common personal relationships. Third, *guanxi* relationships are not a purely emotional attachment. People need to use *guanxi* to achieve certain goals, such as obtaining key information, rare resources, special service, and so on (see Chen, Ellinger, & Tian, 2011).

2.6.2 Emotional Aspect

Chinese people often use the word *ganqing* to indicate the emotional closeness of *guanxi* among parties in a network. *Ganqing* plays a very important role in *guanxi* interactions. This emotional closeness can be used as a key indicator to describe the quality of *guanxi* between two people. The more affection between each other, the better *guanxi* they have. *Guanxi* is not a pure utilitarian relationship; it contains affective commitment and a caring attitude toward others. Sometimes, people rely more on its emotional value than its utilitarian value (Wang, 2007). Individuals' emotional attachments can be improved through social activities such as wining and dining. Through frequent social interaction between parties, affectional bonds between parties strengthen, improving their *guanxi*.

Guanxi has always been regarded in Western research as a Chinese version of relationship marketing (Davies et al., 1995). Unlike simple transactional relationships, *guanxi* has many things in common with relationship marketing: trust and mutual understanding, cooperative behavior, development of networks, long-term orientation, and so on (Wang, 2007). *Guanxi* is quite different from Western relationship marketing, however, because of its unique emotional aspect. First, *guanxi* is a personal relationship that contains an affectional element. Unlike Western networks, which are commercial, *guanxi* is also a social network. People in *guanxi* relationship exchanges not only provide beneficial favors but also affection (feelings, care attitudes, etc.). Relationship marketing is an impersonal relationship that becomes established more on a firm level and is built only for commercial purpose with no personal or emotional aspects. Relationship marketing is much more rational than *guanxi*. Second, relationship marketing is universalistic. This relationship is open to any other commercial partner. Any potential business partners can build this relationship if they are willing to sign the contracts and respect them. But Chinese society is a low trust society(Fukuyama, 1995). Chinese people trust only people with whom they share *guanxi* or are inside their *guanxi* circle. The *guanxi* circle is a highly specific network. The Chinese treat insiders and outsiders totally differently in terms of trust. In *guanxi* relationships, people rely more on oral commitment than written contracts in relationship marketing efforts (see Wang, 2007).

2.7 *GUANXI* AND BUSINESS

The *guanxi* phenomenon is anchored in Chinese daily life. It contains a set of social norms (*renqing* rule) that heavily influence Chinese social behaviors and interpersonal interactions, including business behaviors. Many foreign managers regard *guanxi* as a rule of doing business in China. Indeed, many researches have pointed out that *guanxi* has a big influence in every aspect of the business domain, including relationship marketing, supply chain management, market performance, market channeling, and so on. Business people can benefit from their social networks with either government officials or business partners. This part focuses on *guanxi* and people looking for business interests (include investment, business opportunities, rare resources, etc.) through their *guanxi* networks.

Before we discuss its impact on business performance, one crucial question needs to be raised: because *guanxi* has been described as a relationship at the personal level, how does this personal relationship turn into a benefit at the organizational level?

In business circumstances, *guanxi* refers to the cross-organizational connections between each company's representatives. These persons are also called *channel-boundary personnel*, representing their company directly and communicating frequently with the other company's representatives (Park & Luo, 2001; Zhuang et al., 2010). *Guanxi* in business situations is also a reciprocal relationship based on mutual benefits, so when channel-boundary person A of company A does a personal favor for person B, who is a representative of company B, person B could return this favor by showing favoritism during a business exchange between company A and company B. This is how a corporate exchange can be personalized. In Western cultures, people always make a clear distinction between business interests and private interests, but such "business is business" behavior culture cannot be applied in Chinese firms. In a *guanxi* culture–dominated company, business exchange also involves *renqing* exchange (benefits and emotion). A personal obligation can be paid by business actions, which in turn increases corporate benefits. And, as discussed, unlike trust and commitment, the cornerstone of relationship management, Chinese people rely more on a personal trust—*xinren*—than contract trust or system trust at the organizational level. Personal reliability is always more important than confidence in corporations. So in China, people build personal *guanxi* first, then business relationships can be developed based on this good personal *guanxi*. Whereas, in Western cultures, personal relationships are always built after successful business cooperation.

Even though *guanxi* is in force, personal relationships do play an important role at the firm level; *guanxi* remains a personal asset and can hardly be transformed to an organizational property. *Guanxi*, which is a personal network, can be transferred only interpersonally, not from a person to an organization (Fan, 2002). When an employee leaves his or her company, his or her *guanxi* asset will be separated from the company at the same time. So, organizational *guanxi* is actually based on personal *guanxi* among cross-organizational boundaries staff (e.g., company representatives).

2.7.1 Business With Government *Guanxi*

Previous *guanxi* research (before 2000) focused on *guanxi*'s function in terms of government officials. Because the Chinese legal system is undeveloped and the business infrastructure is far from efficient, small and private companies need to rely on *guanxi* to get protection from risks caused by unstable investment environment. In such a situation, *guanxi* functions as a substitute for formal institutional support (Xin & Pearce, 1996). Companies can get benefits from government *guanxi* in the following four ways:

2.7.1.1 Resource Acquirement

The original Chinese economic system was based on a central planning economy, and still today the Chinese market is not totally opened. State-owned companies still contribute a large part to Chinese industrial output (50% in 1998 and 25% in 2011). Many rare resources, such as land, raw material, and special licenses, are strictly controlled by the central government and local governments. And these resources are usually not open to the public. Only people who have government *guanxi* (insiders of this *guanxi* circle) can access procurement of these rare resources (Davies et al., 1995).

2.7.1.2 Information Access

Because of underdeveloped business infrastructures, the information about government policy, regulation, and market trend is not publicly transparent. Much information is kept confidential, and only insiders have the access to it. Establishing *guanxi* with government officials is an important way to access key information and avoid environmental uncertainty (Davies et al., 1995).

2.7.1.3 Get Protection

In the background of weakened institutional forces and an unstable investment environment in China, especially before the 1990s, a close relationship with important government officials could get protection from unstable conditions and ward against appropriation or extortion (Xin & Pearce, 1996).

2.7.1.4 Antibureaucracy

The Chinese government has been criticized as bureaucratic and lacking efficiency. However, if you have *guanxi* with some officials, you can break this bureaucratic barrier and get a quick response for relevant formalities. *Guanxi* can help you save time and chase quick-moving business opportunities.

Early literature emphasized the *guanxi* between business people and government officials (Gu et al., 2008). This kind of *guanxi* has been regarded as a magic weapon enabling entrance into the Chinese market and providing a company strategic advantage. Such a view was formed during a time of imperfect legal systems and weakened institutional forces. Additionally, business-government *guanxi* was always involved in corruption. Because *guanxi* practice is a process of reciprocal exchange, if you want to get rare resources, rare information, special treatment, or protection, you needed to pay back monetary favors to key government officials. It's a money-power exchange trade, which causes unfair competition and has a negative impact on the whole market. However, as the economy has developed, the Chinese government has paid more and more attentions to laws and regulations in order to build a rational-legal system. In addition, the Chinese market is becoming more competitive with deeper marketization, so its government is decreasing its interference in the market. For these reasons, government *guanxi* is losing its importance for business development.

2.7.2 Business *Guanxi*

Guanxi has been proven to have a positive influence on business results, specifically financial performance including sales growth, sales trends, cost savings, market expansion, market share increasing, supply chain performance including supplier development, strategic purchasing, outsourcing, bullwhip effect reduction, and increasing company reputations. But how does *guanxi* influence business performance? The following points describe *guanxi*'s direct and indirect influences on business performance.

2.7.2.1 Direct Influence

This part presents the business behaviors that can be affected directly by *guanxi* behaviors and discusses how *guanxi* works.

2.7.2.1.1 Trust

Trust plays an important role in Western relationship marketing. Similarly, *guanxi* is highly related to trust. As described previously, *guanxi* exchange is based on social norms of obligation and reciprocity, and people need to respect these norms in order to keep *xinyong* and avoid losing face. Therefore *guanxi* can improve interpersonal trust (Lee et al., 2001; Leung et al., 2005). Trust can effectively avoid business interruptions caused by opportunistic behaviors (Gu et al., 2008).

2.7.2.1.2 Information Sharing

Guanxi reflects emotional feeling toward others. This emotional closeness promotes better interaction among business partners. Together with trust, good interaction encourages business partners to have open communication and to promote information-sharing behaviors. In addition, under *renqing* rules, good *guanxi* will lead to more reciprocal information exchange (Cai et al., 2010), including business opportunities and market trends, helping business performance (Cao et al., 2014; Yi & Ellis, 2000).

2.7.2.1.3 Resource Acquirement

The cooperative firms in *guanxi* networks have the possibility of accessing partners' resources to achieve resource complementarity. Reciprocal behaviors will take place in resource exchanges. Through *guanxi* links, distant people also can have the chance to have cooperative resources exchanges (Park & Luo, 2001).

2.7.2.1.4 Cost Savings

Cost savings related to *guanxi* practice can be produced in three ways: lower transaction costs, lower information research costs, and lower resource research costs. First, interpersonal trust in *guanxi* relationships produces reliability that can eliminate unnecessary administrative process to facilitate future transactions (Gu et al., 2008). Simplified transaction processes save transaction time and cost. Second, *guanxi* promotes cooperative behaviors, and lower transaction costs can be achieved by synergic practices between business partners (Cao et al., 2014). Additionally, because of more frequent information exchange produced by *guanxi* practices, information research cost decreases. Third, because *guanxi* networks permit access to partner resources, resource research costs also will be reduced by resource sharing.

2.7.2.1.5 Satisfaction

Because *guanxi* contains reciprocal exchanges for in-circle members, exchange partners can obtain increasing satisfaction through these mutual benefits. This satisfaction is gained by acquiring necessary information and resources from a partner's company. In addition, the nature of *guanxi* is a close relationship that increases satisfaction naturally (Leung et al., 2005).

2.7.2.1.6 Interdependence

Once a partner invests in a *guanxi* relationship, the other partner has to pay back and invest more into this relationship. Otherwise, he or she will lose face because of violating the *renqing* rule. As the investment in special assets increase, business partners become more dependent on each other.

2.7.2.1.7 Negotiation

Better interaction in *guanxi* relationships can promote better negotiation. Moreover, the affection attachment, good interactions, and interlocking mutual obligations between *guanxi* partners results in less conflict and coercive power use (including reward, referent, expert, etc.) when facing disagreements. *Guanxi* relationships are useful to reduce and resolve conflicts (Chen et al., 2011).

2.7.2.1.8 Flexibility

A close *guanxi* relationship among business partners can achieve a better negotiation and control benefits with a set of reciprocal obligations that one partner can use to influence other's decision behaviors. This control behavior can help companies to anticipate future exchanges and to make real-time exchanges, increasing company's flexibility when facing uncertain environments (Gu et al., 2008).

2.7.2.1.9 Cooperation

Based on the *renqing* rule, reciprocal obligations are based on mutual interest by both partners. Furthermore, trust and emotion mechanisms in *guanxi* increase the willingness to cooperate. Together with *guanxi*'s influence on using noncoercive power and on avoiding conflicts, *guanxi* contributes a lot to firms' cooperating (Zhuang et al., 2010).

2.7.2.1.10 Coordination

Coordination refers to the synchronization of business activities among partners. It's believed that the trust and emotional ties built in *guanxi* can increase the frequency of information exchange, which in turn increases the coordination between *guanxi* partners.

2.7.2.2 Indirect Influence

Regarding key indicators of business performance (such as financial performance and marketing performance), *guanxi*'s influences are not direct but occur through mediators who have been introduced previously.

2.7.2.2.1 Long-Term Orientation

Compared with other countries, Chinese society puts a great value on a long-term orientation (Hofstede & Hofstede, 2001). Satisfaction, mutual trust, and interdependence help to promote companies' future collaboration in the long term.

2.7.2.2.2 Financial Performance

Financial performance is one of the most important indicators of business performance. This includes sales growth, net profits growth, cost savings, and so forth. Cost decreases can be achieved by transaction cost savings, information research savings, and resource research savings. Long-term orientations can increase relationship quality and, together with controlled behaviors in *guanxi* relationships, have a positive effect on financial performance (Lee et al., 2001). In addition, through *guanxi* networks, more business opportunities for financial resources will open for exchange partners. And through the access of key information about market trends and the cooperative behaviors with business partners, companies will find out about real-time market changes and be able to quickly respond. Such agility augments a company's financial performance, especially sales growth (Gu et al., 2008).

2.7.2.2.3 Market Performance

Similar to financial performance, market performance is also a key indicator that reflects business performance. Market performance can be shown by the increase of market share. *Guanxi* has been proven to have a positive impact on market channels (Zhuang et al., 2010) and develops a firm's effectiveness and responsive capability. In this way, a firm's market share will increase. Cooperative and coordinated behaviors in *guanxi* networks can both improve financial performance and increase market share by sharing market information and benefits control (Gu et al., 2008).

2.7.2.2.4 Supply Chain Performance

Supply chain performance can be improved through *guanxi* practices in terms of supplier development, strategic purchasing, and outsourcing (Lee & Humphreys, 2007). Supplier development is achieved through regularly exchanged favors between *guanxi* partners. Long-term orientations, open communication, and a cooperative culture in *guanxi* lead the development of strategic purchasing. And trust fostered in *guanxi* encourages companies to outsource to their business partners. Furthermore, because of close relationships and frequent information sharing, the bullwhip effect will decrease and supply chain performance will be improved (Cao et al., 2014).

Table 2.2 shows *guanxi*'s influence on business performance based on the previous explanations.

Table 2.2 *Guanxi*'s Influence on Business Performance

Guanxi's Key Elements	Mediate Influence on Business Performance	Final Influence on Business Performance
Reciprocal obligation	Trust Information exchange Resource exchange Cost saving Satisfaction Interdependence Cooperation	Long-term orientation Financial performance Market performance Supply chain performance
Emotional closeness	Trust Information exchange Satisfaction Cooperation Coordination	
Interaction	Information exchange Satisfaction Negotiation Flexibility	

2.8 CONCLUSION

Guanxi (Chinese interpersonal relationship) culture plays a very important role in Chinese society. Firstly, as a product of Confucius Culture, *guanxi* is deeply rooted in Chinese daily life. Secondly, due to the inefficiency and ineffectiveness of Chinese business infrastructures and related institutions, Chinese people rely more on personal *guanxi* for commercial protection and risk avoidance.

Guanxi originated in clanship. It referred to family relationship and developed later into social relations. *Guanxi* is established on *guanxi* base (such as kinship, neighbors, coworkers, classmates). However, only *guanxi* cannot necessarily produce active *guanxi* (i.e., using *guanxi* to have things done). *Guanxi* must be cultivated and maintained through a set of social activities like dinning and winning.

The process of maintaining *guanxi* is called *guanxi* practice, in which people exchange *renqing* favor. As a specific *guanxi* exchange resource, *renqing* includes not only tangible things like valuable goods and money, but intangible affections and opportunities as well. *Guanxi* exchange respects a set of social norms which is called *renqing* rule. *Renqing* rule focuses on reciprocity, which means *guanxi* partners are obliged to return favors as necessary. If one partner failed to do so, he or she will lose *xinyong* (personal credit) and *mianzi* (face, social statue, and reputation).

Guanxi contains both a utilitarian aspect and an emotional aspect. On one hand, unlike pure personal relationship, *guanxi* is based on mutual interests, and people establish *guanxi* is for certain beneficial purposes. On the other hand, *guanxi* contains affective commitment and caring attitude toward others, so emotional closeness can be used as a key indicator to describe the quality of *guanxi*. *Guanxi*'s emotional aspect differs it from Western relationship marketing.

As the development of Chinese economy, it is more and more common that people seek business interests (include investment, business opportunities, rare resources, etc.) by using *guanxi* network. In business circumstances, *guanxi* refers to the cross-organizational connections between each company's representatives. It is believed that a personal obligation can be paid by business actions, which in turn increase corporate benefits. In other words, closer *guanxi* (frequent *guanxi* interactions and *renqing* exchanges) between two companies' channel-boundary persons could lead more collaborative behaviors between companies. And these collaborative behaviors (include mutual trust, information sharing, resource acquirement, cost saving, negotiation, etc.) could turn ultimately into a better business performance in terms of finance, marketing, and supply chain. So for Western people who want to invest in China, or doing business with Chinese partners, *guanxi* practice with key personnel is an inevitable process.

REFERENCES

Alston, J. P. (1989). Wa, guanxi, and inhwa: Managerial principles in Japan, China, and Korea. *Business Horizons*, *32*(2), 26–31.

Ambler, T., Styles, C., & Xiucun, W. (1999). The effect of channel relationships and guanxi on the performance of inter-province export ventures in the People's Republic of China. *International Journal of Research in Marketing*, *16*(1), 75–87.

Cai, S., Jun, M., & Yang, Z. (2010). Implementing supply chain information integration in China: The role of institutional forces and trust. *Journal of Operations Management*, *28*(3), 257–268.

Cao, Q., Baker, J., & Schniederjans, D. (2014). Bullwhip effect reduction and improved business performance through guanxi: An empirical study. *International Journal of Production Economics*, *158*, 217–230.

Chen, H., Ellinger, A. E., & Tian, Y. (2011). Manufacturer-supplier guanxi strategy: An examination of contingent environmental factors. *Industrial Marketing Management*, *40*(4), 550–560.

Davies, H., Leung, T. K., Luk, S. T., & Wong, Y. H. (1995). The benefits of "Guanxi": The value of relationships in developing the Chinese market. *Industrial Marketing Management*, *24*(3), 207–214.

Fan, Y. (2002). Questioning guanxi: Definition, classification and implications. *International Business Review*, *11*(5), 543–561.

Fukuyama, F. (1995). *Trust: The social virtues and the creation of prosperity*. New York, NY: Free Press. (pp. 61–67).

Gu, F. F., Hung, K., & Tse, D. K. (2008). When does guanxi matter? Issues of capitalization and its dark sides. *Journal of Marketing*, *72*(4), 12–28.

Guthrie, D. (1998). The declining significance of guanxi in China's economic transition. *The China Quarterly*, *154*, 254–282.

Hofstede, G. H., & Hofstede, G. (2001). *Culture's consequences: Comparing values, behaviors, institutions and organizations across nations*. Sage.

Hwang, K. K. (1987). Face and favor: The Chinese power game. *American Journal of Sociology*, *92*, 944–974.

Lee, D. J., Pae, J. H., & Wong, Y. H. (2001). A model of close business relationships in China (guanxi). *European Journal of Marketing*, *35*(1/2), 51–69.

Lee, P. K., & Humphreys, P. K. (2007). The role of Guanxi in supply management practices. *International Journal of Production Economics*, *106*(2), 450–467.

Leung, T. K. P., Lai, K. H., Chan, R.Y., & Wong, Y. H. (2005). The roles of xinyong and guanxi in Chinese relationship marketing. *European Journal of Marketing*, *39*(5/6), 528–559.

Park, S. H., & Luo, Y. (2001). Guanxi and organizational dynamics: Organizational networking in Chinese firms. *Strategic Management Journal*, *22*(5), 455–477.

Wang, C. L. (2007). Guanxi vs. relationship marketing: Exploring underlying differences. *Industrial Marketing Management*, *36*(1), 81–86.

Xin, K. K., & Pearce, J. L. (1996). Guanxi: Connections as substitutes for formal institutional support. *Academy of Management Journal*, *39*(6), 1641–1658.

Yang, M. M. H. (1994). *Gifts, favors, and banquets: The art of social relationships in China*. Cornell, NY: Cornell University Press.

Yang, Z., & Wang, C. L. (2011). Guanxi as a governance mechanism in business markets: Its characteristics, relevant theories, and future research directions. *Industrial Marketing Management*, *40*(4), 492–495.

Yi, L. M., & Ellis, P. (2000). Insider-outsider perspectives of guanxi. *Business Horizons*, *43*(1), 25–30.

Zhuang, G., Xi, Y., & Tsang, A. S. (2010). Power, conflict, and cooperation: The impact of *guanxi* in Chinese marketing channels. *Industrial Marketing Management*, *39*(1), 137–149.

CHAPTER 3

Interpreting China's Model for Business: Roles of Corruption, Favoritism, Reliability, and Responsibility

Duane Windsor
Rice University, Houston, TX, United States

The contribution of this chapter is to provide a description and an interpretation of China's evolving model for business. The description and interpretation emphasize these four key dimensions of business in the Chinese context: corruption, favoritism (including *guanxi*), reliability (political), and corporate social responsibility (CSR). The author argues that compiling empirical information about these four dimensions within the context of the changing Chinese political economy should help with scholarly understanding of China's model for business. There is a considerable empirical research on Chinese firms (partly listed in the chapter's references), much of it being published by Chinese scholars (national and ethnic), appearing in English-language business and economics literature. The contribution of this chapter is to structure that increasingly large literature into a reasonably synoptic and revealing description and interpretation of the Chinese business model as guided by the party and state.

The methodology of the chapter involves two approaches. The first approach is identification of literature on the four dimensions of the business model—corruption, favoritism, reliability, and CSR—within an interpretive understanding of the Chinese political economy. The second approach is more tenuous, due to the apparent uniqueness of the Chinese context. This chapter positions the identified research within a proposed theory of comparative political economy relevant to China's situation. The term political economy refers to the interaction of political and economic institutions and the influence of this interaction on other social institutions, in a specific country. Each country has a political economy, as just defined. Culture is one such institution, defined as shared norms

The China Business Model. DOI: http://dx.doi.org/10.1016/B978-0-08-100750-1.00003-6

and patterns of behaviors, illustrated by customs and traditions, and cognitive understandings of those norms and behaviors constituting a group or community identity and typically acquired by socialization. Nationality and culture are not necessarily coincident (see Zolfaghari, Möllering, Clark, & Dietz, 2016). Modern China is heir to an ancient civilization and rich cultural tradition, and has the world's largest population. The literature concerning "varieties of capitalism" identifies a reasonably wide range of countries that can be classified under the definition of capitalism; there is no single unified model of capitalism (De Leon, 2015; Detomasi, 2015). However, China falls well outside the typical range of such capitalist political economies in being in transition from former command economy to present state capitalism toward possible future market capitalism.

The proposed positioning involves three key dimensions. One dimension concerns privately owned Chinese firms, as distinct from the state-owned enterprises (SOEs), whether listed on the Shanghai Stock Exchange (SSE) or the Shenzhen Stock Exchange (SZSE) or not. The chapter's particular interest is information available about the motives and behavior of private business owners and managers (Guo, Jiang, Kim, & Xu, 2014). The second dimension concerns the domestic institutional context—political, economic, and social—within which those owners and managers operate. China is a single-party political regime, grounded in Marxism–Leninism–Maoism ideology and practices, if no longer strictly speaking a communist regime. China is neither a communist-style command economy nor a full-blown market economy, but rather is positioned somewhere between the two models in a way that is difficult to define with precision. China may or may not be in true transition to a market economy; it may possibly remain strongly oriented toward communism. The third dimension concerns identifying the most relevant political economies to which China can be compared. China is unique—politically, economically, and socially; so comparisons will be weak at best. The chapter suggests that the BRICS (China being a member of that five-country category) with particular attention to Russia and countries of Southeast and South Asia, especially Vietnam and India are the most reasonable comparison countries, although it is vital to bear in mind China's essential uniqueness and the paucity of readily available comparative data. Much available research tends to focus on specific countries (China, India, Russia, or Vietnam for instance) rather than on cross-country comparisons.

The remainder of the chapter comprises four additional sections. The next section provides some basic relevant information about China's political economy: economic, political, and socio-cultural. The third section provides a conceptual framework for interpreting Chinese conditions. The fourth section discusses research findings about the Chinese business model with emphasis on the roles of corruption, favoritism (including *guanxi*), reliability (political), and CSR. Favoritism is closely intertwined with *guanxi* networking. Reliability involves how party officials view the pro-regime loyalty of business owners and managers. Chinese practice of CSR may arguably be closely influenced by corruption and reliability. The concluding section summarizes the chapter's arguments.

3.1 SOME BASIC, RELEVANT INFORMATION ABOUT CHINA

In March 2016, China's premier Li Keqiang, who has the leading responsibility for the economy, publicly announced that more market-opening reforms will be forthcoming, including (1) reducing the state-owned steel and coal industries, (2) further reforming the financial system to be more market oriented, and (3) further reducing the government's role in business (Ecns.com, 2016; *Houston Chronicle*, 2016). This information helps to confirm that China remains on the path to marketization and privatization.

The emphasis of this chapter is on the motives and behavior of private business owners and managers in the Chinese setting. A secondary interest is on the motives and behavior of the managers of Chinese SOEs, by way of comparison (Bruton, Peng, Ahlstrom, Stan, & Xu, 2015; Zhu, Liu, & Lai, 2016). In the prevailing theory of a firm operating in market economies (whether privately owned or publicly traded), managers seek financial performance results within conditions shaped by their cognitive understanding (Mele & Ogunyemi, 2014), pressures from formal and informal institutions, and pressures from stakeholders and media. These conditions likely generate role dissonance for managers (Benjamin, Nisim, & Segev, 2015).

The "varieties of capitalism" theory accepts a range of such conditions across countries within the Organisation for Economic Co-operation and Development (OECD) (34 in 2015), with extensions to other contexts. Conditions in China approach the extreme limit of this prevailing framing in that cognitive understanding arguably has been shaped by both socio-cultural traditions and explicit social control by a communist party which has effectively suppressed activism and media. Compensation, governance, philanthropy, political influence, regulation, and taxation arguably do not have the same meaning or role in China as in the OECD (adding Singapore and Taiwan as emerging economies which are not in the OECD to Japan and South Korea which are in the OECD), or in the rest of East Asia (Chua & Wellman, 2015; Cumming, Fleming, Johan, & Takeuchi, 2010) including Hong Kong as a special situation (Connor, 2014).

In October 2015, 12 countries agreed to a Trans-Pacific Partnership (TPP) trade agreement: Australia, Brunei, Canada, Chile, Japan, Malaysia, Mexico, New Zealand, Peru, Singapore, United States, and Vietnam. Japan, Singapore, and Vietnam are included; China and Taiwan are not members of this recent TPP agreement.

The World Factbook (U.S. CIA, n.d.) estimated China's population at about 1.367 billion and India's population at about 1.252 billion (July 2015), although a higher growth rate in India might lead to a reversal of these first and second positions sometime in the future. *The World Factbook* identifies the government of China as a Communist state; India is a federal republic. Hong Kong is a special administrative region within the People's Republic of China (PRC), and identified as a limited democracy. This chapter is not directly concerned with Hong Kong enterprises, or the Hong Kong exchanges. China is not ethnically homogeneous; there are various minority groups (as was the case in the now disintegrated USSR).

Measured by estimated 2015 gross domestic product (GDP), in US dollars, China is the world's second largest economy at $11.4 trillion after the United States at $17.97 trillion. Japan ($4.1 trillion), Germany ($3.4 trillion), and the United Kingdom ($2.9 trillion), the next three national economies in size, are much smaller on this measure (Statista, n.d.). The GDP of the 28-country European Union (EU), which is larger than the 19-country eurozone, aggregates to about 13.1 trillion euros. Depending on conversion rate to US dollar, the EU economy is somewhat larger than China's economy (Statista, n.d.). China's growth rate has slowed recently, attributed in part to shifting from investment and manufacturing expansion toward consumption and services for the population (Pylas, 2016).

China is an emerging (or industrializing) market in transition from a command communism approach to a more free market approach. One empirical condition in support of this conventional characterization is emergence of privately owned enterprises (such as Alibaba Group, Dalian Wanda Group, Haier, and Lenovo Group) alongside important SOEs and significantly state-influenced and politically connected private enterprises (Chang & Wong, 2004; Xia & Walker, 2015). However, the present situation is better appreciated as a party model for business rather than a business model, in the sense that one might expect varieties across the OECD. Chief elements of this Chinese model for business involve political reliability (to the party) and CSR practiced through extracted philanthropy, in addition to realities of corruption (commercial and governmental) and favoritism. For example, the warehouses of Rui Hui International Logistics exploded in Tianjin (Binhai New Area). Corruption and favoritism explain how ineffective regulation permitted unsafe conditions to persist until there was a disaster. The Fonterra-Sanlu IJV milk scandal in which melamine was added to milk to mimic proteins led to a terrible scandal in adulterated infant formula powdered product, resulting in the bankruptcy of Sanlu and evidence suggesting absence of testing by Fonterra, a New Zealand company (Chen, Zhang, & Delaurentis, 2014; Pavlovich, Sinha, & Rodrigues, 2016). Here again, within China corruption and favoritism for Sanlu may have been at work, with Fonterra unable to exercise closer supervision of a Chinese partner.

The information provided above gives a general picture of Chinese political economy. That general picture is one of uniqueness, making useful comparisons to the other BRICS or to other countries in Southeast and South Asia difficult, compounded by the difficulty of finding useful cross-country comparative data.

3.2 INTERPRETIVE FRAMEWORK FOR EVALUATING THE CHINESE MODEL FOR BUSINESS

In addition to providing a general description of the Chinese political economy, in a process of evolution toward marketization and privatization within a one-party regime itself evolving away from communism, the author argues that one must formulate a reasonable interpretive framework for evaluating the Chinese model for business. The framework formulated in this section emphasizes corruption, favoritism, reliability, and CSR as aspects of the business model highlighted in recent empirical studies. That empirical literature, however, deals with these aspects essentially separately as standalone considerations. This section seeks to provide a better integration of the four aspects.

The Chinese regime's approach for its economic transition since the reforms under Deng Xiaoping might be characterized as either "state capitalism" or a "socialist market economy." Under either label, there is a dominant state-owned sector and a state-influenced and state-guided as well as regulated privately owned sector. In Russia, for comparison, the state-owned sector was dismantled through privatization by a now displaced democratic regime; and the authoritarian Putin regime has been emphasizing recovery of ownership and control of natural resources (Dufy, 2015; Rutland, 2015). Even a "constitutional democracy" formally defined can be quite illiberal in actual practice (Innes, 2015). One study argues that the Chinese regime, characterized as a "shareholding state," has morphed into a shareholder and institutional investor in the Chinese economy and shifted to financialization of economic management of ownership, assets, and public investments (Wang, 2015). That study characterizes this specific shift as politically endogenous to Chinese conditions.

Put simply, the state controls the economy through a unique vertical economic structure, organized top-down (Li, Liu, & Wang, 2012). In this model, the SOEs control key upstream industries and markets, while downstream industries and markets have been opened to private competition. Li, Liu, and Wang report that the SOEs have outperformed private firms since c.2000, whereas the private firms outperformed the SOEs in the 1990s. Those authors argue that the upstream SOEs have benefited from international trade more than the downstream private firms through the abundance of relatively cheap labor in China. Recent reports suggest that China's manufacturing costs are rising significantly (AlixPartners, 2013), and this increase is one of the drivers for relocation of production activities to other countries viewed as having relatively lower costs (Das, 2015; Hwang & Chen, 2016; Rivoli, 2015; Sacchetto & Andrijasevic, 2015).

The "varieties of capitalism" interpretation, anchored in the OECD, should be expanded to recognize newer varieties of state capitalism. One study distinguishes between the four varieties of state capitalism: (1) wholly owned SOEs; (2) the state as a majority investor; (3) the state as a minority investor; and (4) the state as strategic supporter of specific sectors (Musacchio, Lazzarini, & Aguilera, 2015). China appears to combine these various approaches. One taxonomy of political regimes (Mukand & Rodrik, 2015) uses the three dimensions of property rights, political rights, and civil rights (meaning equality before the law across individuals and minorities). Liberal democracy combines these three dimensions. In this theory of political regimes, elites seek to protect property rights and the majority seeks to obtain political rights. Electoral democracies may not automatically include civil rights as minorities lack the resources and numbers to be effective in bargaining for those rights. Industrialization emphasizes class cleavages; decolonization emphasizes identity cleavages.

This author argues that the Chinese regime dominates key property rights upstream while allowing privatization of nonkey property rights downstream, and the party functions to appear to represent the majority indirectly; civil rights particularly in the form of protest and access to Internet information are regulated for protection of the party.

There are two points of comparison. The BRICS category puts China in a set of emerging countries that meet periodically in an invitation-only summit for governmental discussions. Russia is the closest country within the BRICS for comparison with China. Both Russia and China are formerly communist regimes. The other point of comparison is the countries in Southeast Asia, among which Vietnam as a formerly communist regime is the closest country for comparison with China. North Korea is too extreme an example of a communist regime that continues to be a totalitarian state and uninterested in privatization steps for useful comparison to China. The term BRICs (Kiely, 2015), not including South Africa, was used until 2010, when addition of South Africa resulted in a shift to the term BRICS (Robinson, 2015). While Cuba may be in a similar situation of transition away from communism like China, Cuba is just starting that transition and is relatively isolated in the Caribbean and does not begin to approach the economic importance and population size of China, Russia, or Vietnam (Backer, 2015; Villalobos, 2014–2015). Cuba is thus not a useful comparison case.

A continuum for comparative political economy analysis leaves North Korea at one end-point as the pure totalitarian regime (control passing within a family) engaged in state terrorism and Vietnam as the other end-point as the centralized one-party-state in the hands of pragmatists and technocrats seeking to attract foreign direct investment (FDI) to support economic development. Russia, centralizing control of rich natural resources, is engaged in a strategic policy of revanchism to reverse territorial disintegration. Identifying a mid-point along the continuum, Russia lies somewhat toward North Korea, while China lies somewhat toward Vietnam. The Eastern European countries, once dominated by or part of the disintegrated USSR, are "westernizing"; and the Central Asian countries, once part of the USSR, are also following separate paths little influenced by or connected to the example of China. The importance of the continuum is that it helps to reveal that China is a unique and original case, uniqueness making interpretation and comparison challenging.

There is literature on the various comparison countries, both among the BRICS (Lopes, 2015) and among the countries in the region. Vietnam is also following a path of economic liberalization, in which the country's provinces have been playing an important role in experimentation (Hansen, 2016; Schmitz, Tuan, Hang, & McCulloch, 2015; Yang, Ramstetter, Tsaur, & Ngoc Phan, 2015). North Korea, a militarized one-party state technically still at war with South Korea and its allies (there is an armistice in place) and engaged in nuclear weapons and long-range missile development, suffers periodically from what amounts to state-induced famine and incompetence (1994–2000 and 2010–2012) while a prison population of about 200,000 is subjected to penal starvation (Howard-Hassmann, 2012; H. Lee, 2015). North Korean refugee survey responses suggest that there was some marketization following the 1994–2000 famine (Haggard & Noland, 2010). The same responses suggest increasing inequality, corruption, and internal debate about pathways to social status and income—and widespread dissatisfaction with the regime (Haggard & Noland, 2010). Singapore (Huat, 2015; Rodan, 2015) has used SOEs transforming into global enterprises and sovereign wealth funds (as a strategy) to protect the domestic economy and also support political stability under the center-right People's Action Party (PAP) founded in 1954 by Lee Kuan Yew and in power since 1959. The PAP has a social democratic orientation in its domestic policies.

In Singapore, sovereign wealth funds contribute to government social expenditures without having to increase taxes (Huat, 2015). Sovereign wealth funds globally hold about $6.65 trillion dollars (Alhashel, 2015). Although the motives of fund managers appear to be economic rather than political, there is conflicting evidence concerning whether such funds typically increase economic value for the owning governments or not (Aguilera, Capape, & Santiso, 2016; Alhashel, 2015). Poor fund performance might result in no economic gains or possibly even economic losses to the owning governments, for whom fund managers are agents.

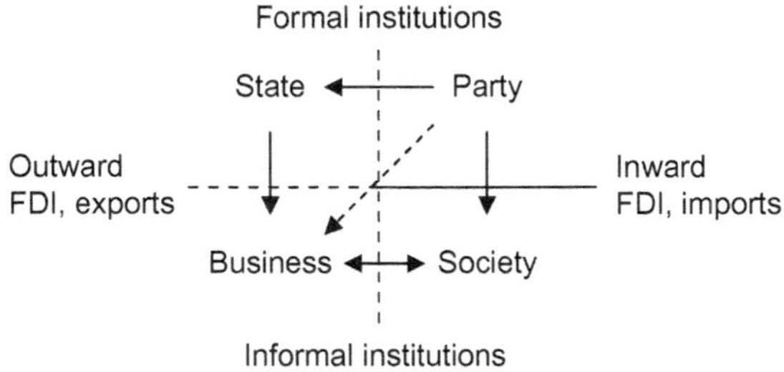

Figure 3.1 Key considerations in interpreting China's model for business.

Fig. 3.1 provides a depiction of the key considerations involved in an interpretation of China's model for business. The figure differentiates between the two formal institutions of party and state, and the two informal institutions of society and business. One can think of party, state, society, and business as four sectors of the Chinese political economy. The term formal institution refers only to the party and the state. The term informal institutions is adopted to convey that in Marxist–Leninist–Maoist ideology, society and any form of private enterprise exist only at the permission and design of the party. The essential attribute of the Chinese situation is that the regime is a modernizing totalitarian one-party state that directly or indirectly attempts to control everything in the country, releasing such control at its discretion. The party dominates the state and dominates society; the party influences business both through the state and through infiltration of corporate governance—shown through a dashed line from party to business. The top elite of the party, advancing to power through nondemocratic processes, is in effective control of the country, with a judiciary (which in reality is not yet independent) and a legislature which in reality can change laws without respect to constitutional principles. As mentioned earlier, the party and state are formal institutions (Holmes, Miller, Hitt, & Salmador, 2013), while there are informal institutions such as kinship networks (Meyer & Lu, 2013) and *guanxi* (personal networks of influence through favors) in business and society, which may reach into the state if not the party. This chapter does not predict how the political system will progress in relationship to market economy development, as prediction is difficult. As Fig. 3.1 depicts, the party is dominant and effectively insulated from other pressures (in theory, if not in practice); pressures operate through the perceptions and preferences of the party leadership.

Interpretation of constructs and behaviors such as business–government relations, corporate political activity, or corporate philanthropy requires conceptual positioning within the motives, goals, and practices of the Chinese one-party-state system. The existing literature appears to contain conflicting views concerning the motives and goals of the regime with respect to political reform and anticorruption reform (Chen & Cao, 2016; Jiahong, 2016; Kipnis, 2016; Ortmann & Thompson, 2016; Tian & Slocum, 2016; Yang, 2016). Rather the motives and goals of the regime are to maintain party control of the country through the process of economic development, requiring a controlled and guided market-like economy—at least, as long as possible. It is in this sense that there is a modernized version of a totalitarian regime characterized by one set of authors as authoritarian capitalism (Hofman, Moon, & Wu, 2015). This modernization of control reflects the history of the party since taking power in 1949. Totalitarianism is now pragmatic with respect to means. Yet, the Chinese regime undertakes to acquire key resource positions abroad as in Africa (Hudson, 2014).

Economic arrangements reflect regime political preferences: "... monopoly control in the Chinese political economy is not simply an economic phenomenon but also a phenomenon deeply embedded in a comprehensive system of power that draws from the legacy of a centrally planned economy and from Chinese societal traditions" (Duan & Saich, 2014, letter). The state controls strategic sectors and releases nonstrategic sectors to private actors through a kind of "bifurcated capitalism" varying considerably by sector (Hsueh, 2016). Ideological orientation and strategic control will presumably tend to attenuate over time with new generations of more pragmatic leaders (Wu, 2015).

This chapter generally follows the political history interpretation provided by Yang (1998) and the economic history interpretation provided by Coase and Wang (2013). The Mao era was from 1949 (establishment of the PRC) to September 1976 (when Mao Zedong died). This era was a communist-style command economy dominated by a full-blown totalitarian one-party communist regime under Mao's personal and ideological control (Yang, 1998, p. 137). The defining characteristic of a communist regime is the rationalization of revolutionary actions and policies through Marxist–Leninist interpretation. The Chinese communists explained revolutionary history as two stages: democratic revolution (achieved in 1949) and socialist revolution (initiated in 1956) (Yang, 1998, p. 138). Coase and Wang date post-Mao reform from the end of 1976 and transition to a market economy by the end of the 1990s, with China joining the World Trade Organization (WTO) in 2001. Ramo (2004) termed this reform process the "Beijing Consensus" to characterize a state-dominated Chinese economic development model different from the "Washington Consensus" among the IMF, World Bank, and US government promoting market-oriented reforms.

Coase and Wang suggest two phases of reform efforts. The central regime in Beijing initiated the first phase in 1978 with the explicit goal of revitalizing the state sector and thereby saving socialism. Hua Guofeng, Mao's designated successor who arrested the "Gang of Four" and ended the Cultural Revolution, emphasized heavy industry investment. At the end of 1978, Deng Xiaoping and Chen Yun came to power in place of

Hua Guofeng and changed direction. At the same time, left alone by the regime, private farming, township and village enterprises, urban private businesses, and Special Economic Zones were transforming the economy through grassroots initiatives. The student democracy movement (Tiananmen Square protest) occurred in 1989, then in 1992, after Deng Xiaoping's southern tour, regional competition generated a market economy. There was a price reform in 1992, a tax reform in 1994, and privatization of SOEs in the mid-1990s (Li, Vertinsky, & Zhou, 2004). The result, according to Coase and Wang (2013), was a more integrated common national market. There are 32 provinces, 282 municipalities, 2862 counties, 19,522 towns, and 14,677 villages according to Coase and Wang's figures. Competition meant multiple economic experiments throughout the country (see Dai, Alon, & Jiao, 2015, on the pharmaceutical industry in China).

Coase and Wang (2013) argue that the Chinese regime is communist only in name, and has transitioned to a one-party state and the most recent presidents are no longer charismatic "strongman" leaders. Radical ideology has been succeeded by a more pragmatic political philosophy. Deng reduced stress on class struggle, emphasized efficiency and prosperity, supported rule of law but not criticism of the regime, and increased economic and spiritual attention to the Western advanced countries (Yang, 1998, p. xii). A speech by Deng (Party Center's work conference, December 13, 1978) entitled *Liberate Our Minds, Seek Truth From Facts, and United to Look Forward* emphasized that "Any party, any country, or any nation, if its mind is bound by doctrines and superstitions, cannot advance, and it will lose its vital life and eventually die away" (Yang, 1998, pp. 204–205).

Yang (1998, p. xiii) criticized the "... ultimate futility of trying to combine a market economy with a Leninist political system." There is an active debate concerning whether China's political regime is moving toward a constitutional democracy. One view is that China is an authoritarian regime seeking to preserve a one-party monopoly of power by promoting economic liberalization (Bell, 2015; Chen & Kinzelbach, 2015; Minzner, 2015). Another team of authors recently characterizes the regime as authoritarian capitalism (Hofman et al., 2015). An alternative view is that the foundations for future democracy can be discerned in a process of development (Miquel, Qian, Xu, & Yao, 2015; Owen, 2015). Assessment is difficult (Cooper & Farooq, 2015), in part because what appear to be "democracies" may be in reality "illiberal" as has been argued about Hungary (Innes, 2015). The task in this chapter is less to assess political development and more to characterize China's business model in this transition process (see Huang & Chen, 2016). In this regard, I emphasize a timeless methodological point made by Yang (1998, p. 84): "Politics entails complexity and paradox, and is not always subject to simple laws of causality as contemporary politicians claim and later political observers believe." Although in late 1978, Deng stressed "truth from facts" he reportedly regarded this principle as the "essence of Marxism" when it might be characterized as "a traditional Chinese teaching" (Coase & Wang, 2013). During a speech in early 1979 (Party Center's theoretical conference, March 30, 1979) entitled *Persist in the Four Cardinal Principles* Deng emphasized the socialist road, the proletarian dictatorship, Communist Party leadership, and Marxism–Leninism–Maoism thought (Yang, 1998, pp. 207–208). More recently, the Chinese regime has turned more to military-naval development and territorial claims, as occurring in the South China Sea (Dittmer, 2015).

3.3 ASSESSMENT OF FOUR DIMENSIONS OF BUSINESS MOTIVES AND BEHAVIOR

Fig. 3.1 in the Section 3.2 provided a perspective on the Chinese political economy emphasizing the formal institutions of party and state and the informal institutions of business and society. The party remains dominant both politically and ideologically in Chinese life. This perspective is applied in this section to four basic considerations affecting business motives and behavior: corruption, favoritism, reliability, and responsibility. State, party, and business in China are infected with corruption, which may be pervasive below the party's top elite. Kinship networks and *guanxi* create favoritism and nepotism, which may be emulated by foreign firms attempting to curry influence. Politics are about reliability in terms of loyalty to the party. Responsibility is defined in China in terms of "philanthropic" contributions deemed desirable directly or indirectly by party officials, but this definition does not automatically correspond to Western conceptions.

A survey of over 600 business students in Canada found a significant difference between female Canadians in particular and Chinese from either the mainland or Taiwan. The Chinese considered it more appropriate to use ethically questionable negotiation strategies. However, Canadian males were also more in that direction than Canadian females (Xiao & Ma, 2015). How to evaluate such findings is unclear: mainland Chinese,

Taiwanese, and Canadian males view ethically questionable negotiation strategies as more appropriate than do Canadian females. The findings are thus neither strictly cultural (Chinese vs Canadians) nor strictly gender (males vs females). Underlying the findings may be difficult to assess conflict between conceptions of economic rationality (the purpose of negotiation is to win something) and business ethics (there are rules governing negotiation) lacks resolution in the literature (Windsor, 2015a). While China's political economy is essentially unique, it does not follow that Chinese businesspersons necessarily are also unique as a result.

Managers may develop their own operational philosophies focused on practical matters of turf, reputation, and coalition building (Windsor, 2015b). For example, consider the situation of the SOEs in China. There are three conflicting views toward taxation of SOEs (Cui, 2015). One view is that taxation is meaningless, because the government as sole shareholder can directly demand distribution of profits. The second view is that SOE taxation should aim at making SOEs and private firms competitive, instead of affording an advantage to SOEs. The third view is that SOE taxation forces profit distributions. Cui provides evidence that Chinese SOEs including centrally owned SOEs engage in extensive tax lobbying and tax planning, as one would expect of private firms.

This possible conflict between the expectations of the party and state and the motives and behavior of businesspersons—in state-owned or privately owned enterprises—may inform how businesspersons engage with corruption, favoritism, reliability, and responsibility. Each dimension is addressed in a separate subsection below. For each subsection, the author provides a general or broad definition of the dimension followed by a specific and narrower formulation for China. Chinese motives and behavior should be interpreted in light of the general definition being applied to Chinese conditions.

3.3.1 Corruption

An aspect of business and government in China is reportedly a pervasive corruption (Gao, 2011; White, 2015). Corruption takes the form of bribery in various forms of government officials and also personnel of commercial entities. Corruption specific to China is the pervasiveness and the particular forms of bribery, extortion, gifting, and so forth. Detailed information is difficult to obtain in any country, because corruption is secret and illegal. Table 3.1 provides Transparency International (TI)'s 2014 corruption perception index (CPI) and 2011 bribe payers index (BPI)

Table 3.1 Transparency International's 2014 Corruption Perceptions Index (CPI) and 2011 Bribe Payers Index (BPI) estimates for selected countries and territories

Country by CPI rank order	CPI 2014 score (0–100 scale)	CPI 2014 rank (175 entities)	BPI score 2011 (0–10 scale)	BPI rank 2011 (28 entities)
China's region				
Singapore	84	7	8.3	8
Japan	76	15	8.6	4
Hong Kong	74	17	7.6	15
Taiwan	61	35	7.5	19
South Korea	55	43	7.9	13
BRICS (Brazil, Russia, India, China, South Africa)				
South Africa	44	67	7.6	15
Brazil	43	69	7.7	14
India	38	85	7.5	19
China	36	100	6.5	27
Russia	27	136	6.1	28

Source: http://www.transparency.org/cpi2014 and http://www.transparency.org/bpi2011.
Notes: A score of 100 (CPI) or 10 (BPI) means zero domestic corruption or zero bribing abroad, respectively; a score of 0 means pervasive domestic corruption or always bribing abroad, respectively.
CPI: Denmark best (92, 1/175), New Zealand second best (91, 2/175), North Korea and Somalia tied at worst (8, 174/175). Cuba (46, 63/175), Mongolia (39, 80/175), Vietnam (31, 119/175), Kazakhstan (29, 126/175).
BPI: Netherlands and Switzerland tied at best (8.8, 1/28).

estimates for the five BRICS and a number of countries (including Hong Kong) in China's region. TI reports CPI data annually and BPI data periodically. The CPI estimates perceptions of in-country corruption of public officials; the BPI estimates perceptions of out-of-country bribery by the country's businesses. Within each category (China's region and BRICS), countries are listed in order of the 2014 CPI score and rank; then for each country the table displays the 2011 BPI score and rank. China is perceived to be less corrupt than Russia, but somewhat more corrupt than India. Other listed countries in China's region and Hong Kong are much less corrupt than South Africa. On the BPI, China and Russia are the two worst of 28 entities (including Hong Kong). The table notes show some comparison countries for CPI and BPI. North Korea and Somalia are tied for the worst in the world on CPI. Vietnam and Kazakhstan are more corrupt than China, while Mongolia is about as corrupt as India. Cuba is about as corrupt as South Africa.

A 2008 random sampling method survey of 1604 residents of Shanghai assessed citizens' perceptions and attitudes concerning the government's anticorruption campaign (Li, Gong, & Xiao, 2016). The study identified two findings that affected a respondent's expectation for positive anticorruption outcomes: (1) the perceived unfairness of income distribution increased expectation; and (2) acceptance of power intrusion into income distribution decreased expectation. A study of self-reported direct personal bribes paid by art students at examinations and in college admissions attributed individual willingness to bribe a personal characteristic and not to attributes of the admissions process (Liu & Peng, 2015). Students from middle-income families reported higher propensity to bribe than students from either poor or rich families. Gender had no effect. A 2011 nationwide survey found that citizens benefiting from economic growth may tolerate corruption (Li, Xiao, & Gong, 2015). A large state sector in a growing economy means considerable investment in public construction, which is likely the most corrupt sector in China (Shan, Chan, Le, Xia, & Hu, 2015). The authors of that study used semi-structured interviews with 14 experts and a questionnaire survey of 188 respondents. Another study using qualitative investigation of corruption cases and statistical analysis of a unique dataset of corruption rates to conclude that natural resource dependency significantly increases propensity for corruption among state employees (Zhan, 2015).

The available data suggest that corruption is pervasive in China, and that this condition likely affects businesses in various ways. While China is somewhat more corrupt than India, it is less corrupt than Russia or Vietnam. The Chinese regime is conducting a serious anticorruption campaign. In September 2014, a Chinese court found GlaxoSmithKline (GSK), a British pharmaceutical company, guilty of systematic bribery of doctors and fined the company about $490 million (£297 million) and gave GSK's former head of Chinese operations a suspended sentence—as reported in multiple news services.

3.3.2 Favoritism

Favoritism, occurring in various forms, such as nepotism, tying arrangements, *guanxi*, is partiality on grounds considered to be social-welfare-harming in a competitive market economy which should aim at efficiency in resource allocation and distribution of goods and services. This general conception of favoritism, which may occur in any number of countries in various forms, may take specific forms in China requiring detailed empirical investigation. Relationships, political and private, may provide the specific forms of favoritism in Chinese business. *Guanxi* (roughly "relationships") is exchange of personal favors, in a network of personal relationships regarded as more important than either laws or formal agreements such as contracts (Goh & Sullivan, 2011). There is an increasing literature on *guanxi* in business. *Guanxi* may operate throughout China, although less is likely known about party and government circles (Chen, Chang, & Lee, 2015; Hu, Schaufeli, & Taris, 2016; Murray & Fu, 2016; Warren, Dunfee, & Li, 2004).

A study about a decade ago of a sample of 790 newly and partially privatized firms reported that almost 27% of the CEOs were former or current government bureaucrats (Fan, Wong, & Zhang, 2007). As with other empirical findings on Chinese firms, such information should be placed in comparative cross-country context. Difficulty in assessing empirical findings for China is the absence of such detailed cross-study comparisons. The authors reported that firms with politically connected CEOs underperformed financially by almost 18% when compared to nonpolitically connected firms—based on comparison of 3-year post-IPO stock returns reflecting poorer earnings and sales growth and change in returns on sales. The first-day stock return for the IPO was also negative. Politically connected CEOs were more likely to appoint other former or current government bureaucrats to the board of directors. The essential implication of such findings is that in 2007 political connections were of importance and resulted in relatively poorer performance of newly and partially privatized firms. Nonpolitically connected firms performed better financially following privatization. There is a similar study for Vietnam listed firms (Phung & Mishra, 2016).

Clearly, the specific data in Fan et al. (2007) is likely to be significantly out of date after a decade, without current data available that replicates the specific approach. Furthermore, a regulatory change reportedly occurred in China to prohibit bureaucrats from being members of boards of listed firms: Han and Guangli (2015) tested for the market reaction to the change. There was a positive cumulative abnormal return for firms with politically connected directors affected by the regulatory change relative to a matched sample; and the effect of resignation announcement by a politically connected director is also positive and higher than the effect for resignation of a nonconnected director. The agency cost of the political connection outweighs the business value of the political connection. Reportedly consistent poor performance of China's stock markets has been attributed to political connections. A study of samples of publicly traded privately owned firms finds 74% are politically connected and also that such firms are more likely to report significant financial performance deterioration following IPOs (Zhou & Li, 2016). Findings supporting the importance of political connections are reported in Wu and Cheng (2011). Chinese experience might be compared to commercial bank performance in Malaysia (Poon, Yap, & Lee, 2013).

There are a few studies of Chinese auditors that bear on favoritism. One study conducted two experiments with 174 Chinese auditors (Du, Ronen, & Ye, 2015). The first experiment investigated auditor awareness of attempts to manage earnings induced by a delisting rule. The authors conclude that the auditors believe that the classification of investment transactions could be appropriate in order to avoid losses. The second experiment investigated the role of *guanxi* between managers and auditors. The authors conclude that *guanxi* does undermine auditors' ability to correct earnings management attempts. Given *guanxi*, auditors are less likely to recommend adjustments, but, increased regulatory penalty does improve auditors' willingness to challenge managers' decisions. A reading of these findings is that in absence of sufficiently harsh penalties auditors default to *guanxi*. Another study examined auditor choice (Guedhami, Pittman, & Saffar, 2014). Public firms with political connections are more likely to appoint a Big Four auditor, for the purpose of improving accounting transparency to outside investors. One should bear in mind, however, that Big Four auditors in China are affiliates rather than direct offices (Rapoport, 2015). Affiliates are generally owned and managed independently, and operate within the national regulatory setting of the country. The study on political connections also found that the relationship to Big Four auditors is stronger for connected firms with ownership structures favorable to insiders. The connected firms with Big Four auditors exhibit less earnings management and other positive attributes such as higher valuations and cheaper equity financing (see also Liu, Li, Zeng, & An, 2016; Tsai, 2012).

A study of a sample of 1435 Chinese foundations during 2005–11 (Johnson & Ni, 2015) found no relationship between the presence of state employees on an NGO's staff and private donations. The presence of state employees was used as a measure of political *guanxi*. The study did, however, find a small but positive relationship between amount of government funding of an NGO and private donations. The authors interpret government funding as a signal of legitimacy of the NGO. The implication is that donors are seeking to develop a robust civil society of legitimate and high-quality NGOs rather than seeking future favors from government.

This subsection has assembled information on the dimension of favoritism in relations between the Chinese party-state and enterprises, both state-owned and privately owned. It seems reasonably clear that there is a complicated relationship between political connections and business activities in China. Politically connected firms may perform more poorly than nonpolitically connected firms. Political connections involve a conflict or tradeoff between agency costs of the connections and the value of favoritism.

3.3.3 Reliability

For purposes of this chapter, reliability is a perception of businesspersons' compliance with party and state expectations. This reliability may have different specific meanings in each country. In China specifically, reliability means the party's perception that an individual is sufficiently loyal to the regime itself in addition to being compliant with expectations such as paying taxes. An important purpose of the current anticorruption campaign, whether effective or not (C. Lee, 2015), may be to place individuals in charge of SOEs and state-influenced enterprises who demonstrate political reliability to the party (Wei & Davis, 2014). The Chinese censorship system arguably aims not at individual dissent or content but at suppressing collective action against the regime (King, Pan, & Roberts, 2013). Evidence suggests that reported earnings quality for politically connected firms is significantly poorer (Chaney, Faccio, & Parsley, 2011), and not due to firms with poor earnings quality establishing political connections more often as a substitute for performance. Rather, politically connected firms can disclose lower quality information because of lesser need to respond to market pressures. Also, such firms apparently do not face a higher cost of debt, which does occur for nonpolitically connected firms (Chaney et al., 2011). These findings for China seem to echo cross-national evidence reported for 47 countries. Otherwise, standalone data for China—frequently the only data that can be conveniently located—is of course difficult to interpret contextually. Politically connected firms have higher leverage and higher market shares, but underperform on accounting measures (Faccio, 2006, 2010). Differences between politically connected and unconnected firms vary with level of corruption and degree of economic development in each country (Faccio, 2006, 2010).

Empirical studies tend to confirm that political connections affect firm-level actions and outcomes (Zhu & Chung, 2014, report on political connections and business groups in Taiwan). One study found that politically connected boards were negatively associated with top executive pay and dispersion between top executive pay and average employee pay; the study also found that politically connected boards weaken the pay–performance relationship (Chizema, Liu, Lu, & Gao, 2015). A study of earnings forecasts by financial analysts, based on firm-level data from 17 jurisdictions around the world (1997–2001), found that analysts had greater difficulty predicting earnings of politically connected firms (Chen, Ding, & Kim, 2010). In jurisdictions with relatively high corruption, the firm's political connections have stronger influence on earnings forecast accuracy. This study suggests that anticorruption measures can reduce the negative effect of political connections. Another study across 22 countries finds significant effect of political connections on M&A activities and postmerger performance, the effect being dependent on the institutional setting (Brockman, Rui, & Zou, 2013). In countries with strong legal systems or low corruption, politically connected bidders underperform by about 15% abnormal stock returns over a 3-year period. In countries with weak legal systems or high corruption, politically connected bidders outperform by more than 20% on the same basis. The postmerger performance difference is greater for domestic mergers than for cross-border mergers.

It is important to bear in mind that party and government may seek to influence even private enterprises, and derive benefits from marketized state ownership through FDI (Alon, Leung, & Simpson, 2015; Cui & Jiang, 2013; Miska, Witt, & Stahl, 2016). A longitudinal study of 973 Chinese publicly listed firms finds that advantages to firms with marketized state ownership (central and local levels of government) are contingent on firms being affiliated with certain institutional structures such as state business groups reallocating resources member firms (Li, Cui, & Lu, 2015).

In China's business model, the role of reliability is assurance to the party that businesspersons are loyal in the sense of supporting the regime. Such assurance may occur through direct and partial state ownership, political connections, and various economic incentives (such as subsidies) or possibilities for sanctions of firms. China's business model may be highly unique in how reliability is defined and enforced. One possible effect is that the greater the reliability, the more the party and state may be willing to move further in marketization and privatization. Partial state ownership, political connections, and incentives may substitute for direct state ownership and may help generate incentives leading to businesspersons to support the regime.

3.3.4 Responsibility

This chapter draws a distinction between CSR as a general orientation and corporate philanthropy as a specific practice. CSR is generally defined by many scholars as voluntary choices to contribute social benefits beyond legal requirements. Thus, paying taxes is not voluntary CSR; making donations in support of various causes is voluntary. This general conception of CSR must be assessed within the special context of China's model for business (Hofman et al., 2015; Li & Zhang, 2010). The specific question in China is whether CSR activities, including donations, are wholly voluntary or at least partly function as responding to political connections or seeking political influence. Many scholars define CSR as voluntary actions in the public interest not required by law. This widely adopted definition, however, effectively makes CSR synonymous with altruism, while philanthropy is defined somewhat more narrowly as donations of corporate monies and employee volunteers. The author views CSR more broadly as the avoidance of irresponsibility (that is, violations of ethics and laws causing harm to society and/or other stakeholders of the firm) on the one hand and good citizenship contributions to social benefit on the other hand. Absence of irresponsibility may have a more important influence on social welfare than does practice of altruism (Windsor, 2013). The latter is a net addition to social welfare only if there has been ethical or legal violations causing harm to society and/or other stakeholders; otherwise altruism may be only a minor reduction in the harm caused.

3.3.5 CSR and Business Ethics

A study of CSR across 50 companies in seven Asian countries (India, Indonesia, Malaysia, the Philippines, Singapore, South Korea, and Thailand), based on analysis of Web site reporting, found considerable variation across countries in CSR explained by factors in each national business system rather than by stage of development (Chapple & Moon, 2005). The study found also that multinational enterprises (MNEs) are more likely to adopt CSR than purely domestic firms. CSR profile, however, reflects profile of the host country of operation rather than the home country or origin.

For China, studies of 292 employees from 53 companies and 224 middle-level managers from 40 companies found that ethical leadership and external stakeholder pressure significantly and positively influence CSR implementation (Tian, Liu, & Fan, 2015). The effect of external stakeholder pressure weakens with higher level of ethical leadership and strengthens with lower level of ethical leadership. These findings suggest that ethical leadership is the dominant consideration.

The findings raise the issues of the philosophical orientation of business leaders and the role of moral education of those business leaders (Windsor, 2015a, 2015b). In China, how to understand responsibility and concepts of duty, obligation, power, and right must be studied in context (Lu & Koehn, 2015). Coase and Wang (2013) report that premier Wen Jiabao was impressed with Adam Smith's *The Theory of Moral Sentiments* (1759), appearing in various Chinese translations. Those authors express the view that Adam Smith appeals to the Chinese because there is an affinity with traditional (pre-communist) Chinese thought on economy and society. Viewed in this way, China might be returning to its traditional cultural foundations. The only philosophical competition with or substitute for communist ideology arguably lies either in pre-Maoist Chinese philosophers or in modern market economics theory. The three dominant pre-Maoist Chinese philosophies are Daoism (or Taoism), Confucianism, and Legalism (Ma & Tsui, 2015). Legalism seems better characterized as political realism in a condition of competing and warring states; individual morality is irrelevant and impersonal systems should guide personal selfishness to benefit the state in effect indirectly (Goldin, 2011; Pines, 2014). Ma and Tsui (2015) analyzed articles reporting interviews with fifteen Chinese business leaders to determine relationship between their leadership practices and the three traditional philosophies. Applying any of these traditional philosophies to business ethics and leadership practices involves both contextualization and decontextualization (Liu & Stening, 2016). Contextualization means placing specific Chinese moral concepts back into original context for accuracy of understanding and interpretation. Decontextualization means adjusting those concepts to the modern business environment in China (Liu & Stening, 2016).

There is no available evidence discovered by this author concerning the beliefs of Chinese businesspersons (whether in state-owned or privately owned enterprises). The three options appear to loyalty to the prevailing party ideology, interest in pre-Maoist Chinese philosophies, or the economic rationality of business (Windsor, 2015a, 2015b). What is important to appreciate is that Chinese business executives likely choose for themselves among these options; and the empirical distribution of choices may affect business–government interactions in China.

3.3.6 Corporate Philanthropy

Philanthropy in China is reportedly low relative to India, but significantly higher than in Russia (Cunningham, 2016). In 2014, philanthropy in China was 0.1% of GDP; the proportion in India was 0.4% of GDP (see Ren & Ye, 2016). However, in Russia philanthropy was only one-tenth of the GDP proportion in China (Cunningham, 2016). In India, a statute from 2013 requires corporate philanthropy of some 8000 domestic and foreign firms above certain minimum requirements (Godfrey, Branigan, & Khan, 2016). While philanthropy in the United States was 2% of GDP, as reported by Cunningham (2016), the United States or other developed countries do not seem to be proper comparison standards. Comparative data may be located in a recent handbook on global philanthropy (Wiepking & Handy, 2015). A recent study of the 100 largest donors in China completed during September 2014–August 2015 (the China Philanthropy Project) provides information about the economic elite (Cunningham, 2016). According to this study, tax breaks are not much of a factor in China. Rather, top donors appear to desire to cement personal and family legacies. Education was the leading recipient. Giving appears to be generally local and single-cause focused. The top 100 donors provided $3.8 billion in donations or pledges amounting to 0.03% of GDP. Beijing is a net recipient of this top donation set, receiving 15.7% of 2015 total donations; and 87.3% of this total was given by donors with corporate headquarters not located in Beijing. In the reverse direction, Beijing located donors gave 86.5% of their donations and pledges to organizations outside of Beijing.

3.4 CONCLUSION

The contribution of the chapter is to identify information about four key dimensions of the business model in China: corruption, favoritism, reliability, and CSR. No other work known to the author provides an integrated framework of this kind for assessing where businesses stand in China's evolution toward marketization and privatization. The framework facilitates insight into Chinese businesses, both state-owned and privately owned enterprises.

This chapter has used a theory of comparative political economy to position interpretation of China's transition from communist-style command economy to a more market economy opening to international trade and globalizing Chinese MNEs (He, Chakrabarty, & Eden, 2016). The comparison benchmarks may be the other BRICS particularly Russia and other countries in Asia and Southeast Asia, with particular attention to Vietnam. North Korea is too extreme an instance for reasonable comparison to China. Singapore and Taiwan are also relevant in China's region; Hong Kong is a special subject in being more market oriented and politically liberal than but politically dominated by China. The Chinese setting appears to be unique, making direct comparisons relatively difficult. Hence, the methodology of comparison has relatively limited value in assessing the Chinese business model. Comparison is not useless, but rather must be viewed as relatively distant from Chinese conditions. Russia and Vietnam may be closer than India, Singapore, or Taiwan.

Several important suggested findings bear emphasizing. The Chinese economy appears to be still vertically structured. SOEs dominate the upstream economy, with privatization progressing more downstream in consumption of goods and services. The party dominates the state, and the regime still considerably controls or influences the private economy in multiple ways. While one can argue that the party is no longer "communist" in the classical sense, leadership appears to be still in a state of transition from Marxism–Leninism–Maoism to pragmatism. This trend presently remains more pronounced in the economic sphere than in the political sphere, possibly due to increasing decentralization to the provinces and subprovincial units. The regime still manages political thought and dissent, although the strategy has been characterized as one of permitting individual dissent to release pressure while preventing collective mobilization against the regime.

The chapter assessed four dimensions of the model of business with emphasis on the motives and behavior of business managers: corruption, favoritism (with emphasis on *guanxi*), reliability (meaning loyalty to the regime), and responsibility separated into CSR and philanthropy. Business owners and managers will tend to emphasize financial performance and develop their own operational philosophies partly influenced by but partly independent of either official ideology or traditional Chinese philosophies. This characterization invokes in part the inherent nature of market competition on the one hand and the inherent realities of turf, reputation, and coalition within organizations. *Guanxi* in the private sphere and political connections in the party-state sphere are under empirical investigation as ways in which networking functions within a one-party regime operating a vertical structured, bifurcated variety of capitalism. State capitalism, or market socialism, remains the dominant factor in this approach to date. Studies of Chinese businesses will remain, for the present, subject to the problem of having to be positioned within the conditions of the Chinese political economy.

REFERENCES

Aguilera, R., Capape, J., & Santiso, J. (2016). Sovereign wealth funds: A strategic governance view. *Academy of Management Perspectives*, *30*(1), 5–23.

Alhashel, B. (2015). Sovereign wealth funds: A literature review. *Journal of Economics and Business*, *78*, 1–13.

AlixPartners. (April 2013). *The AlixPartners Manufacturing-Sourcing Outlook: As the US closes the cost gap with other locations, nearshoring decisions remain complex*. <http://www.alixpartners.com/en/LinkClick.aspx?fileticket=l1diPmnb044%3D&tabid=635>.

Alon, I., Leung, G. C. K., & Simpson, T. J. (2015). Outward foreign direct investment by Chinese national oil companies. *Journal of East-West Business*, *21*(4), 292–312.

Backer, L. C. (2015). The Cuban Communist Party at the center of political and economic reform: Current status and future reform. *Northwestern Interdisciplinary Law Review*, *8*, 71–129. Draft version July 2014 available March 15, 2015, at SSRN. <http://ssrn.com/abstract=2473351 or http://dx.doi.org/10.2139/ssrn.2473351>.

Bell, D. (2015). *The China model: Political meritocracy and the limits of democracy*. Princeton, NJ: Princeton University Press.

Benjamin, O., Nisim, S., & Segev, G. (2015). Corporate social responsibility as shaped by managers' role dissonance: Cleaning services procurement in Israel. *Journal of Business Ethics*, *130*(1), 209–221.

Brockman, P., Rui, O. M., & Zou, H. (2013). Institutions and the performance of politically connected M&As. *Journal of International Business Studies*, *44*(8), 833–852.

Bruton, G. D., Peng, M. W., Ahlstrom, D., Stan, C., & Xu, K. (2015). State-owned enterprises around the world as hybrid organizations. *Academy of Management Perspectives*, *29*(1), 92–114.

Chaney, P. K., Faccio, M., & Parsley, D. (2011). The quality of accounting information in politically connected firms. *Journal of Accounting and Economics*, *51*(1), 58–76.

Chang, E. C., & Wong, S. M. L. (2004). Political control and performance in China's listed firms. *Journal of Comparative Economics*, *32*(4), 617–636.

Chapple, W., & Moon, J. (2005). Corporate social responsibility (CSR) in Asia: A seven-country study of CSR web site reporting. *Business & Society*, *44*(4), 415–441.

Chen, C., Zhang, J., & Delaurentis, T. (2014). Quality control in food supply chain management: An analytical model and case study of the adulterated milk incident in China. *International Journal of Production Economics*, *152*, 188–199.

Chen, C. J., Ding, Y., & Kim, C. F. (2010). High-level politically connected firms, corruption, and analyst forecast accuracy around the world. *Journal of International Business Studies*, *41*(9), 1505–1524.

Chen, D., & Kinzelbach, K. (2015). Democracy promotion and China: Blocker or bystander? *Democratization*, *22*(3), 400–418.

Chen, M. H., Chang, Y. Y., & Lee, C. Y. (2015). Creative entrepreneurs' guanxi networks and success: Information and resource. *Journal of Business Research*, *68*(4), 900–905.

Chen, Z., & Cao, Y. (2016). Chinese private corporate philanthropy: Social responsibility, legitimacy strategy, and the role of political capital. *Chinese Sociological Review*, *48*(2), 108–136.

Chizema, A., Liu, X., Lu, J., & Gao, L. (2015). Politically connected boards and top executive pay in Chinese listed firms. *Strategic Management Journal*, *36*(6), 890–906.

Chua, V., & Wellman, B. (2015). Social networks in East and Southeast Asia I: National characteristics, institutions, network capital, and guanxi. *American Behavioral Scientist*, *59*(8), 903–913.

Coase, R., & Wang, N. (January/February 2013). *How China became capitalist*. <http://www.cato.org/policy-report/januaryfebruary-2013/how-china-became-capitalist>.

Connor, J. (October 1, 2014). *Hong Kong: Economic freedom belies Crony capitalism*. <http://sevenpillarsinstitute.org/news/economics/hong-kong-economic-freedom-belies-crony-capitalism>.

Cooper, A. F., & Farooq, A. B. (2015). The Advocacy of democratic governance by India and China: Patterns of consistency/inconsistency between declaratory and operational practices. *India Quarterly: A Journal of International Affairs*, *71*(3), 221–238.

Cui, L., & Jiang, F. (September 2013). State ownership effect on firms' FDI ownership decisions under institutional pressure: A study of Chinese outward investing firms. *Chinese Management Insights*, *2*(3), 80–85. <http://www.iacmr.org/v2en/CMI/Vol2Issue3/eCMI_6.pdf>.

Cui, W. (2015). Taxation of state owned enterprises: A review of empirical evidence from China. In B. Liebman & C. Milhaupt (Eds.), *Regulating the visible hand? The institutional implications of Chinese state capitalism* (pp. 109–131). Oxford: Oxford University Press.

Cumming, D., Fleming, G., Johan, S., & Takeuchi, M. (2010). Legal protection, corruption and private equity returns in Asia. *Journal of Business Ethics*, *95*(2 Suppl.), 173–193.

Cunningham, E. (January 2016). *China's most generous: Understanding China's philanthropic landscape*. Cambridge, MA: China Philanthropic Project, Ash Center for Democratic Governance and Innovation, Harvard Kennedy School. Retrieved from <http://chinaphilanthropy.ash.harvard.edu/china-philanthropy-report.pdf>.

Dai, W., Alon, I., & Jiao, H. (2015). Financial marketization and corporate venturing in China: The impact of provincial-level institutions on the pharmaceutical sector. *Journal of Entrepreneurship in Emerging Economies*, 7(1), 2–22.

Das, D. K. (2015). Multinational corporations and the transforming operational environment in China. *Thunderbird International Business Review*, *57*(4), 271–280.

De Leon, C. (2015). Integrating varieties of capitalism and welfare state research: A unified typology of capitalisms. *Contemporary Sociology: A Journal of Reviews*, *44*(2), 248–249.

Detomasi, D. (2015). The multinational corporation as a political actor: "Varieties of Capitalism" revisited. *Journal of Business Ethics*, *128*(3), 685–700.

Dittmer, L. (2015). China's new leadership and global role. In E. Berman & M. S. Haque (Eds.), *Asian leadership in policy and governance* (pp. 21–43). Bingley: Emerald Group Publishing Limited.

Du, N., Ronen, J., & Ye, J. (2015). Auditors' role in China: The joint effects of *guanxi* and regulatory sanctions on earnings management. *Journal of Accounting, Auditing & Finance*, *30*(4), 461–483.

Duan, P., & Saich, T. (May 2014). *Reforming China's Monopolies*. Boston, MA: Harvard Kennedy School, RWP14-023.

Dufy, C. (2015). Redefining business values in Russia: The boundaries of globalisation and patriotism in contemporary Russian industry. *Europe-Asia Studies*, *67*, 84–101.

Ecns.com. (March 16, 2016). *Q&A transcription of premier Li Kiqiang's press conference*. <www.ecns.cn/2016/03-16/203164.shtml>.

Faccio, M. (2006). Politically connected firms. *American Economic Review*, *96*(1), 369–386.

Faccio, M. (2010). Differences between politically connected and nonconnected firms: A cross-country analysis. *Financial Management*, *39*(3), 905–928.

Fan, J. P. H., Wong, T. J., & Zhang, T. (2007). Politically connected CEOs, corporate governance, and post-IPO performance of China's newly partially privatized firms. *Journal of Financial Economics*, *84*(2), 330–357.

Gao, Y. (2011). Government intervention, perceived benefit, and bribery of firms in transitional China. *Journal of Business Ethics*, *104*(2), 175–184.

Godfrey, J., Branigan, E., & Khan, S. (2016). Old and new forms of giving: Understanding corporate philanthropy in India. *Voluntas: International Journal of Voluntary and Nonprofit Organization*, 1–25. (online before print).

Goh, A., & Sullivan, G. (February 24, 2011). *The most misunderstood business concept in China*. Beijing, China: US-Pacific Rim International, Inc. Retrieved from <http://www.businessinsider.com/the-most-misunderstood-business-concept-in-china-2011-2>.

Goldin, P. A. (2011). Persistent misconceptions about Chinese "Legalism." *Journal of Chinese Philosophy*, *38*(1), 64–80.

Guedhami, O., Pittman, J. A., & Saffar, W. (2014). Auditor choice in politically connected firms. *Journal of Accounting Research, 52*(1), 107–162.

Guo, D., Jiang, K., Kim, B. -Y., & Xu, C. (2014). Political economy of private firms in China. *Journal of Comparative Economics, 42*(2), 286–303.

Haggard, S., & Noland, M. (2010). Reform from below: Behavioral and institutional change in North Korea. *Journal of Economic Behavior & Organization, 73*(2), 133–152.

Han, J., & Guangli, Z. (July 24, 2015). *Politically connected boards, value or cost: Evidence from a natural experiment in China.* Available at SSRN <http://ssrn.com/abstract=2635741> or <http://dx.doi.org/10.2139/ssrn.2635741>.

Hansen, A. (2016). Review: Politics in contemporary Vietnam: Party, state and authority relations. *Journal of Contemporary Asia, 46*(1), 143–146.

He, X., Chakrabarty, S., & Eden, L. (2016). The global emergence of Chinese multinationals: A resource-based view of ownership and performance. *Asian Business & Management, 15*, 1–31.

Hofman, P. S., Moon, J., & Wu, B. (2015). Corporate social responsibility under authoritarian capitalism: Dynamics and prospects of state-led and society-driven CSR. *Business & Society*, 1–21. (online before print).

Holmes, R. M., Miller, T., Hitt, M. A., & Salmador, M. P. (2013). The interrelationships among informal institutions, formal institutions, and inward foreign direct investment. *Journal of Management, 39*, 531–566.

Houston Chronicle. (March 17, 2016). China: Leader promises more reforms to open markets. Thursday, B3 (Business).

Howard-Hassmann, R. E. (2012). State-induced famine and penal starvation in North Korea. *Genocide Studies and Prevention*, 7(2) Article 3, 147–165. Retrieved from <http://scholarcommons.usf.edu/cgi/viewcontent.cgi?article=1035&context=gsp>.

Hsueh, R. (2016). State capitalism, Chinese-style: Strategic value of sectors, sectoral characteristics, and globalization. *Governance, 29*(1), 85–102.

Hu, Q., Schaufeli, W. B., & Taris, T. W. (2016). Extending the job demands-resources model with guanxi exchange. *Journal of Managerial Psychology, 31*(1), 127–140.

Huang, D., & Chen, C. (2016). Revolving out of the Party-State: The *Xiahai* entrepreneurs and circumscribing government power in China. *Journal of Contemporary China, 25*(97), 41–58.

Huat, C. B. (2015). State-owned enterprises, state capitalism and social distribution in Singapore. *The Pacific Review, 29*(4), 499–521.

Hudson, R. (April 7, 2014). *Chinese investments in Africa: The ethics of transparency.* <http://sevenpillarsinstitute.org/news/chinese-investments-africa-ethics-transparency>.

Hwang, Y. -S., & Chen, D. (2016). A reversal theory in internationalization: Case of Korean jewelry inside China. *Chinese Management Studies, 10*(1), 82–101.

Innes, A. (2015). Hungary's illiberal democracy. *Current History, 114*(770), 95–100.

Jiahong, H. (2016). Reorganization of anti-corruption agencies in China. *Journal of Money Laundering Control, 19*(2), 106–108.

Johnson, J. M., & Ni, N. (2015). The impact of political connections on donations to Chinese NGOs. *International Public Management Journal, 18*(4), 514–535.

Kiely, R. (2015). The BRICs, state capitalism and globalization: Challenge to or triumph of the West?. In R. Kiely (Ed.), *The BRICs, US "decline" and global transformations* (pp. 33–64). London: Palgrave Macmillan.

King, G., Pan, J., & Roberts, M. E. (2013). How censorship in China allows government criticism but silences collective expression. *American Political Science Review, 107*(2), 1–18.

Kipnis, A. B. (2016). Modernity and the Chinese moral crisis. *The China Journal, 75*(1), 121–127.

Lee, C. (July 13, 2015). *China and corruption: The case of GlaxoSmithKline.* <http://sevenpillarsinstitute.org/news/china-and-corruption-the-case-of-glaxosmithkline>.

Lee, H. (2015). Inevitable reform? The politico-economic choices facing North Korea under Kim Jong-Un's rule. *North Korean Review, 11*(1), 82–100.

Li, H., Gong, T., & Xiao, H. (2016). The perception of anti-corruption efficacy in China: An empirical analysis. *Social Indicators Research*, *125*(3), 885–903.
Li, H., Xiao, H., & Gong, T. (2015). The impact of economic well-being on perceptions of anti-corruption performance: Evidence from China. *Policy and Society*, *34*(2), 97–109.
Li, M. H., Cui, L., & Lu, J. (2015). Marketized state ownership and foreign expansion of emerging market multinationals: Leveraging institutional competitive advantages. *Asia Pacific Journal of Management*, 1–28. (online before print).
Li, S., Vertinsky, I., & Zhou, D. (2004). The emergence of private ownership in China. *Journal of Business Research*, *57*(10), 1145–1152.
Li, W., & Zhang, R. (2010). Corporate social responsibility, ownership structure, and political interference: Evidence from China. *Journal of Business Ethics*, *96*(4), 631–645.
Li, X., Liu, X., & Wang, Y. (October 2012). *A model of China's State capitalism*. <https://www.usitc.gov/research_and_analysis/documents/Wang_A_Model_of_Chinas_State_Capitalism.pdf>.
Liu, Q., & Peng, Y. (2015). Determinants of willingness to bribe: Micro evidence from the educational sector in China. *Journal of Economics and Statistics (Jahrbuecher fuer Nationaloekonomie und Statistik)*, *235*(2), 168–183.
Liu, T. Q., & Stening, B. W. (2016). The contextualization and de-contextualization of Confucian morality: Making Confucianism relevant to China's contemporary challenges in business ethics. *Asia Pacific Journal of Management*, *33*(3), 821–841.
Liu, Y., Li, X., Zeng, H., & An, Y. (2016). Political connections, auditor choice and corporate accounting transparency: Evidence from private sector firms in China. *Accounting & Finance*, 1–29. (online ahead of print).
Lopes, G. P. (2015). The Sino-Brazilian principles in a Latin American and BRICS Context: The case for comparative public budgeting legal research. *Wisconsin International Law Journal*, *31*, 1–45. Retrieved January 25, 2016, from <http://www.migalhas.com.br/arquivos/2015/6/art20150601-02.pdf>.
Lu, X., & Koehn, D. (2015). On responsibility in China: Understanding and practice. *Journal of Business Ethics*, *127*(3), 607–622.
Ma, L., & Tsui, A. S. (2015). Traditional Chinese philosophies and contemporary leadership. *The Leadership Quarterly*, *26*(1), 13–24.
Mele, D., & Ogunyemi, A. O. (October 2014). Human quality treatment in SMEs run by Christian owner-managers. *Academy of Management Annual Meeting Proceedings*, 16741. <http://dx.doi.org/10.5465/AMBPP.2014.16741>. (abstract).
Meyer, M. W., & Lu, X. (September 2013). Managing the indefinite boundaries of Chinese business firms. *Chinese Management Insights*, *2*(3), 70–74. <http://www.iacmr.org/v2en/CMI/Vol2Issue3/eCMI_6.pdf>.
Minzner, C. (2015). China after the reform era. *Journal of Democracy*, *26*(3), 129–143.
Miquel, G., Qian, N., Xu, Y., & Yao, Y. (April 2015). *Making democracy work: Culture, social capital and elections in China*. National Bureau of Economic Research. No. w21058.
Miska, C., Witt, M. A., & Stahl, G. K. (2016). Drivers of global CSR integration and local CSR responsiveness: Evidence from Chinese MNEs. *Business Ethics Quarterly*, *26*(3), 317–345.
Mukand, S., & Rodrik, D. (September 2015). *The political economy of liberal democracy*. NBER Working Paper No. 21540. <http://www.nber.org/papers/w21540>.
Murray, J. Y., & Fu, F. Q. (2016). Strategic guanxi orientation: How to manage distribution channels in China? *Journal of International Management*, *22*(1), 1–16.
Musacchio, A., Lazzarini, S. G., & Aguilera, R. V. (2015). New varieties of state capitalism: Strategic and governance implications. *Academy of Management Perspectives*, *29*(1), 115–131.
Ortmann, S., & Thompson, M. R. (2016). China and the "Singapore Model." *Journal of Democracy*, *27*(1), 39–48.

Owen, D. A. (2015). The impact of economic development on political interest across social classes in China: Turning the Chinese dream into a Chinese reality? *Journal of Chinese Political Science*, *20*(2), 185–202.
Pavlovich, K., Sinha, P. N., & Rodrigues, M. (2016). A qualitative case study of MNE legitimacy: The Fonterra-Sanlu IJV corporate milk scandal in China. *International Journal of Emerging Markets*, *11*(1), 42–56.
Phung, D. N., & Mishra, A. V. (2016). Ownership structure and firm performance: Evidence from Vietnamese listed firms. *Australian Economic Papers*, *55*(1), 63–98.
Pines, Y. (2014, December 10). Legalism in Chinese philosophy. Stanford Encyclopedia of Philosophy. <plato.stanford.edu/entries/chinese-legalism>.
Poon, W. C., Yap, A. K. -H., & Lee, T. -H. (2013). The outcome of politically connected boards on commercial bank performance in Malaysia. *Modern Applied Science*, 7(1), 35–50. Available online at <http://www.ccsenet.org/journal/index.php/mas/article/view/23117> and at SSRN <http://ssrn.com/abstract=2490269>.
Pylas, P. (January 24, 2016). Panel eyes solutions for market turbulence. *Houston Chronicle*, *115*(103), A5. Sunday.
Ramo, J. C. (2004). *The Beijing consensus*. London: The Foreign Policy Centre. <http://fpc.org.uk/fsblob/244.pdf>.
Rapoport, M. (February 6, 2015). SEC, Big four accounting firms in China settle dispute deal over refusal to turn over audit documents lifts threat of suspension. *Wall Street Journal* Retrieved from <http://www.wsj.com/articles/sec-big-four-accounting-firms-in-china-settle-dispute-1423237083>.
Ren, Q., & Ye, M. (2016). Donations make people happier: Evidence from the Wenchuan Earthquake. *Social Indicators Research*, 1–20. (online before print).
Rivoli, P. (2015). Made in Bangladesh, Cambodia, and Sri Lanka: The labor behind the global garments and textiles industries. *Labor History*, *56*(1), 103–105.
Robinson, W. I. (2015). The transnational state and the BRICS: A global capitalism perspective. *Third World Quarterly*, *36*(1), 1–21.
Rodan, G. (2015). The ruling elite of Singapore: Networks of power and influence. *Journal of Contemporary Asia*, *45*(2), 354–356.
Rutland, P. (2015). Petronation? Oil, gas, and national identity in Russia. *Post-Soviet Affairs*, *31*(1), 66–89.
Sacchetto, D., & Andrijasevic, R. (2015). Beyond China: Foxconn's assembly plants in Europe. *South Atlantic Quarterly*, *114*(1), 215–224.
Schmitz, H., Tuan, D. A., Hang, P. T. T., & McCulloch, N. A. (2015). Drivers of economic reform in Vietnam's provinces. *Development Policy Review*, *33*(2), 175–193.
Shan, M., Chan, A. P., Le, Y., Xia, B., & Hu, Y. (2015). Measuring corruption in public construction projects in China. *Journal of Professional Issues in Engineering Education and Practice*, *141*(4), 05015001. Retrieved from <https://www.researchgate.net/publication/276092147_Measuring_Corruption_in_Public_Construction_Projects_in_China or draft version http://eprints.qut.edu.au/82770/3/82770a.pdf>.
Statista. (n.d.). Retrieved January 24, 2016, from <http://www.statista.com/statistics/268173/countries-with-the-largest-gross-domestic-product-gdp/> and <http://www.statista.com/topics/921/european-union/>.
Tian, Q., Liu, Y., & Fan, J. (2015). The effects of external stakeholder pressure and ethical leadership on corporate social responsibility in China. *Journal of Management & Organization*, *21*(4), 388–410.
Tian, X., & Slocum, J. W. (2016). Managing corporate social responsibility in China. *Organizational Dynamics*, *45*(1), 39–46.
Tsai, B. -H. (2012). Political interference and earnings manipulation in Chinese firms. *Chinese Economy*, *45*(6), 84–102.
U.S. Central Intelligence Agency (CIA). (n.d.). *The World Factbook*. <https://www.cia.gov/library/publications/resources/the-world-factbook/geos/in.html>.

Villalobos, K. M. (2014–2015). Digital oppression in Cuba and China: A comparative study of ICCPR violations. *Journal of Transnational Law & Policy*, *24*, 161–203.

Wang, Y. (2015). The rise of the "shareholding state": Financialization of economic management in China. *Socio-Economic Review*, *13*(3), 603–625.

Warren, D. E., Dunfee, T. W., & Li, N. (2004). Social exchange in China: The double-edged sword of guanxi. *Journal of Business Ethics*, *55*(4), 355–372.

Wei, L., & Davis, B. (October 26, 2014). China's assault on corruption enters executive suite. *Wall Street Journal (Online)*, 1–3.

White, L. T. (2015). Political mechanisms and corruption. In G. C. Chow & D. H. Perkins (Eds.), *Routledge handbook of the Chinese economy* (pp. 280–302). Abingdon, Oxon: Routledge.

Wiepking, P., & Handy, F. (Eds.). (2015). *The Palgrave handbook of global philanthropy*. New York: Palgrave Macmillan.

Windsor, D. (2013). Corporate social responsibility and irresponsibility: A positive theory approach. *Journal of Business Research*, *66*(10), 1937–1944.

Windsor, D. (2015a). Economic rationality and a moral science of business ethics. *Philosophy of Management*, *15*(2), 135–149.

Windsor, D. (2015b). Philosophy for managers and philosophy of managers: Turf, reputation, coalition. *Philosophy of Management*, *14*(1), 17–28.

Wu, J., & Cheng, M. L. (2011). The impact of managerial political connections and quality on government subsidies: Evidence from Chinese listed firms. *Chinese Management Studies*, *5*(2), 207–226.

Wu, S. (2015). Development lessons from China: A political-economic perspective on how neopatrimonial states may achieve high economic growth. *Canadian Journal of Development Studies*, *36*(3), 283–295.

Xia, F., & Walker, G. (2015). How much does owner type matter for firm performance? Manufacturing firms in China 1998–2007. *Strategic Management Journal*, *36*(4), 576–585.

Xiao, H., & Ma, Z. (2015). Business ethics in Canada, China, and Taiwan: A three-culture study on the perceived ethicality of negotiation strategies. *Nankai Business Review International*, *6*(2), 106–127.

Yang, B. (1998). *Deng: A political biography*. Armonk, NY: M. E. Sharpe.

Yang, C. -H., Ramstetter, E. D., Tsaur, J. -R., & Ngoc Phan, M. (2015). Openness, ownership, and regional economic growth in Vietnam. *Emerging Markets Finance and Trade*, *51*(Suppl. 1), S224–S233.

Yang, G. (2016). Still a century of the Chinese Model? Exploring dimensions of democratic centralism. *Chinese Political Science Review*, *1*(1), 171–189.

Zhan, J. V. (2015). Do natural resources breed corruption? Evidence from China. *Environmental and Resource Economics*, 1–23. (online before print).

Zhou, H., & Li, G. (January 19, 2016). *Political connections: An explanation for the consistently poor performance of China's stock markets*. Available at SSRN <http://ssrn.com/abstract=2718005 or http://dx.doi.org/10.2139/ssrn.2718005>.

Zhu, H., & Chung, C. -N. (2014). Portfolios of political ties and business group strategy in emerging economies: Evidence from Taiwan. *Administrative Science Quarterly*, *59*(4), 599–638.

Zhu, Q., Liu, J., & Lai, K. H. (2016). Corporate social responsibility practices and performance improvement among Chinese national state-owned enterprises. *International Journal of Production Economics*, *171*, 417–426.

Zolfaghari, B., Möllering, G., Clark, T., & Dietz, G. (2016). How do we adopt multiple cultural identities? A multidimensional operationalization of the sources of culture. *European Management Journal*, *34*(2), 102–113.

CHAPTER 4

Evolution of Responsible and Sustainable Corporate Identity for Chinese Firms

Harish C. Chandan[1] and Riturpana Das[2]
[1]Argosy University, Atlanta, GA, United States
[2]Adamas University, Kolkata, West Bengal, India

4.1 INTRODUCTION

Chinese economy is a mixture of state-owned enterprises and private companies. A transition from state-controlled to market economy has contributed to the runaway economic growth, leading to environmental pollution due to lack of corporate social responsibility (CSR) practices by firms, and lack of regulation and monitoring by the government. In China, CSR is driven by the central government creating a policy and regulatory framework for introducing and promoting the adoption of corporate sustainability (CS) reporting. The CSR practices are evolving rapidly, led by the state-owned enterprises (SOEs) (V.H. Ho, 2013).

Historically, North America and Western Europe lead the world in CSR practices. The Western-centric perceptions of CSR, however, need to be modified when being applied to China: what constitutes CSR and how organizations act responsibly. The practice of CSR and stakeholder engagement relies on specific institutional elements, which are structurally possible and normatively legitimate CSR practices. Various state regulations, industrial norms, civil organizations, and community groups may result in different CSR sense making and practices (Yin & Zhang, 2012). A firm's approach to CSR is context-specific due to social environment, cultural ethics, political structure, government regulations, peer-pressure, and economic considerations (Hou & Li, 2014).

This chapter summarizes the evolution of CSR practices in China. The roles of cultural ethics (national and organizational), normative and structural aspects (political structure, and government regulations), competitive forces (consumer-driven and peer-pressure), corporate philanthropy, and

The China Business Model. DOI: http://dx.doi.org/10.1016/B978-0-08-100750-1.00004-8

social environment are reviewed. The current Chinese CSR/sustainability practices are discussed in terms of the international CSR standards (UN Global Compact (UNGC), G4-Global Reporting Initiative (G4-GRI), and ISO 26000).

4.2 HISTORICAL PERSPECTIVE ON THE EVOLUTION OF CSR IN CHINA

People's Republic of China was established in 1949 with a centrally planned economic system and SOEs. In 1978, China instituted an economic reform, opening up to the rest-of-the world policy. The CSR concept was introduced into China from the West in late-1980s. The theoretical foundation of CSR research in China began c.1990 and CSR was defined as the enterprise's obligation to face the social needs and all kinds of social problems, to safeguard the state, the society and the fundamental interests of people, while ensuring its own survival (Li, Zhang, & Check-Teck, 2013).

As China transitioned from the state-controlled to market economy, its a strong emphasis on rapid economic growth for over 30 years, has led to excessive environmental pollution, social injustice, social inequality, income inequality, rural poverty, corruption, and social protests. The Chinese leaders are very sensitive to the social disorder (*luan*) that has previously led to social unrest during many dynasties and governments in the history of Chinese civilization. All segments of society are called upon to share responsibility to finance, monitor, and deliver social services to build a modern and harmonious China. Since 2005, the business sector has been recognized as a key to deliver better social services through CSR (Lu, 2009; See, 2009).

The economic reform of building market-oriented economy began in 1993, leading to a rapid growth of private firms at the expense of environment pollution and ethical treatment of customers. China's economy has been more export-oriented since the beginning of economic reforms. Economic globalization brought the multinational corporations (MNCs) into China, and as the MNC's implemented certification and audit procedures on production regulations, such as Social Accountability International, SA8000, the focus on CSR increased. The CSR audits of Chinese suppliers of the MNC's motivated Chinese firms to begin CSR practices. This practice of CSR was not only to maximize the profit of shareholders, but also benefit all stakeholders, including employees, consumers, creditors, debtors, small- and medium-sized competitors, the local community and environment, vulnerable groups, and the whole of society (Li, Zhang, Mao, & Min, 2012; Selmier, 2013).

China joined the World Trade Organization (WTO) in 2001. A triangle model of CSR was proposed, consisting of the mandatory legal level, the adherence to standard level, and the strategic and moral level that reflect managers' value judgment; CSR was considered as the third responsibility beyond economic and legal responsibility. Some Chinese scholars defined CSR similar to the West: as a four-dimensional CSR concept, involving economic, legal, ethical, and discretionary (or philanthropic) dimensions (Carroll, 2004,1991).

In 2005, Chinese President Hu Jintao instituted a "Harmonious Society (*jianshe héxié shèhuì*)" policy as China's socio-economic development process in order to reduce social disparities in China. This new vision was aimed at building a society that placed people first, including the employees and creditors. This vision combines economic growth with social and environmental concerns, and emphasizes the increased level of CSR in China beyond mere compliance with regulatory norms. Between 2006 and 2011, the enforcement of China's company law (CCL) contributed to some progress relevant to CSR, including data on the performance of directors' duties toward stakeholders. Enforcement of CSR-related legal requirements still involves some political interference. Public awareness of the social problems that CSR can impact, improvements in the legal system, and business disclosure of social and environmental issues will contribute toward better CSR (Zhao, 2012).

In 2006, the Company Law of the People's Republic of China was amended. This law requires companies to abide by social ethics, business ethics, to be honest and trustworthy, as well as to fulfill social responsibilities, including sustainable development. The CSR was defined as the combination of economic responsibility and legal responsibility, abiding by laws about environment, resources, and the rights and interests of stakeholders while defending the benefits as well as the sustainable development of the society. Another definition of CSR, for the purpose of sustainable development, was divided into three hierarchies: the legal responsibility that must be fulfilled, the economic and ethical responsibility that need to be fulfilled, and the charitable responsibility that is voluntarily fulfilled (Wong, 2009).

Since 2006, the Chinese government has promoted building a harmonious society, which has led to a greater focus on reporting of CSR and sustainability. Shenzhen and Shanghai Exchange-listed companies are required to issue sustainability reports, and the Shenzhen Exchange provides training on data collection and CSR-report writing for listed companies. *China's New Social Policy* assesses the social impact created by the market-oriented changes in China's social policies, and contests the idea that market-oriented development can result in a more sustainable society (Zhao & Lim, 2009). There is an overlap between the objectives of a harmonious society and CSR, and the new social policy may lead to increased CSR engagement in China. Toward the end of his tenure in 2011, Hu appeared to extend the ideology to an international dimension, with a focus on international peace and cooperation—said to lead to a "harmonious world," whereas Hu's successor, Xi, Jinping has used the Harmonious Society philosophy more sparingly, in favor of emphasizing his vision of the Chinese Dream. Harmonious Society is unlikely to promote CSR in China's growing private sector because policy measures that affect the "constraints" driving CSR are bound by other political considerations (See, 2009). Innovation of CSR processes is necessary for overall efficiencies of economy, society, and environment (Wang, Qin, & Cui, 2010).

The CSR practices of foreign multinational enterprises in China can contribute to China's national priority of building a harmonious society. Based on personal reflections, extensive literature review, and 8 years of experiential field work in China, it was found that only 4 out of 20 multinational enterprises surveyed were committed to fostering green growth, improving livelihood, and promoting a general integration of Chinese business into global markets through social innovations and collaborative projects. Many CSR programs were found to superficially complement China's harmonious society policy (Lam, 2014).

In 2008, the Chinese Academy of Social Sciences established a set of CSR reporting guidelines, which is now highly recommended by Central Government officials. There was a notable increase in the subsequent CSR articles written by Chinese university researchers. Most of the articles employed an empirical research methodology to study CSR in various sectors. There were no comparative studies found between China and other countries that may perform better in CSR. It is likely that the Chinese academics may be under some political pressure not to compare Chinese CSR unfavorably with foreign examples (Memon, Chanar, & Robson, 2015). Based on a synthesis of Carroll's CSR model and the strategic legitimacy approach, the political capital influences corporate philanthropy (Chen & Cao, 2016).

The China Enterprise Management Association defines CSR as the responsibility that *must* be fulfilled was the economic and legal responsibility, the responsibility that *should* be fulfilled was the ethical responsibility, the responsibility that is *voluntarily* fulfilled was the charity responsibility. Another definition of CSR in China considers three levels: the basic responsibility, including economic and legal responsibility for the shareholders, the employees and the government; responsibility related directly to the development of enterprise, including responsibility for employees and consumers; charitable responsibility related directly to the development of the enterprise, including responsibility for the environment and the public. The nongovernmental organizations (NGOs) can serve to monitor corporations for sustainability practices, but, in China most of the influential NGOs that serve to monitor corporations are established by, or dependent on, government agencies. China needs to develop independent NGOs in order to apply greater checks on this power and allow the social and economic system to run more smoothly (Yu, 2015).

From 1953 onwards, the concept of CSR in the West has experienced five stages of evolution: social ethics-oriented stage, differentiation and prosperity stage, stakeholder stage, business-oriented stage, and sustainable development stage. After about 20 years of development, going through the evolution of the introduction period, chaotic period, plus the legal and ethical responsibility period, the concept of CSR in China achieved unification with the West with an orientation of sustainable development in the late-2000s (Chu, Chatterjee, & Brown, 2013). There are some differences between CSR concepts in China and the West. The CSR concept in the West had a social or ethical orientation in 1950–60s. It was further expanded in 1970s' and shifted toward a business-oriented concept, based on the stakeholder theory in 1980s. It was not until 1990s' that CSR concept incorporated a notion of sustainable development. In China, the CSR practices evolved from the legal dimension of CSR (low-level CSR). The next higher level of CSR in China is business-oriented (medium-level). The ethics and sustainability-oriented CSR is considered the highest level of CSR in China (Yang and Guo, 2014).

4.3 EVOLUTION OF CSR INTO CS IN CHINA

CSR and CS are related concepts. With increased globalization and social awareness due to the evolution of web 2.0 (social media networks, user-generated content, and open source approaches), the notion of

CSR has evolved into the present CS within the context of "global commons," "stakeholder involvement," and "innovative global partnerships" (Kolk, Hong, & Dolen, 2010; Pirnea, Olaru, & Moisa, 2011). The concept of CSR has evolved into a broader CS perspective to include the three pillars of profit, people, and planet (Wempe & Kaptein, 2002). The ultimate goal of CS is to "meet the needs of the present without compromising the ability of future generations to meet their own needs" (Bruntland Report, 1987).

CSR is a voluntary business initiative that represents a way of managing a business in a sustainable and ethical manner to achieve the triple bottom line—financial, environmental, and social. CSR promotes sustainable development. It is a partnership between the business, government, civil society, investors, and all the other stakeholders including employees and customers. Its voluntary initiative encourages companies to implement responsible business practices, develop new business models, innovations, and new technologies—leading to sustainable manufacturing processes and green supply chain management. CSR nudges companies to conduct business ethically and beyond compliance within the laws governing product safety, environmental protection, corruption, human rights, labor rights, and giving back to society. CSR inspires firms to watch the interests of both the shareholders and other stakeholders including employees, consumers, suppliers, and local communities. CSR involves not just providing jobs but also the quality of life (Lin, 2010).

CSR is often used as a synonym to reference "sustainability," "responsible business conduct," or "business and human rights," balancing the triple bottom line (profit, people, and planet). CS, however, is rooted in the wider concept of sustainable development, which can be characterized as a normative concept like freedom, democracy or social justice (Kraus & Britzelmaier, 2012). This sustainability is a dynamic process of change and constant improvement with intermediate achievable targets (Delai & Takahashi, 2011).

According to European Union, CSR refers to "Companies taking responsibility for their impact on society. The European Commission believes that CSR is important for the sustainability, competitiveness, and innovation of EU enterprises and the EU economy. It brings benefits for risk management, cost savings, access to capital, customer relationships, and human resource management." The EU-CSR strategy is based on UNGC, UN Guiding Principles on Business and Human Rights, ISO 26000: Guidance Standard on Social Responsibility, International Labor Organization (ILO) Tripartite Declaration of Principles Concerning Multinational Enterprises on Social Policy, and OECD Guidelines for

Multinational Enterprises. CSR is a voluntary effort led by a company and is supported by complementary public (government) regulation. Companies become socially responsible by following the law and integrating the social, environmental, ethical, consumer, and human rights concerns into their business strategy and operations. CSR is beneficial to the enterprise in its risk management, cost savings, access to capital, customer relationships, HR management, and its ability to innovate. CSR makes companies more sustainable and innovative, which contributes to a more sustainable economy. CSR builds a more cohesive society (EU-CSR, 2015; EU Multi Stakeholder Forum, 2015).

4.4 CSR/CS THEORETICAL FRAMEWORK IN CHINA

Historically, the CSR framework includes four domains—economic, legal, ethical, and philanthropic. The hierarchy of the importance of the four domains can be described by a pyramid, intersecting circles, or concentric circles. The Pyramid model of CSR includes four levels with the economic level as the base of the pyramid. The next levels, in order of importance are legal, ethical, and philanthropic activities from bottom to the top of pyramid. In both the pyramid and concentric circle models, the hierarchy of domains is economic, legal, ethical, and philanthropic and there is no overlap between various domains. In the Intersecting circle model, the four circles of domains intersect and show overlap. All three models describe economic responsibility as the core responsibility. A firm must be economically profitable, must obey the laws, be ethical and be a good corporate citizen by contributing to society. The pyramid model does not include the influence of culture, peer-pressure, social needs, environmental responsibility, and political structure on CSR activities (Carroll, 1991, 2004; Geva, 2008).

Adapting these CSR models in developing countries, such as China, needs some adjustments to reflect the culture, needs of the society and political structure. The philanthropic domain in both the pyramid and concentric circles models is in the last position. Philanthropy needs to be a higher priority in the CSR model to account for social needs and political structure. Philanthropy in a developing country can help toward improving infrastructure, schools, hospitals and housing developments. CSR in developing countries of both Asia and Latin America are more concerned with life threating diseases such as AIDS, improving working condition, wages, and poverty. A more-inclusive CSR framework is necessary to address the social and environmental problems in a region, such as deforestation, unemployment, income, inequality, and crime. CSR, must be understood in the context of cultural ethics, institutional infrastructure, and political structure within a country. The national culture plays an important role in implementing and managing CSR practices in an organization National culture is the collection of shared values among people that determines how they perceive and reacts to its environment. Therefore, the concept of CSR, rooted in organizational culture, is highly influenced by the national culture. The short-term and long-term goals of the organization, peer-pressure, social pressure, and the evolving global sustainability norms further influence a firm's CSR practices.

Based on multiple case studies of 16 Chinese firms, it was found that the Chinese understanding of CSR is largely grounded within the context of ethical and discretionary actions. Early CSR research focus in China was on ethical issues. It has expanded to social, environmental, and stakeholder concerns (Moon & Shen, 2010). The governmental leadership, the ethical leadership, and cultural traditions in Chinese CSR determine the focus of CSR in China. The absence of a conducive, socially normative environment and positive peer pressure, and misalignment between CSR and organizational design further contribute to the lack of a systemic and institutionalized approach to CSR in China (Yin & Zhang, 2012). The context-specific drivers of CSR/CS are illustrated in Fig. 4.1.

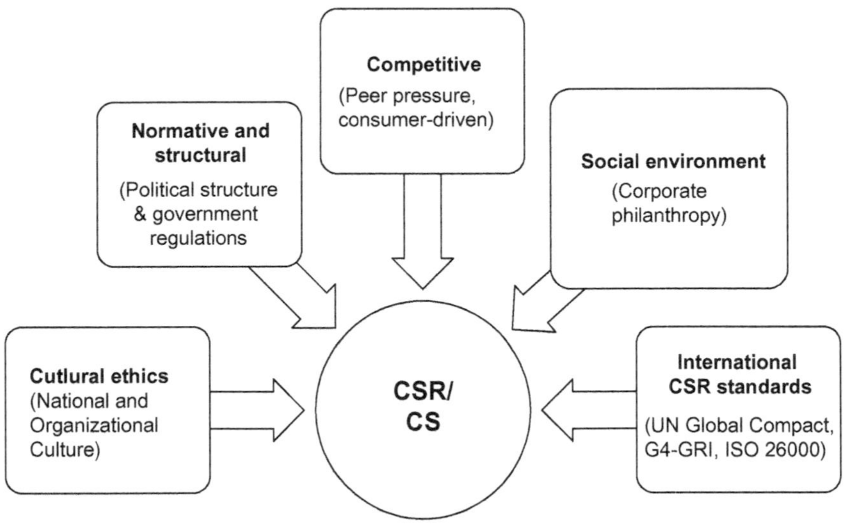

Figure 4.1 Context-specific drivers of CSR/CS in a country.

In China, CSR is not as driven by the consumer as it is in the United States. The SOEs play a large role in setting examples for CSR practices, and much corporate responsibility is driven by governmental organizations; Philanthropy and volunteerism is slowly emerging again in China. During the early years of Communist China, volunteerism was limited to people helping out their own family members in accordance with the saying "Charity begins at home." *Culturally, volunteering to help others beyond one's family is emerging again in the post-socialist China and* many wealthy Chinese have established private foundations. For example, during the Sichuan earthquake in 2008, many Chinese businesses made donations to help the victims. Companies focus their philanthropic efforts on what the government wants and provide that on a voluntary basis. Companies in China often find that employee volunteerism encourages a sense of camaraderie that boosts employee morale at the workplace (Mullich, 2011).

A management model for organizations to use when implementing CSR (both nationally and internationally) includes compliance with regulations, analysis of existing policies and performance in CSR. This requires identifying several factors including key aspects of business that influence the local community and the existing problems with the local community. One then has to define goals, strategies, and operational plans, provide necessary human and material resources, and develop a plan of action for implementation of programs and plans. During implementation, one has to measure and report the results to the internal and external stakeholders in order to influence the perception and attitudes toward CSR. This management tool will allow an organization to continually seek new ways of differentiating itself from its competitors—especially in the 21st-century business paradigm. CSR is affectively achieved by employing management strategies that are designed to create unique operating capabilities and a culture that embraces CSR. An organization's culture should be considered when implementing CSR responsibilities (Bakić, Kostić, & Nešković, 2015).

4.5 INTERNATIONAL STANDARDS FOR CSR/CS

The major international CSR/CS standards include SA8000, UNGC, and G4-GRI and ISO 26000. The SA8000 is one of the "world's first auditable social certification standards for decent work places, across all industrial sectors. It is based on the UN Declaration of Human Rights, conventions of the International Labor Organization (ILO), UN and national law, and spans industry and corporate codes to create a common language to measure social performance. It takes a management systems approach by setting out the structures and procedures that companies must adopt in order to ensure that compliance with the standard is continuously reviewed. Those seeking to comply with SA8000 have adopted policies and procedures that protect the basic human rights of workers" (SAI, 2015).

4.5.1 UN Global Compact

Launched in 2000, UNGC is the largest international corporate sustainability initiative (CS). It is a public–private initiative with over 12,000 signatories, based in 145 countries. The UNGC proposes 10 principles in the 4 core areas of human rights, labor, environment, and anticorruption. The companies that adopt the Global Compact publish "Communication on Progress" (COP) through their annual report, CS report or a CSR Report. The UNGC helps ensure that business activity adds value to the bottom-line, to people, communities, and the planet. The COP is issued annually as part of a Sustainability- or CSR Report. It is certified to qualify for the Global Compact active level. The self-assessed COP includes a statement from the CEO regarding continued support for the UNGC and its 10 principles, a description of actions on relevant policies related to human rights, environment, anticorruption, and includes a measurement of outcomes (G4-GRI, 2015).

The UNGC engages civil society, investors, educators, consumers, and policymakers to help create an enabling environment for responsible business. It recommends five CSR practices: operating responsibly in alignment with universal principles, taking strategic actions that support the society around them, pushing sustainability deep into the corporate identity, commitment at the highest level, reporting annually on their efforts, and engaging locally where they have a presence. The UNGC is a holistic approach, recommending that responsible businesses enact the same values and principles wherever they have a presence and that good practices in one area do not offset harm in another (Cetindamar, 2007; Rothlin, 2010; UN Global Compact, 2015).

The ultimate goal of CSR is to embed social responsibility into the DNA of companies on a voluntary basis. The main role of the regulatory agencies should be to provide guidance and firms should comply voluntarily. Laws should help monitor enforcement. The media needs to be engaged in CSR; it must play a more-proactive role—documenting developments, progress, and setbacks. There should be open platforms for exchanging dialogue, best practices and collaboration among stakeholders.

Firms should follow international CSR frameworks including the UN Guiding Principles on Business and Human Rights. Firms should publish substantive CSR reports voluntarily following the international standards (EU, 2015; EU Multi Stakeholder Forum, 2015).

The UNGC global opportunity report identifies and ranks 15 sustainability opportunities, according to public and private sector interest and potential impact on societies and business. With the new sustainability mindset, the global sustainability challenges and risks can be seen as opportunities. The report recommends an open innovation platform where stakeholders worldwide can explore and capture sustainability opportunities and solutions across risk domains and regions. These include: extreme weather, lack of fresh water, unsustainable urbanization, noncommunicable disease, and fossil fuels (Global Opportunity Report, 2015).

4.5.2 G4-Global Reporting Initiative (GRI)

The interpretation of the CSR/CS concept and reporting framework is context-specific. In preparing CSR/CS reports, key challenges include reporting content selection, data collection and transparency in reporting (Searcy & Buslivich, 2014). The G4-GRI sustainability reporting guidelines offer reporting principles, standard disclosures and an implementation manual for the preparation of sustainability reports by organizations—regardless of their size, sector, or location. These guidelines provide an international reference for the disclosure of governance approach and environmental, social, and economic performance and impacts of organizations. These guidelines were developed through a global multistakeholder approach including inputs from business, labor, civil society, financial markets, and governmental agencies in several countries. The G4-GRI offers the guidelines for CSR or CS reporting, based on UNGC. Globally, G4-GRI is the most widely used and comprehensive sustainability reporting standard (G4-GRI, 2015). The G4-GRI is aligned with the guidelines of Organization for Economic Co-Operation and Development (OECD) for multinational enterprises, the UNGC Principles, and the UN Guiding Principles on Business and Human Rights. By using the GRI Guidelines, reporting organizations disclose their most critical impact, both positive and negative, upon the environment, society, and the economy. G4-GRI-based reports generate reliable, relevant, and standardized information. This helps to assess opportunities and risks, and enable more informed decision-making within the organization and among its stakeholders. Some firms use third-party sustainability reporting such as the Dow Jones

Sustainability Index (DJSI). The DJSIs are based on RobecoSAM's internationally recognized Corporate Sustainability Assessment methodology (DJSI, 2015). RobecoSAM has developed the DJSI in order to help us identify those companies that are best equipped to recognize and respond to emerging opportunities and risks resulting from global sustainability trends (DJSI, 2015).

Any company that does not submit a COP for two consecutive years is labeled as "inactive" on the UNGC website. In October 2015, the United Nations delisted 335 companies including China Petroleum and Chemical Corporation. By delisting companies, the Global Compact is demonstrating its credibility and interest in upholding its standards of corporate responsibility. The Global Compact is a voluntary initiative, but it is important for companies to take their sustainability commitment seriously and demonstrate performance. To regain their "active" status, delisted companies are simply required to submit the missing COP (World Watch Institute, 2015).

4.5.3 International Standard, ISO 26000

ISO 26000 provides guidance, rather than requirements, so it cannot be certified to, unlike other well-known ISO standards. Instead, it helps clarify what social responsibility is, helps businesses and organizations translate principles into effective actions, and shares global best practices relating to social responsibility. It is aimed at all types of organizations regardless of their activity, size, or location. The standard was launched in 2010, following 5 years of negotiations between many different stakeholders across the world. Representatives from government, NGOs, industry, consumer groups, and labor organizations around the world were involved in its development, which means it represents an international consensus. Other related international standards include ISO 14000—Environmental management, ISO 50001—Energy management, and ISO 45001—Occupational Health and Safety (ISO, 2015).

4.6 CSR/CS REPORTING IN CHINA

CSR reporting focuses on the disclosure of information regarding sustainability practices, environment, human rights, and anticorruption (UN Global Compact, 2015). The information reported, however, is all too often determined by what the company itself deems important. To improve the reliability of CSR information and to enhance stakeholders' confidence, CSR reports are now often reviewed by third parties including certified public accountants. According to accounting experts, key factors in Chinese CSR were identified, with data obtained from interviews and analyzed using the decision making trial and evaluation laboratory (DEMATEL). The dimensions and subfactors of China's CSR were established, to determine the impact of each dimension, and to ascertain the mutual impact among the subfactors, from which to construct an influential network relation map. Based on the analysis of these expert interviews, it is suggested that CSR improvements should be made in the following order: (1) Safe Production, (2) Product Quality, (3) Environmental Protection, and (4) Employee Promotion. These four CSR dimensions were found to be mutually influential. The "Safe Production" dimension was the most influential dimension (Chen and Chi, 2015).

Leading Chinese and global companies operating in China communicate their CSR practices to the Chinese and global stakeholders on their websites. It was found that the companies follow one of the three approaches to CSR reporting: ad-hoc public philanthropy, strategic philanthropy, and ethical business practices. Chinese and global companies present their CSR principles and practices differently because of their different relations with major Chinese and global stakeholders. The nature of the CSR communication was determined more by whether a firm is targeting businesses or consumers, than whether the firm is Chinese or global (Lu & Hingmei, 2009).

Large Chinese firms have increasingly adopted formal CSR reporting, especially the SOEs. For example, COSCO, the Chinese shipping giant, was awarded Model Practice Company by the UNGC in 2010. In 2013, Chinese Academy of Social Sciences released a blue book (official report), on the state of CSR in China, which recommended improved reporting guidelines. Because the purpose of CSR reporting is to share information about a business's social and environmental impact with the public., the publication of such reports often leads to transparency, enhanced awareness and better sustainability practices. According to a Chinese sustainability consultant Syntao, State Grid was the only company in China to file a CSR report in 2006. Six years later, in 2012, 1722 Chinese companies filed CSR reports. According to Syntao, 22.6% of central government-led enterprises issued CSR reports in 2012, compared with only 9.4% of private enterprises. This suggests that the CSR reporting in China trend is being driven by SOEs, which are owned by the central government. Publishing CSR reports, however, does not necessarily mean that these reports are presenting a full and accurate picture of the firm's operations and it is not clear whether publishing an increasing number of CSR reports has resulted in more sustainable business practices. For example, Baogang Group, a steel company in Inner Mongolia claims to have invested tens of millions of dollars a year in environmental protection and waste processing. It has been publically recognized for its CSR and sustainability activities. In early 2013, however, the company was reported to emit large amounts of heavy metals and other chemicals into the air, leaking into surface and ground water. Studies carried out in one of the worst affected villages confirmed there were unusually high rates of cancer, along with high rates of osteoporosis and skin and respiratory diseases and the radiation levels are ten times higher than in the surrounding countryside. Another example of discordant CSR reporting is, China National Petroleum Corporation (CNPC). CNPC has received awards for its outstanding performance in CSR reporting. In 2013, it was sued by All-China Environment Federation (ACEF) because its emissions polluted soil and ground water in Jilin province. A few leading CSR companies in China have already adopted internationally accepted frameworks. For example, Baosteel, a state-owned iron and steel company based in Shanghai, has disclosed information according to GRI standards since 2006. Moreover, as a high energy-consumption enterprise, it also reported information related to energy consumption, water consumption, greenhouse gas emissions, and wastewater discharge, which are beyond the standard requirements. According to Syntao's report, among 2012 reports, only 17% supplied such critical information (M. Ho, 2013; Marquis & Chen, 2013).

Based on interviews with 30 executives from 20 foreign MNE's in China, 95% focused on the legal compliances of charity, internal employee conduct, internal technical and operational efficiency of environmental activities in their CSR programs. The firm's main priority was the economic responsibility. The CSR programs are used to gain political legitimacy with the Chinese government and CSR is used as a public relations management tool to create good brand images in the local and international media, without ensuring their Chinese suppliers' CSR performance or paying the cost of the environment being damaged by their Chinese suppliers. The CSR practices in China must be driven through corporate commitment as the system in China allows many companies to easily bypass the legal environmental requirements at low cost (Lam, 2011; Tan, 2009).

4.6.1 Role of Chinese Government in CSR Reporting

In China, the government plays a major role in how business firms comply with CSR reporting. Based on a database that includes all CSR reports issued by approximately 1600 publicly listed Chinese firms between 2006 and 2009, it was found that government signaling is an important mechanism of political influence. The firms strategically respond to government signals on monitoring CSR activities. The private-versus-state ownership, executives serving on political councils, political legacy, and financial resources affect the likelihood of firms issuing CSR reports. State-owned firms are more likely to issue CSR reports. In addition, the government monitoring leads to firms issuing substantive CSR reports (Marquis & Qian, 2014).

Corporations in China are increasingly expected by the public and government to be more socially responsible. A mandate from the government for CSR reporting does not necessarily lead to high quality CSR reporting. The firms publishing high quality CSR reports tend to have better financial characteristics including market valuation, ownership, and leverage. Based on data from 613 CSR reports by corporations listed on both the Shenzhen and Shanghai stock exchanges (SSE). The CSR behavior of listed corporations in China was evaluated using in-depth and multifaceted quality CSR scores (overall, and segregated into macro-social, content, and technology). The CSR report quality scores were gathered from HEXUN (website) and the financial and stock market information from the China Stock Market and Accounting Research (CSMAR) database. It was found that the quality of a (mandatory) CSR report was positively related to corporate financial characteristics, including: market capitalization (corporate size), shareholders' concentration of powers, and corporate financial leverage (implying bondholders/debtors' influence). It was also found that CSR reporting was not associated with corporate profitability or with state-ownership. The presence of independent directors (in China) seems to have negative influence (Li et al., 2013). Based on a recent review of the CSR literature in China and an in-depth critique of two major Chinese CSR studies conducted by the Chinese Academy of Social Sciences, it was found that Chinese firms tend to use self-developed CSR indicators instead of international CSR standards (Guan and Naronha, 2013).

The issues of CSR in China are evolving from a latent to an emerging stage but have not been consolidated and institutionalized.

The CSR responses and performance levels of corporations are evolving from defensive and compliance stages to a managerial stage but are far from the strategic and civil stages. The multiple dimensions and dynamics of CSR can be explored using an aggregate methodology of observation, comparison and estimation, and a fuzzy analytic hierarchy process can be constructed. In a case study of a state-owned corporation, it was concluded that CSR has a dual nature, consisting of both objective and subjective aspects.

Corporations need to be adaptive in taking social responsibilities that are appropriate to their context and capacity. Both the national and corporate approaches are necessary for CSR risk mitigation and capacity building (Zeng, Xu, Yin, & Tam, 2012; Zhao, Zu, Li, & Li, 2014).

CSR is often understood as the voluntary actions firms take beyond legal compliance. In China, however, both the national and subnational governments in China advance CSR. This reflects broader governance trends that embrace "soft law" and quasi-voluntary standards to nudge companies toward and beyond minimum regulatory goals. It is not clear how the "soft law" will work within the formal legal institutions and traditional regulatory monitoring and enforcement structures, which are weak in China. The interaction of the national and subnational CSR policies in China and the role of alternate regulatory tools are still evolving (M. Ho, 2013; V.H. Ho, 2013).

4.7 CSR/CS ACTIVITIES OF CHINESE FIRMS IN VARIOUS SECTORS

CSR activities in China are driven by several factors, including structural and normative factors (political structure and government regulations), competitive factors (peer-pressure and consumer-driven), social environment (corporate philanthropy), cultural ethics (national culture and organizational culture), and international CSR standards including UNGC, G4-GRI, and ISO 26000 (Kolk et al., 2010). A statistical analysis of 146 questionnaires showed that Chinese state-owned companies implement four types of CSR practices under the ISO 26000 framework including employee rights, consumer issues, fair operation, and labor practices. Chinese state-owned companies lead CSR practices, except those related to charity and employee rights. Corporate philanthropy, or charity, is a specific CSR dimension in China, but it is usually implemented based on guidance from the government. Normative drivers like regulations motivate most CSR practices. The consumer issues-related CSR practices are driven by the competition. Peer-pressure from external institutional to drive CSR practices is relatively low (Zhu & Zhang, 2015).

As part of CSR activities, many corporations in China contribute toward social development. Based on a review of 52 corporate foundations set up in China, it was found that the corporate philanthropy in China is at an early stage of development; Corporate philanthropists participate in social development mainly through donation to government and government-organized NGOs. The corporations are more enthusiastic about supporting infrastructure projects and the Chinese nonprofit sector needs to become more professional (Zhou, 2015). The Chinese firms are becoming more sensitive to codes of conduct in curbing the labor abuses and codes of conduct represent a privatized form of global labor regulation. They are effective in some respects, but are ineffective in others, improving labor standards in the global production system, for example. Based on an in-depth case study about the implementation of codes of conduct at a Chinese supplier for Reebok, a leading global footwear brand, it was found that the effectiveness of codes of conduct in curbing labor abuses must be understood in terms of overlapping international, industrial, national, and local contexts (Yu, 2015).

International pressure groups and customer expectations are forcing the Chinese textile and apparel industry to implement CSC900T, which is based on a consumer-oriented and sustainable development philosophy. The CSC9000T standard has similar features as the standards SA8000 and ISO 26000. The main focus is on social aspects but has relatively vague environmental guidelines and lack of third-party audits. An initial internal focus is placed on education and company policies. The role of the Chinese government and authorities is to strengthen and legitimize the industry (Chen, Larsson, & Mark-Herbert, 2014).

Based on the responses of food company managers in 161 companies in China, a company's attitude (defensive/passive/proactive) to CSR influences its performance with respect to food risks: A food company experiences less risk with better CSR performance. Of course, food risk management is influenced by budget allocated, the managers' perception of the importance of food risk management, and their actions to affect organizational behavior to reduce food risks. CSR, however, tends to mitigate any food risks due to the goodwill generated by CSR activities of the firm (Zhang, Gao, & Morse, 2015).

Table 4.1 lists the top 15 Chinese companies ranked by Fortune 500 Global. Most of them are state-owned and have joined Global Compact and are active in reporting the COP.

Table 4.1 Top 15 Chinese companies ranked by Fortune 500 Global

	Chinese company	Fortune 500 Global Rank	Ownership	Joined global compact	Next COP in
1	Sinopec (oil)	2	State	2004	2016
2	China National Petroleum (Petro China)	4	State	2007	2016
3	State Grid (utilities)	7	State	2006	2016
4	Industrial and Commercial Bank of China (ICBC)	18	State	2012	2016
5	China Construction Bank	29	State	n/a	Yes
6	Agriculture Bank of China	36	State	n/a	n/a
7	China State Construction Engineering	37	State	n/a	n/a
8	Bank of China	45	State	n/a	
9	China Mobile Communications	55	Private	2007	2016
10	SAIC Motor	60	State	n/a	n/a
11	China Railway Engineering	71	State	n/a	n/a
12	China National Offshore Oil	72	State	n/a	n/a
13	Noble Group (Trading)	77	Private	n/a	n/a
14	China Railway Construction	79	State	2010	2016
15	China Development Bank	87	State	2006	2016

Source: Fortune 500 Global. (2015). <http://fortune.com/global500/> Retrieved on December 29, 2015.

Sinopec is the top-ranked Fortune 500 Global Company and is state-owned. It became a participant in UNGC in November 2004, being one of the first Chinese institutions to join UNGC. Since 2005, Sinopec has established a comprehensive CSR assurance system to comply with UNGC's 10 principles in the areas of human rights, labor, the environment, and anticorruption. Its annual sustainable development report has been submitted to UNGC and released to the public since 2006 (Sinopec, 2015).

The China National Petroleum Company (CNPC) is technically a private corporation. However, CNPC is a state oil company of the People's Republic of China, a central SOE that is the direct successor to the Ministry of Petroleum Industry. Although there is an official split between the Chinese Communist Party (CCP) and the Chinese national oil companies, they do maintain a symbiotic relationship: many of the key company executives also hold positions in the Central Committee of the CCP.

CNPC reports on its sustainability initiatives and compliance with various human rights, labor, and environmental standards. Self-reporting alone only reflects a company's self-analysis of its current programs. It does not provide an independent source of analysis, and does not provide a standard to which the company should aspire in its future activities. In order to show its commitment to international norms, CNPC should consider opening itself to third-party auditing under SA8000, or explicitly adopting the external obligations created by the VPs and the Global Compact (Wolfe & Evans, 2011). Thirteen out of 15 top Chinese companies as ranked by Fortune 500 Global are state-owned. The two private companies are China Mobile Communications (9th) and Noble Group (13th) (Fortune 500 Global, 2015).

China Mobile was the first telecommunications company in China to release a CSR report in 2007. It is ranked 9th in the Fortune 500 Global list and is privately owned. It changed the name of the report to "sustainability report" in 2010, and integrated sustainability management with operational management. In 2011, DJSI recognized China Mobile for the fourth consecutive year and were still the only company from Mainland China listed on the DJSI. China mobile actively engages their stakeholders, including: employees, shareholders and investors, government authorities and regulators, customers, value chain partners and community, and environment.

Many MNCs in China equate the concept of CSR with stakeholder management. The stakeholders are defined as: shareholders, employees, government, community, customers, suppliers, and environment. The key responsibilities toward shareholders include financial returns, information disclosure and transparency, sustainable growth and legal compliance. For employees, the key responsibilities included competitive wage and salary, employee engagement in CSR programs, training, and career development. Toward government, key responsibilities include public–private partnership/collaboration, government capacity building, alignment with government initiatives and concerns, legal compliance, and tax payment. For community, the responsibilities involve investment in community education, cross-sector collaboration, community engagement and dialogue. Toward customers, they are: product quality and service excellence, customer engagement in CSR programs, CSR education, and meeting customer expectations. For suppliers, responsibilities include win–win partnership and inclusion of social- and environmental criteria in supplier selection. With regards to environment, there are responsibilities to green workplace/factory, environmental policies, environmental education and management (Yin, Rothlin, Li & Caccamo, 2013). Firms with more-concentrated block ownership are less likely to issue CSR reports (Trifilova, Bessant, Fu, & Gosling, 2013; Zheng, Balsara, & Huang, 2013).

4.8 CONSUMER RESPONSE TO CSR IN CHINA

The CSR practices of a firm positively influence the consumers purchase intention of products and services. In China, consumers who have a high level of awareness and trust of CSR, transform good CSR record into positive corporate evaluation, product association and purchase intention. Across different product categories, the consumer response to CSR varies: Firms selling experience products (vs search and credence products) tend to gain positive product association and purchase intention through CSR practices and middle-age consumers with good income tend to respond to CSR more positively (Tian, Wang, & Yang, 2011). For Chinese consumers, a good CSR record is more likely to be transformed into positive corporate evaluation, product association and purchase intention if they have a high level of awareness and trust of CSR. Consumer responses to CSR vary across different product categories. Middle age and income level consumers respond to CSR more positively (Zhilong, Wang, & Yang, 2011).

The consumers in China are becoming increasingly aware of the CSR. Based on the factor analysis in a study of 4980 sports lottery consumers, two factors were identified associated with consumer perceptions of CSR in China's lottery administration—Regulatory/Prevention Responsibilities and Product Development Responsibility. These two factors influenced the consumer behavior of relative and absolute expenditure, purchasing frequency and time commitment The originally Western CSR construct seems possible to generalize in China, but consumers across all regions perceive two, rather than four components: combining economic and legal responsibilities (labeled "required CSR"), and combining ethical and philanthropic responsibilities ("expected CSR"). Consumers expect local Chinese firms to take more responsibility than foreign firms, particularly for required CSR (Kolk, Dolen, & Ma, 2015).

4.9 PERCEIVED BENEFITS OF CSR/CS—COMPANY IMAGE AND FINANCIAL PERFORMANCE

CSR helps with the public relations management of a firm. In a survey on CSR accountability and transparency of corporate communication/public relations executives in China, four topical areas were investigated: drivers for CSR engagement, areas of practice, importance of CSR communication, and preferred channels of communication. It was found there was a strong concern for corporate image and culture in pursuing CSR. Among the society's many problems, disaster relief was given an overwhelming priority, perhaps to earn goodwill with the government. The Chinese firms did most of the CSR communication on their website and Internet media (Wang & Chaudhri, 2009).

CSR activities are often considered as cost to a company and there is not a clear-cut financial payoff. Based on a study of 30 domestically listed Chinese Petroleum enterprises, it was found that the CSR increased their enterprise value in both the short term and long term. CSR investment of the petroleum enterprise had positive correlation with equity return, profit margin and growth rate of major business, and liquidity ratio. It had negative correlation with debt-to-asset ratio and no relationship with enterprises ownership (Xiantao, Wang, & Jian, 2014).

Many multinationals operate their subsidiaries in China. Although CSR is still new to China, being socially responsible nevertheless brings financial benefits. To achieve sustainability with a stakeholder-based CSR assessment, foreign invested enterprises need to improve on awareness and communication between different stakeholders (Shengtian, Fu, & Li, 2010). The MNC's CSR practices can influence the firm's performance in the host country at the subsidiary level. Their global and local CSR strategies must adjust based on local cultures and economic levels. It was found that the MNCs' CSR performance influences the performance of the subsidiary in China and there are moderating effects of institutional and geographic distances. The subsidiaries' CSR is associated positively with their profit in China. The greater the cultural, economic and geographic distances between the home countries and China, the less likely a subsidiary will benefit from CSR (Zou & Zhao, 2015).

4.10 CONCLUSIONS

There are differences in the process of CSR development between China, Europe, and the United States. The differences are due to the history, economics, and development of corporations (Hou & Li, 2014). The largely western concept of CSR is beginning to emerge in China in a unique way that is context-specific (Wang, 2015). The drivers of CSR in a country can be viewed in a framework of environmental constraints and discretionary responses. The evolution of reporting CS practices for firms in

China has to be viewed within the context of planned economy where the state plays a major role in economic strategy and policy management (Wong, 2009). The Shanghai and Shenzhen stock exchanges emphasize to the listed firms the importance of CSR practices in manufacturing operations and green supply chains. A global movement for social and environmental sustainability reporting has encouraged companies to be more transparent in documenting their social and environmental impacts. Such information disclosure makes companies more aware of their own impact on environment and society, and they are more open to monitoring by the government, society, and investors. The UNGC is an international forum to promote and self-report CS in the four core areas of environment, human rights, labor standards, and anticorruption The UNGC and G4-GRI are becoming the internationally accepted frameworks for companies to follow when measuring and reporting on their environmental and social performance (Bitanga & Bridwell, 2010).

CSR practices in China are converging with those of the West regarding sustainable development. The CSR research in China started in the late 1980's and the CSR concept has been evolving for over 30 years. The Corporate Social Responsibility (CSR) reports are now called "Corporate Sustainability (CS)" reports (Yang and Guo, 2014). There are differences in the process of evolution of CSR in China, Europe, and the United States. The differences result due to the political structure, social environment, economics, and development of corporations (Hou & Li, 2014). China's former global image of cheap labor, sweatshops, human rights abuses, cutting corners, unethical practices, substandard products, and serious environmental pollution, is changing toward people- and planet-friendly. Many local CSR initiatives have emerged in China, including environmental laws and regulations, governmental instructions and guidelines, NGOs and standards (Lin, 2010). Since 2005, the business sector in China has been recognized as a key sector to deliver better social services through CSR. The most important driver of the development of CSR in China is the Chinese government itself (Lam, Lam, & Lam, 2010). The government is interested in establishing competitive business environments, promoting social cohesion, and fostering collective responsibility for the betterment of society through business practices. Chinese policymakers have encouraged more corporations to practice CSR in China through the provision of a better institutional environment. The CSR/CS can become a social change agent in China when enlightened public concerns are brought back to business operations through the involvement of nongovernment organizations, local government, local citizens, and a greater degree of transparency of information and international reporting guidelines (Bai, Sarkis, & Dou, 2015).

The majority of the CSR reporting so far has, however, been mainly symbolic due to the lack of monitoring mechanisms and enforcement by the government. Most companies do not follow the international CSR reporting standards and indulge in "greenwashing," without actually practising sustainability (Larson, 2013). Chinese firms tend to issue complicated reports using self-made criteria that can be confusing, rather than being transparent. Chinese CSR reports must adhere more closely to international standards that make them verifiable for stakeholders, both domestic and overseas, and independent, third-party verification of CSR reports can enhance this credibility (Memon et al., 2015).

REFERENCES

Bai, C., Sarkis, J., & Dou, Y. (2015). Corporate sustainability developments in China: Review and analysis. *Industrial management and Data Systems*, *115*(1), 5–40.

Bakić, T. V., Kostić, S. C., & Nešković, E. (2015). Model for managing corporate social responsibility. *Management (1820-0222)*, *74*, 47–56. http://dx.doi.org/10.7595/management.fon.2015.0002.

Bitanga, J., & Bridwell, L. (2010). Corporate social responsibility and the United Nations Global Compact. *Competition Forum*, *8*(2), 265–269.

Bruntland, G. H. (1987). Our common future. *Report of the world commission on environment and development* (pp. 1–247). United Nations.

Carroll, A. B. (1991). The pyramid of corporate social responsibility: Toward the moral management of organizational stakeholders. *Business Horizons*, *34*(4), 39–48.

Carroll, A. B. (2004). Managing ethically with global stakeholders: A present and future challenge. *Academy of Management Executive*, *18*(2), 114–120.

Cetindamar, D. (2007). Corporate social responsibility practices and environmentally responsible behavior: The case of the United Nations global compact. *Journal of Business Ethics*, *76*(2), 163–1761. http://dx.doi.org/10.1007/s10551-006-9265-4.

Chen, F., & Chi, D. J. (2015). Application of a new DEMATEL to explore key factors of China's corporate social responsibility: Evidence from accounting experts. *Quality and Quantity*, *49*(1), 135–154.

Chen, T., Larsson, A., & Mark-Herbert, C. (2014). Implementing a collective code of conduct—CSC9000T in Chinese textile industry. *Journal of Cleaner Production*, *74*, 35–43.

Chen, Z., & Cao, Y. (2016). Chinese private corporate philanthropy: Social responsibility, legitimacy strategy, and the role of political capital. *Chinese Sociological Review*, *48*(2), 108–136.

Chu, C. L., Chatterjee, B., & Brown, A. (2013). The current status of greenhouse gas reporting by Chinese companies. *Managerial Auditing Journal*, *28*(2), 114–139.

Delai, I., & Takahashi, S. (2011). Sustainability measurement system: A reference model proposal. *Social Responsibility Journal*, 7(3), 438–471.

Dow Jones Sustainability index (DJSI). (2015). *RobecoSAM corporate sustainability assessment*. <http://www.sustainability-indices.com> Retrieved on December 18, 2015.

EU Multi Stakeholder Forum on Corporate Social Responsibility. (2015). *Executive summary of 2015 CSR forum*. February 3–4. <http://ec.europa.eu/growth/industry/corporate-social-responsibility/index_en.htm> Retrieved on December 18, 2015.

European Union (EU). (2015). *Corporate social responsibility*. <http://ec.europa.eu/growth/industry/corporate-social-responsibility/index_en.htm> Retrieved on December 18, 2015.

Fortune 500 Global. (2015). <http://fortune.com/global500/> Retrieved on December 29, 2015.

Geva, A. (2008). Three models of corporate social responsibility: Interrelationships between theory, research, and practice. *Business & Society Review (00453609)*, *113*(1), 1–41. http://dx.doi.org/10.1111/j.1467-8594.2008.00311.x.

G4-Global Reporting Initiative (GRI). (2015). *GRIG4-Part 1-Reporting principles and standard disclosures.pdf, GRIG4-Part2-Implementation manual.pdf*. <https://www.globalreporting.org/standards/g4/Pages/default.aspx> Retrieved on December 18, 2015.

Global Opportunity Report. (2015). *Your guide to opportunities*. <https://www.unglobalcompact.org/docs/publications/Global_Opportunity_Report.pdf>.

Guan, J., & Noronha, C. (2013). Corporate social responsibility reporting research in the Chinese academia: A critical review. *Social Responsibility Journal*, *9*(1), 33–55.

Ho, M. (2013). Key challenges facing the SRI indices development in China. *Society and Business review*, *8*(1), 6–17.

Ho, V. H. (2013). Beyond regulation: A comparative look at state-centric corporate social responsibility and the law in China. *Vanderbilt Journal of Transnational Law*, *46*, 375–442.

Hou, S., & Li, L. (2014). Reasoning and differences between CSR theory and practice in China, the United States and Europe. *Journal of International Business Ethics*, 7(1), 19–30.

International Standards Organization (ISO). (2015). <http://www.iso.org/iso/home/standards/iso26000.htm> Retrieved on December 31, 2015.

Kolk, A., Dolen, W.V., & Ma, L. (2015). Consumer perceptions of CSR: (how) is China different? *International Marketing Review*, *32*(5), 492–517.

Kolk, A., Hong, P., & Dolen, W.V. (2010). Corporate social responsibility in China: An analysis of domestic and foreign retailers' sustainability dimensions. *Business, Strategy and the Environment*, *19*, 289–303.

Kraus, P., & Britzelmaier, B. (2012). Corporate sustainability management: Evidence from Germany. *Journal of Global Responsibility*, *3*(2), 248–262.

Lam, M., Lam, A., & Lam, L. (2010). The importance of non-government organizations in the corporate social movement in China. *The International Journal of Humanities*, 7(12), 101–114.

Lam, M. L. L. (2011). Challenges of sustainable environmental programs of foreign multinational enterprises in China. *Management Research Review*, *34*(11), 1153–1168.

Lam, M. L. L. (2014). Toward a 'harmonious society' through corporate social responsibility. *Journal of Public Affairs*, *14*(2), 105–115.

Larson, C. (2013). *"Corporate social responsibility" reports in China: Progress or greenwashing?* <http://www.bloomberg.com/bw/articles/2013-12-12/corporate-social-responsibility-reports-in-china-progress-or-greenwashing>.

Li, H., Zhang, J. J., Mao, L. L., & Min, S. D. (2012). Assessing corporate social responsibility in china's sports lottery administration and its influence on consumption behavior. *Journal of Gambling Studies*, *28*, 515–540.

Li, Y., Zhang, J., & Check-Teck, F. (2013). Towards a theory of social responsibility reporting: Empirical analysis of 613 reports by listed corporations in China. *Chinese Management Studies*, 7(4), 519–534.

Lin, L. W. (2010). Corporate social responsibility in China: Window dressing or structural change? *Berkley Journal of International Law*, *28*(1), 64–100.

Lu, T., & Hingmei, L. (2009). Corporate social responsibility communication of Chinese and global corporations in China. *Public Relations Review*, *35*(3), 199–212.

Lu, X. (2009). A Chinese perspective; business ethics in China now and in the future. *Journal of Business Ethics*, *86*(4), 451–461.

Marquis, C., & Chen, Y. (2013). *Environmental reporting in China still likely to be greenwash.* <https://www.chinadialogue.net/article/show/single/en/6543-Environmental-reporting-in-China-still-likely-to-be-greenwash>.

Marquis, C., & Qian, C. (2014). CSR reporting in China: Symbol or substance? *Organization Science, 25*(1), 127–148.

Memon, Z.A., Chanar, Z.A., & Robson, M. G. (2015). Finding 'corporate social responsibility' research trends and content in Chinese universities: A literature review. *International Journal of Technology Management & Sustainable Development, 14*(3), 179–204.

Moon, J., & Shen, X. (2010). CSR in China research: Salience, focus and nature. *Journal of Business Ethics, 94*, 613–629.

Mullich, J. (2011) *Corporate social responsibility emerges in China.* <http://online.wsj.com/ad/article/chinaenergy-responsibility>.

Pirnea, I. C., Olaru, M., & Moisa, C. (2011). Relationship between corporate social responsibility and social sustainability. *Economy Trans Disciplinary Cognition, 14*(1), 36–43.

Rothlin, S. (2010). Towards a socially responsible China: A preliminary investigation of the implementation of the global compact. *Journal of International Business Ethics, 3*(1), 3–13.

Searcy, C., & Buslivich, R. (2014). Corporate perspective on the development and use of sustainability reports. *Journal of Business Ethics, 121*, 149–169.

See, G. K. H. (2009). Harmonious society and Chinese CSR: Is there really a link? *Journal of Business Ethics, 89*(1), 1–22.

Selmier, W. T., II (2013). Political resistance in Chinese mergers and acquisitions: An interview with Ted Tokuchi. *Business Horizons, 56*(6), 743–748.

Shengtian, H., Fu, W., & Li, X. (2010). Achieving sustainability with a stakeholder-based CSR assessment model for foreign invested enterprises in China. *Journal of International Business Ethics, 3*(1), 41–555.

Sinopec. (2015). <http://english.sinopec.com/media_center/news/20110622/15712.shtml> Retrieved on December 27, 2015.

Social Accountability International, SAI. (2015). SA8000. <http://www.saintl.org/index.cfm?fuseaction=Page.ViewPage&PageID=937> Retrieved on December 30, 2015.

Tan, J. (2009). Institutional structure and firm social performance in transitional economies: Evidence of multinational corporations in China. *Journal of Business Ethics, 86*, 171–189.

Tian, Z., Wang, R., & Yang, W. (2011). Consumer response to corporate social responsibility (CSR) in China. *Journal of Business Ethics, 101*, 197–212.

Trifilova, A., Bessant, J., Fu, J., & Gosling, J. (2013). Sustainability-driven Innovation and the Climate Savers' Programme: Experience of international companies in China. *Corporate Governance, 13*(5), 599–612.

United Nations (UN) Global Compact. (2015). <https://www.unglobalcompact.org/what-is-gc/strategy> Retrieved on December 18, 2015.

Wang, J., & Chaudhri, V. (2009). Corporate social responsibility engagement and communication by Chinese companies. *Public Relations Review, 35*(3), 247–250.

Wang, J., Qin, S., & Cui, Y. (2010). Problems and prospects of CSR development in China. *International Journal of Business and Management, 5*(12), 128–134.

Wang, X. C. (2015). Corporate social responsibility vs. basic corporate responsibility: Sustainability reporting of Chinese listed agribusinesses. In *Proceedings of international OFEL conference on governance, management and entrepreneurship, Zagreb, April* (pp. 297–312).

Wempe, J., & Kaptein, M. (2002). *The balanced company: A theory of corporate integrity*. Oxford: Oxford University Press.

Wolfe, W. M., & Evans, A. S. (2011). China's energy investments and the corporate social responsibility imperative. *Journal of International Law & International Relations, January*, 83–107.

Wong, L. (2009). Corporate social responsibility in China: Between the market and the search for a sustainable growth development. *Asian Business and Management, 8*(2), 129–148.

World Watch Institute. (2015). *Vision for a sustainable world*. <http://www.worldwatch.org/node/4713> Retrieved on December 22, 2015.

Xiantao, L., Wang, D., & Jian, L. (2014). Empirical analysis of the correlation between CSR of petroleum enterprises and financial performance in China. *Pakistan Journal of Statistics, 30*(5), 837–856.

Yang, L., & Guo, Z. (2014). Evolution of CSR concept in the West and China. *International Review of Management and Business Research, 3*(2), 819–826.

Yin, J., Rothlin, S., Li, X., & Caccamo, M. (2013). Stakeholder perspectives on corporate social responsibility(CSR) of multinational companies in China. *Journal of International Business Ethics, 6*(1–2), 57–71.

Yin, J., & Zhang, Y. (2012). Institutional dynamics and corporate social responsibility (CSR) in an emerging country context: Evidence from China. *Journal of Business Ethics, 2012*(111), 301–316.

Yu, X. (2015). Upholding labour standards through corporate social responsibility policies in China. *Global Social Policy, 15*(2), 167–187.

Zeng, S. X., Xu, X. D., Yin, H. T., & Tam, C. M. (2012). Factors that drive Chinese listed companies in voluntary disclosure of environmental information. *Journal of Business Ethics, 109*, 309–321.

Zhang, D., Gao, Y., & Morse, S. (2015). Corporate social responsibility and food risk management in China; a management perspective. *Food Control, 49*, 2–10.

Zhao, J. (2012). The harmonious society, corporate social responsibility and legal responses to ethical norms in Chinese Company Law. *Journal of Corporate Law Studies, April*, 163–200.

Zhao, L., & Lim, T. S. (2009). China's new social policy-initiatives for harmonious society. *Series on Contemporary China, Vol. 20*. World Scientific Publishing. <http://www.worldscibooks.com/eastasianstudies/7355.htm> Retrieved on December 19, 2015.

Zhao, Y., Zu, B., Li, Z., & Li, C. (2014). Corporate social responsibility assessment: A multidimensional and dynamic perspective. *Mining Technology, 123*(4), 230–239.

Zheng, L., Balsara, N., & Huang, H. (2013). Regulatory pressure, blockholders and corporate social responsibility disclosures in China. *Social Responsibility Journal, 10*(2), 226–245.

Zhilong, T., Wang, R., & Yang, W. (2011). Consumer responses to corporate social responsibility (CSR) in China. *Journal of Business Ethics, 101*, 197–212.

Zhou, H. (2015). Corporate philanthropy in contemporary China: A case of rural compulsory education promotion. *Voluntas: International Journal of Voluntary & Nonprofit Organizations, 26*(4), 1143–1163.

Zhu, Q., & Zhang, Q. (2015). Evaluating practices and drivers of corporate social responsibility: The Chinese context. *Journal of Cleaner Production, 100*, 315–324.

Zou, P., & Zhao, J. (2015). How multinational' social performance influences performance of subsidiary in China: The role of distance. In *Proceedings of the multidisciplinary academic conference*, October 1 (pp. 1–8).

PART II

Financial Innovation and Application

CHAPTER 5

The Equity Gap Amongst Technology-Based Small Firms: Practices and Challenges for Government-Backed Venture Capital in China

Javed G. Hussain[1], Jun Li[2] and Jonathan M. Scott[3]
[1]University of Birmingham, Birmingham, United Kingdom
[2]University of Essex, Colchester, United Kingdom
[3]Teesside University, Middlesbrough, United Kingdom

5.1 INTRODUCTION

China has formulated and charted its long-term economic reforms to liberalize and move its economy toward the market-oriented system. Its policy to increase the efficiency and market responsiveness of state-owned enterprises and to develop private enterprises has helped to intensify competition and has motivated all sectors to respond to internal and external demand. The government has considered competition and modernization of working practices a prerequisite to break out from the status quo to become a more progressive economy. Therefore government reforms and liberalization since 1978 has led to "miracle growth" (Li & Wang, 2014) in the Dragon over the past several decades. The unstable financial environment, demand-deficient world markets, and reductions in the stock market have, however, all contributed to a halting of growth and affecting all sectors of the Chinese economy over the last few years. Ever since then, the Chinese government has realized the importance of SMEs (Hussain, Millman, & Matlay, 2006) and particularly the external and internal challenges for SMEs and technology-based small firms (TBSFs). Whilst China remains competitive in low-skill based production, there is now a recognition that research, innovation, and technology development are all essential to compete within a global market. To be sustainable and to ensure that China's bandwagon continues to roll, Li (2015) suggests that the momentum

The China Business Model. DOI: http://dx.doi.org/10.1016/B978-0-08-100750-1.00005-X

for growth needs to be driven by entrepreneurship, investment in research, and knowledge-driven innovation. China's surge in growth has been attributed to the low-technology manufacturing model that has enabled impressive export growth. Yet, it is a system that is not sustainable in forthcoming decades. Wen Jiabao, the former Chinese Premier, in his speech to the 18th National Congress in 2012, suggested that low-technology enterprises give rise to "unstable, unbalanced, and unsustainable development."

There appears to be a strong realization amongst policymakers since 2006 that China needs to move forward from the labor intensive manufacturing stage to one that supports the infrastructure of enterprises with innovation and technology. The Chinese government initiated a "Medium and Long-Term National Plan for Science and Technology Development (2006–20)" (MLNP) to empower entrepreneurs in adapting innovation at all stages of production. The government's policy was to inspire entrepreneurs to develop an indigenous or home-grown capacity for original technology, knowledge, to assimilate knowledge and technology acquired from abroad within its manufacturing and service sector. Facilitating infrastructure and an environment that are both conducive to innovation, however, requires new types of financing that support innovative TBSFs in the early stage that the underdeveloped seed and early-stage market fails to offer. Thus the equity gap for TBSFs has been identified as a crucial factor in precommercial and emerging industries.

A prerequisite for the growth and enhancement of any entrepreneurial ecosystem is to have a well-developed, vibrant financial ecosystem that provides risk capital for viable enterprises. Cassar (2004) suggests that adequate finance has implications for the start-up, success and failure of enterprises. China's capital markets are underdeveloped, so the TBSFs are particularly constrained—a phenomenon often associated with developing economies where private enterprises encounter barriers to accessing external debt and equity finance. Chinese entrepreneurs, specifically those that are technology-based, have faced institutional challenges in their access to equity finance. To deal with market imperfections and the conservatism of banks, the Chinese government and policymakers initiated a number of policies to mitigate the finance gap and to encourage high-technology firms to take on high risk and reward initiatives. One notable challenge identified was access to equity finance and consequently the government launched the venture capital guiding funds (VCGFs) in 2008 to meet the financial needs of high-technology firm entrepreneurs. Li (2015) suggests that the government's rationale for providing risk capital was the belief that there is a positive relationship between access to risk capital, innovation, and the growth of TBSFs.

Internationally, it has been reported that the absence of risk capital negatively impacts on survival, longevity, and growth of SMEs (Aldrich, 1999; Christensen, Raynor, & Anthony, 2003; Marlow & Patton, 2005). The same results are supported by Newman, Gunessee, and Hilton (2011). Though support for technology-orientated entrepreneurs has grown globally, it is still contested whether public risk capital provision has enhanced or inhibited the creation and growth of TBSFs (Rigby & Ramlogan, 2013). Of the two schools of thought, one supports government intervention to address issues of market imperfections to overcome the equity gap, whilst the other suggests that government intervention leads to geographical distortions. It has been suggested that programmes supported by governments have the potential to distort the function of the market (Lerner, 2009). On the supply side, State intervention through providing finance can stimulate original innovation or can encourage the adaption of available technology but can also cause a number of challenges. This chapter examines the financing of innovation and technology-based entrepreneurs in China by first exploring the context of State intervention in China and considering structural economic issues. Next, through a literature review, it captures the issues related to entrepreneurs' equity gap (specifically within China), and considers mitigating initiatives, responses, and supply-side State intervention strategies. It examines the necessity for State intervention and its implications for creating market imperfections and the efficiency of the State in narrowing the finance gap for TBSFs.

The chapter then provides an overview of the literature and government strategies to support TBSFs through government-backed venture capital funds (GVCFs), followed by an evaluation of these funds and their impact upon China's objectives to meet the demands of emerging high tech enterprises. Section 5.4 considers some guiding principles for venture capital funds in adapting to the demand of entrepreneurs, and Section 5.6 of the chapter presents the overarching conclusions.

5.2 LITERATURE REVIEW

Venture capitalists enable budding entrepreneurs and established companies to realize their full potential which they might not otherwise be able to achieve due to internal and external financial constraints. Empirical studies have established that technology firms with high growth potential face an equity gap due to market failure, which has spurred debate about the value, impact, and case for state intervention (Alperovych, Groh, & Quas, 2016). The aim of State venture capital funds is to mitigate the impact of market failure for start-ups, given that commercial banks are reluctant to support enterprises with a high level of uncertainty and risk. Private venture capital funds concentrate on providing high risk equity capital but they tend to favor promising high risk, while reward investments usually offer returns in the short-to-medium term.

Hellmann and Puri (2000) and Kortum and Lerner (2000) suggest that private venture capital funds are more suited to the seed- and growth-financing stage and would not necessarily fill the equity gap for the medium to longer term. High-growth technology firms often have high risks and have longer time horizons to develop, so they encounter finance constraints. Therefore state intervention becomes important to address market failure (Brander, Du, & Hellmann, 2015), to safeguard economic prosperity and jobs. Governments are not purely motivated to correct market failures by injecting entrepreneurial capital. The State intervenes—promoting economic growth, create employment, and encourage adaptation of technology to improve productivity, reduce pollution, and above all to generate greater tax revenues to promote economic and social cohesion. The State-backed funds do bridge the equity gap but they also could potentially crowd out private venture capital providers. State-backed funds could also encourage economically nonviable projects that are not sustainable over the long term leading to welfare losses for the country. Critics argue that government funded only ventures do not "add value" (Grilli & Murtinu, 2014, 2015) and such ventures tend to be inefficient (Alperovych, Hübner & Lobet, 2015). Furthermore, state intervention gives rise to "collusion and regulatory capture" (Lerner, 1999). State funded ventures are often accused of lacking transparency and conducting political malpractice for personal gain (Becker, 1983; Peltzman, 1976) negatively impacting on economic activity. Earlier studies (Kortum & Lerner, 2000) reported that venture capital finance facilitates firms to innovate. Subsequent studies, however, (Caselli, Gatti, & Perrini, 2009; Engel & Keilbach, 2007; Lahr & Mina, 2012; Popov & Roosenboom, 2012; Ueda & Hirukawa, 2008) reject Kortum and Lerner's (2000) findings and suggest that VCGFs do not foster new innovations, instead investing in the existing firms with innovative projects. There is limited research from a number of countries testing the performance of public venture capital funds and even these studies offer mixed results. Studies carried out in the United States, Europe, and Israel suggested that some state-supported venture capital funds have generated positive results (Li, 2015). For example, the Small Business Investment Research (SBIR) programme established in the United States in 1982 proved to be successful in creating awareness and success of TBSFs. Lerner (1999), comparing firms which received SBIR support with those who did not, reported that though some firms were not successful in securing finance at first they learned from experience and subsequently they were successful in securing funds from venture capital funds the following year. The process of preparing information to apply for funds from venture capitalists during the first time enabled firms to carry out self-appraisal. The appraisal served as a catalyst for TBSFs to secure external funds. The success in securing external equity was, however, more skewed toward the TBSFs which already had accessed external equity previously from venture capitalists, possibly due to greater familiarity with the requirements of venture capitalist firms and the investment-ready nature of equity seekers. Analysis of other publicly supported venture capitalist schemes in the United States, such as the Small Business Investment Companies (SBICs) that aimed to increase the supply of equity funds, had mixed conclusions (Clarysse, Knocjaert, & Wright, 2009; Li, 2015). Baygan's (2003) analysis of SBICs found that publicly funded equity funds failed to meet the requirement of sectors most in need. Li (2015) draws upon their conclusions (Baygan, 2003; Clarysse et al., 2009) to suggests that publicly supported venture capitalists are competing in sectors which are already well funded and hence do not necessarily increase the overall supply of funds, suggesting that the equity-deficient sectors' or enterprises' demand remains unmet.

The UK equity gap is most severe for firms engaged in cutting-edge technology (Pierrakis & Mason, 2008; Storey & Westhead, 1997), thus hindering innovation, growth, and job creation. It is suggested that technology firms have the capacity to create employment but they are restricted due to lack of access to finance (Cowling, Liu, & Ledger, 2012; North, Baldock, & Ullah, 2013). European-wide initiatives have attempted to overcome the finance gap by establishing government-backed venture capital (GVC) schemes. To examine the impact of GVC schemes, the National Endowment for Science, Technology and the Arts (NESTA) conducted a study in 2009 that examined 782 enterprises backed by 6 government-supported venture capital funds for the period 1995–2008. Its evaluation reported that there was some positive impact on the recipients of publicly backed equity on the performance of firms in comparison with the control sample. However, the effect of GVC is transient. At an early stage of the enterprise, there is a positive impact on job creation and growth;

however, the effect declines after 3 years but has a marked improvement after 6 years. The study suggests that GVC-supported firms' performance exhibits a cyclical pattern. These enterprises, when invested in, go through investment capacity building, develop infrastructure, deplete funds, seek additional investment, and then they take off. The pattern is consistent with the central tenet of the financial growth cycle of firms with high growth potential that, at the same time, exhibit high risk (North et al., 2013). Therefore the review of enterprises' performance suggests that justification exists for government-supported technology firms as they make a positive contribution toward the economy. On the other hand, critics of GVC schemes argue that they tend to have high costs, crowd out the private sector and to be an expensive method of creating jobs. This view is countered by the National Audit Office (NAO) (2009) which found that 84% of respondents in their survey reported that, once they received funds from GVCs, they also were able to secure additional funds, so GVCs could be considered as an enabling fund. These findings suggest that GVC financial support serves as a signal of confidence to finance providers and validates the status of the enterprise that, in turn, enables it to attract external finance. The other criticism reported by NAO (2009) was that the government-supported funds tended to have a bias toward the South East of England and had high administrative costs (Mason, Lynton, & Stephen, 2016). The House of Commons Accounts Committee (2010) similarly suggested that GVC-supported TBSFs lacked efficiency, their structure is skewed against the taxpayers' interest and gives rise to geographical and regional inequalities. Mason and Pierrakis (2013) describes financing of TBSFs by GVC as a "drip feed" that stifles innovation and growth. The experience of the United Kingdom compared to Canada is not dissimilar. Analysis of a Labour Government fund initiative carried out by Cumming and MacIntosh (2006) reported there was no evidence that the fund leads to a significant increase in the supply of venture capital. These results are consistent with Da Rin, Nicodano, and Sembenelli (2006), whose survey amongst 14 European countries reported that GVC spending proportionately displaced private venture capital. Harrison and Mason (2000) suggested that GVC could cause significant and notable regional disparities by enabling concentration in certain geographical localities. In addition, instead of increasing the supply of funds the GVCs may crowd out private funds. Cumming (2014) challenges these findings by examining the data for the period 1989–2011 for GVC in 13 European countries and thus refuting the assertion that GVCFs crowd out the private sector. In fact, the Canadian government supports its TBSFs through its venture finance initiatives and it has been argued that their competitiveness does not diminish.

In this regard, according to Wonglimpiyarat (2015), the competitiveness of Canada is innovation-driven and is supported by government venture finance. Furthermore, the Canadian government's commitment is evidenced by its launch of its Venture Capital Action Plan (VCAP) in 2013. The Canadian government anticipates that the fund will motivate private sector venture capital, leading to an increase in the supply of funds that will promote technology-based projects in TBSFs. GVC initiatives have often been criticized for their lack of entrepreneurial attributes, undercapitalization, and short-term objectives (Lerner, 2009; Li, 2015; Murray, 2007). The suggestion is that at this stage of setting up GVCs, there is a notable lack of clarity in the rationale, size, and intentions of the funds. Government initiatives are not dictated by local, regional, and political interests rather than the economic rationale that results in GVCs' underperformance. European studies have suggested a marked underperformance of enterprises funded by GVCs (Baldock, 2016) but such studies used "outmoded funding models" to evaluate the benefits of such schemes over the medium- to long-term. Evidence from Belgium (Manigart, Baeyens, & Van Hyfte, 2002) suggested that the right type of fund is more important, rather than the distinction between private versus public providers. Proponents of GVCs (e.g., Rigby & Ramlogan, 2013) argue, however, that information asymmetry and external market failures necessitate the need for government intervention in the form of GVC subsidies. The venture capital providers—whether private or public—are a blend of markets or ecosystems for finance which serve a range of clients at different stages of their operations. Thus a "one-size-fits-all" policy would be misguided. Nevertheless, despite their fragmented nature, Li (2015) draws upon Hood's (2000) Scottish experiences and suggests that GVC initiatives need to have a rationale, clarity of objectives, and accountability, and should attract and retain high caliber experienced management teams who understand the commercial realities and functioning of public sector ethos. To date, the literature on venture capital has focused mainly on United States and Europe (Bruton & Ahlstrom, 2003) predominantly provided by private investors. Literature specifically evaluating government-backed initiatives within China are notable by their absence, creating a major gap in the extant literature. The aim of this chapter is to contribute toward addressing this relevant topic.

5.3 EVALUATION OF VENTURE CAPITAL FUNDS IN CHINA

Since China's institutional environment differs from the West, it warrants a closer examination of the growth of private and public venture capital funds to support high-growth technology enterprises. Bruton and Ahlstrom (2003) suggested that China was, and remains, a complex economy for venture capital (VC) operations, despite the reforms which took place in the 1980s. Due to their different cultural, legal, and enterprise models, there are marked differences in the type of VCs in China and the West. China's economy emerged from the command economy and has transitioned for several decades, leading to a rapid change in its financial and enterprise environment. At an early stage, China lacked private venture capital funds as we know them in the West but informal providers of finance existed for the high-technology sector, to a limited extent. To overcome this deficit, State-supported venture capital institutions emerged after the 1980s (Xiao, 2002) but, although these were not initially a policy to reform and promote technology-orientated industry, since 1985 the growth of VCs has mirrored the economic upsurge of China (Ahlstrom, Bruton, & Yeh, 2007).

China's challenge to overcome the equity gap for high-tech firms must be examined within the context of its cultural, political, and institutional contexts. Cultural norms and practices are embedded within institutions that inform the actions of firms, the Government, and individuals. The equity gap amongst high-growth firms has been considered to have a negative impact on innovation, growth, and private investment: a particular challenge for economies such as China transitioning from a command economy to a mixed economy. To overcome finance gaps within Chinese technology firms, venture capital has been considered as an essential tool to stimulate growth, a policy that is consistent with the 18th National Congress of the Communist Party, which aspired to promote "technology and innovation" as core policy to generate economic prosperity. China remains committed to innovate in order to "promote social productive forces" to compete internationally (Hao, Sun, Tian, & Pan, 2015). The venture capital industry is informed by history, the financial environment, and institutional structures (Cetindamar, 2003). China's underdeveloped capital markets necessitated its Government to intervene by establishing public venture capital funds to promote the supply of equity for high-technology firms—at least over the short-to-medium term (Hood, 2000). Public venture capital institutions serve as stimuli to promote confidence and a signal that the Government is supportive and committed to overcome the equity gap not currently being filled by the private sector (Li, 2015).

The policy objective of public venture capital in China was to accelerate the flow of capital in overcoming the equity gap that may accelerate the adoption of high-technology methods through innovation. The Communist Party formally supported science and technology (S&T) through venture capital funds in 1985 that led to the formation of the China New Technology Venture Capital Corporation (CNTVC), endowed with US$10 million of funds (40% from the State Science and Technology Commission and 23% from the Ministry of Finance). The objective of the fund was to support high-technology firms in dedicated industrial zones, but failed due to a lack of skills and experience of fund providers that was eventually closed in 1997. Learning from this experience, and improved economic conditions, both within China and internationally, boosted China's VCs by 2000. China still has relatively limited domestic sources of venture finance for high-technology firms that continue to rely on the Government and wealthy citizens to support high risk, high-technology firms. To overcome the historical underdevelopment of its financial environment, the Chinese government established the Innovation Fund for Small Technology firms (InnoFund) in 1999 to promote and foster innovation, and the adaptation of technology, to enhance knowhow, and enhance international competitiveness. Establishing the fund signaled the Government's intention to support innovative TBSFs by providing grants, loans, and equity finance, thus resulting in large private venture capital inflows that has helped TBSFs accelerate their research and innovation activities. By 2005, China noted almost US$1.17 billion inflow of foreign venture capital investment, a figure that compares favorably with that of nearly US$325 million in 2002 (Pukthuanthong & Walker, 2007). Despite the development of the VC market in China, new TBSFs still struggled with accessing external finance and the equity gap facing new TBSFs remained. For example, VC firms invested an average of RMB 32 billion annually between 2004 and 2006, but 44% of VC was invested in firms in the stage of expansion and 26% in firms in the stage of maturity.[1] The lack of external equity investment means that high-tech SMEs were over-dependent on informal financial sources from individuals and firms' employees (Xiao, 2011). To help technology firms overcome the constraint of the equity gap, the Ministry of Finance and Ministry of Science and Technology jointly issued the Interim Regulation on the Management of the Venture Guiding Fund (VCGF) in 2007. This was

[1] See China Statistical Yearbook on Science and Technology 2013, p. 176.

followed by the launch of US$6.5 billion Venture Capital Fund, specifically designed to assist start-ups in "sunrise" industries to enhance China's competitiveness and productivity.

The other impediment to promoting public sector initiatives was the outdated tax and regulatory system that was not robust enough to provide protection or legal recourse for investors from fraud (Bruton, Ahlstrom, & Singh, 2002). Furthermore, venture capitalist groups encountered information asymmetry, hence the need to monitor and steer the sector and provide a framework for the industry. By 2007, to respond to law and tax concerns, the Chinese government initiated changes to tax policies to overcome venture capitalist providers' concerns. The Government facilitated second board markets to provide venture capitalist exit routes; as part of the same strategy the government launched the Small and Medium Enterprise Board of the Shenzhen Stock Exchange (SSE) in 2004 followed by the establishment of a Growth Enterprise market within SSE in 2009.

Xiao (2002) suggests that China needs to overcome issues such as transparency, information asymmetry, and the financial information deficit required by fund providers to make lending decisions. To regulate VCGFs and maintain their relevance, the National Development and Reform Commission, the Ministry of Finance, and the Ministry of Commerce issued a joint directive in 2008 that regulates the establishment and management of VCGFs. The directive states that the role of Government is not to be the lead investors but to use public finance as leverage to attract and direct private sector funds in the high-tech industries of the future which are designated as the priority areas. It is anticipated that this model has the capacity to foster greater willingness to take on high-risk, high-reward enterprises that could speed up industrialization and innovation to compete internationally in highly competitive industries, offering a range and quality of products. Secondly, there is a realization within the Government that the expertise expected of VC fund managers is often lacking within its employees to manage the activities of VCGF. To overcome this constraint, VCFGs invest in private VCs and act as private investors. This model of participation brings together private sector expertise and knowhow (nationally and internationally) and, instead of competing with private sectors, VCFGs complement them and act as private investors. Such cooperation enables private venture capital professionals to carry out the identification, screening, and due diligence for their investment decisions.

5.4 PUBLIC VENTURE CAPITAL—VENTURE CAPITAL GUIDING FUND

The Chinese government uses four VCGF models to achieve its set objectives: (1) *The funds-of-funds* model is designed to mimic private investor behavior and limits government exposure to risk, liability, and interference with fund decision-making. The funds-of-funds invest in a portfolio of VCs and diversify their exposure to certain sectors or industries, and the surplus generated from some VCs is used to cushion losses incurred in others. (2) The *Coinvestment model* aims to invest in Government priority areas and share risk through joint investment in high-tech small firms not otherwise supported by private VCs. It is often complemented by the VC investment subsidy model to encourage VCs to invest in early-stage small high-tech firms, normally about 5% of the investment, which carry high risks. (3) The *Investment Guarantee* encourages VC funds to identify early-stage high-tech firms, mentor and support them free of charge, and then apply for a development grant of RMB 1 million to recover its research and development costs subject to investing in the company when the 2-year mentoring period ends. At this stage, the VCFG provides a financing guarantee to VCs that it will provide another grant of up to RMB 2 million in order to subsidize production and marketing costs. (4) The *Financing Guarantee* enables VC funds to borrow debt finance from banks and small investors as their risk is minimized, enabling high-tech small firms to achieve optimal capital structure and incur low cost, as the cost of debt is lower than cost of equity.

5.5 GOVERNMENT-BACKED VENTURE CAPITAL—IMPACT

Governments play a dominant role in the promotion of the venture capital industry. GVC schemes are widely used in the United States, Canada, and Europe and globally to encourage access to finance for TBSFs. As with European and other developed economies, the Chinese government has recognized the potential of venture capital to steer its economy from labor intensive to a knowledge economy. In 2008 the emerging industries were identified to be supported through the GVCFs) and increase the supply of finance through venture capital for start-up high-technology firms. The results reported suggest that VCGFs gained greater penetration amongst high-technology businesses and have further increased the supply of funds. By 2009, 43 venture capital funds used *funds-of-funds* methods to support

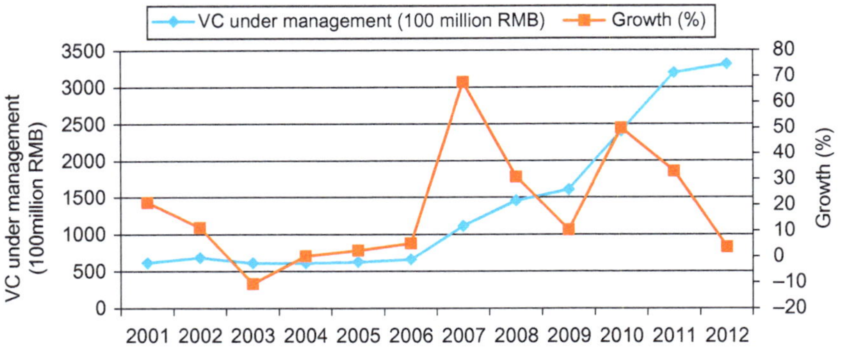

Figure 5.1 Venture capital under management, 2001–12. *MOST online database.*

projects worth RMB 309 million. Ding and Li (2015) reported that these funds were increased to RMB 2.382 billion by 2011, and there is now over RMB 6 billion available to support high-technology firms. Fig. 5.1 illustrates the trend over the period 2001–12. The upward trajectory of funds under venture capital management demonstrates the success of VCGFs which is in line with the economic trends of Chinese economy.

Although the data demonstrate impressive VC growth and the importance, the Chinese government attaches to VCs as a tool mitigating the finance gap for TBSFs, the measure of VCs' impact remains elusive. It has been argued that the increase in the availability of VC funds provide us with no evidence whether government-supported sources, VCGFs, complement or crowd out private venture capital providers (see Harrison & Mason, 2000; Li, 2015). However, the review of financing model schemes above indicates that VCGFs work with private venture capital providers and not necessarily in competition with them.

Measuring the performance of VCGFs remains a challenge as governments tend not have explicitly stated objectives. Within regions, industries, and entire countries, VCGFs serve multiple aims and objectives at regional and local levels, thus complicating evaluation tools for the impact. These challenges are universal. To evaluate the impact VCGFs in Europe and Canada, empirical studies reported mixed results about the efficiency and the effectiveness of the government-backed venture capital schemes (Li, 2015). In China, evaluation of the VCGFs commenced in 2008, but findings remain incomplete at this stage and Li (2015) reported that none of the funds have reached the end of their life. Therefore the impact of Government-supported VCs is unclear.

One of the stated objectives of GVCFs was to provide access to seed capital for new start-ups. Li (2015) suggests that there is inconclusive evidence to confirm the achievement of this objective. Reporting for the period 2003–12, seed capital averaged 10.8% of the funds allocated for new start-ups or seed capital. During the overall 10-year period, for 7 years investment in the seed stage was below this average. These findings suggest that the objective of the fund was not achieved, highlighting the risky nature of new start-ups and problems encountered in targeting and supporting new start-ups. These results neither confirm nor refute the assertion that Government-backed VC crowded out private VCs.

The performance of VCGFs is determined and influenced by a number of factors. The experience of fund managers, the mission of the sponsor, the cost structure of projects, and the exit routes and strategy adopted by VCGFs impacts upon performance (Carter & Van Auken, 2015). Indeed, a bespoke strategy to fund specific sectors, a certain deal size, over a specific time frame, and the ability to make follow-on investments within a geographical region all could improve the effectiveness of CVGFs to mitigate the finance gap for TBSFs (Lerner, 2009; Li, 2015). In the United Kingdom, Government has initiated support for high-tech firms to serve local needs or follow the trend in the sector. Similar evidence is reported in China, where the Government has established VCGFs to support start-ups in the high-technology industries in creating jobs and economic activity leading to the creation of high-tech clusters. A precursor to this strategy is the education and experience of scientific personnel to work within the cluster. In the case of China, not all the regions have conducive environments to promote high-technology firms due to underdeveloped infrastructure that fails to retain or attract skilled labor (Zhang, Peng, & Li, 2008). Local social capital, traditions, educational and training provisions, and infrastructure serves as a gravitational force for the concentration of a sector that leads to formation of a cluster. An attempt through the use of VCGFs to attract firms to form a cluster, without the accompanying supporting infrastructure, often fails (Li & Geng, 2012) suggesting that not all the regions have economies of scale or the business ecosystems to establish VCGFs. For instance, Ding and Li (2015) find that key innovation-oriented intermediaries, consisting of productivity promotion centers, S&T business incubators, university-based science parks, and technology transfer centers, were mainly concentrated in three regions of Beijing-Tianjin, Shanghai-Jiangsu-Zhejiang, and Guangzhou-Shenzhen. As compared with these three regions, many other regions lacked an innovation ecosystem that helps innovation to flourish.

Once China's central government approved the policy of supporting new start-ups and high-technology firms through VC, local governments enthusiastically promoted VCGFs. Their focus, however, has been regional and local and they tended to support certain industries through the use of "funds-of-funds" methods. Local initiatives supported by VCFGs, according to The Ministry of Science and Technology (MOST) survey, reported that 87% of VCGFs required VC fund partners to invest in specific industries locally; 61% set a minimum threshold above which applications would be supported. The survey also reported that local governments supporting VCGFs were more restricted in terms of local conditions placed on VCs to access grants from local governments. These results were validated by the Zero2IP survey of 2011 that reported that over 60% of support through the use of *funds-of-funds* accompanied the condition to invest locally,[2] countering the spirit and rationale for establishing VCGFs. Conditions imposed by the local government adversely affect support for regions or industries where they have competitive advantage.

Competition between local government and the region to attract private VC using the VCGF as a vehicle was tense, despite not all the regions having a sufficiently large concentration of firms in the high-technology sector to warrant sufficient opportunities for investment. The problem could be traced to the initial economic reforms in China that were aimed at decentralizing decision-making. Through decentralization, the authority was devolved in a number of areas, such as public finance for local economic and social development, from the central government to provincial and local governments. The mushrooming of VCGFs across the country, particularly in the less developed regions, may divert funds toward commercially less viable firms, leading to economic losses for the country. Li (2015) suggested that VCGFs and the local government policy of incentives and conditions offered to support local industry distort market operations, leading to the creation of a mismatch between supply and demand; possibly compromising the funds' independence and performance without aiding the creation of a cluster. The creation and promotion of a cluster, according to Porter (1998), depends on the depth, complexity and business environment. Ready factors of production supported by financial services and the businesses in the accompanying sectors support one

[2] See a report in China Jingji Daobao on January 7, 2012, "the butterfly effect of government guiding funds to reshape the driver of regional development," at http://www.ceh.com.cn/ceh/cjxx/2012/1/7/97382.shtml Accessed 15.12.14.

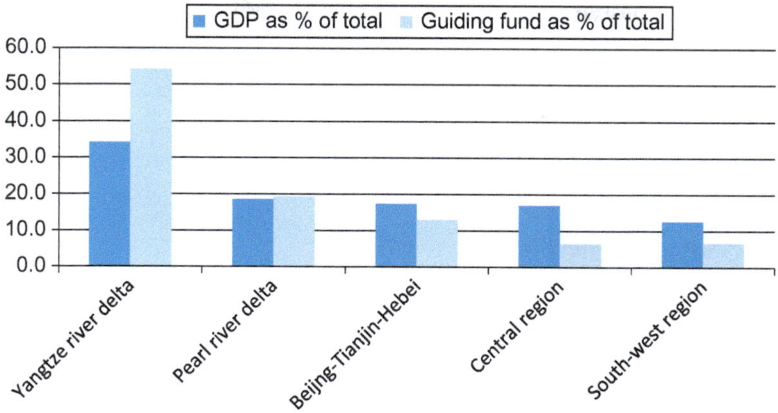

Figure 5.2 Spatial distribution of investments by VCGFs, 2012. *MOST online database.*

another. Such conditions are not fulfilled when there are too few firms operating within a cluster.

Spatial distribution of venture capital is an issue for Western and Asian economies alike. It has been observed that venture capital funds' activities and presence is often parallel to the sectors' spread and follows space, place, and capital flows (Mason et al., 2016). Space allows interaction and flow of ideas; financial institutions tend to have their own defined geographies within which they operate; and flows refer to financial intuitions' geographical areas where their lending funds originate from. Neither in the United Kingdom, Europe, Canada, United States, or other countries the public venture capital manage to reverse the spatial concentration of venture capital. Analysis of data gathered by the MOST online database in Fig. 5.2 suggests during 2012 that there was approximately 54% of VCGFs investment activity taking place along the Yangtze River Delta, a well-developed, region that contributes 34% of China's GDP. In comparison, the South-West and Central region attracted around 6–7% share of VCGFs. This distribution in terms of numbers also shows a skewness toward the South. During 2012, out of 299 VCGFs approved at the national level, only 9 projects approved originated from the West region and 99% of total funding approved of RMB 5 million went to the Southern region and 1% to the West region, demonstrating the geographical disparity of the distribution of venture capital. China's North and South divide mirrors the United Kingdom (Harrison, Mason, & Robson, 2010). The distinctive geography of VCGFs in China is a product of historical clustering of venture capital orientated industry, and small and high-tech small businesses locating in certain regions. The clustering of venture capital funds in certain cities is not unique to China, as a similar trend is also observed in Germany (see Fritsch & Schilder, 2008). Spatial concentration is due to economies of scale, local knowledge, and cost related benefit arising for venture capital funds when investing a given region.

5.6 CONCLUSION

China has aspired to improve its competitiveness through enhanced technological and commercial knowledge to transform its inefficient and labor intensive industries in a short span of time to compete with Western technology-orientated advanced economies. To achieve this objective, China has realized there is a need to overcome the funding gap for start-ups, high risk and high growth small technology companies, especially at the early stage of the venture development.

Given China's evolving political history, financial institutions, labor, and the environment, lacks technological skills to engage with complex high risk business propositions. Therefore there is unmet demand for finance for TBSFs. Too often this, technology orientated, niche was served by informal finance sources but that too failed to build sufficient capacity to meet the needs of the sector in an ever-shrinking global world. To promote technology-orientated industry and entrepreneurship, the Government has recognized, since the 1980s the importance of venture capital and promoted its use. The Government has supported the establishment of large VCGFs nationally and similar schemes at a local level to narrow the finance gap, especially to promote technology-orientated enterprises. The Chinese State intervenes through the use of funds-of-funds and coinvestment methods; their objective is not to displace private venture capital funds but to complement them. The question of whether government-backed funds helped to reduce the equity gap for high-tech firms remains yet to be tested. However, there is some evidence that supports the creation and operation of VCGFs to overcome the equity gap for small high-technology firms in China. In particular, VCGFs have successfully supplanted informal networks to support premarket and more risky phase of firms' journeys, thereby rapidly adapting innovation and technology to enterprises to compete in an increasingly globalized market. However, finance alone is not the precursor to innovation. There is now a growing realization amongst policymakers and practitioners within China and internationally that GVCFs are only effective if they operate within an entrepreneurial ecosystem that nurtures and sustains the cycle of conception, creation and promotes its growth. This means that local governments should focus more on the development of the local entrepreneurial ecosystem rather than on imposing strict terms and conditions that restrict the movement of VC. Also, local government should realize that VCGFs alone are not the instrument to plug the equity gap either. They may make their public-backed VC initiatives more effective by supporting the development of business angel networks as a supplement to VCGFs.

REFERENCES

Ahlstrom, D., Bruton, G. D., & Yeh, K. S. (2007). Venture capital in China: Past, present, and future. *Asia Pacific Journal of Management*, *24*(3), 247–268.

Aldrich, H. (1999). *Organizations evolving*. London: Sage.

Alperovych, Y., Groh, A.P., & Quas, A. (2016). *When can government venture capital funds bridge the equity gap?* <http://papers.ssrn.com/sol3/papers.cfm?abstract_id=2718061> Accessed 13.03.16.

Alperovych, Y., Hübner, G., & Lobet, F. (2015). How does governmental versus private venture capital backing affect a firm's efficiency? Evidence from Belgium. *Journal of Business Venturing*, *30*(4), 508–525.

Baldock, R. (2016). An assessment of the business impacts of the UK's Enterprise Capital Funds. *Environment and Planning C: Government and Policy*http://dx.doi.org/10.1177/0263774X15625995.

Baygan, G. (2003). *Venture capital policy review: United States. No., 2003/12*. Paris: Organisation for Economic Cooperation and Development (OECD) Publishing.

Becker, G. S. (1983). A theory of competition among pressure groups for political influence. *The Quarterly Journal of Economics*, *XCVIII*(3), 371–400.

Brander, J. A., Du, Q., & Hellmann, T. (2015). The effects of government–sponsored venture capital: International evidence. *Review of Finance*, *19*(2), 571–618.

Bruton, G. D., & Ahlstrom, D. (2003). An institutional view of China's venture capital industry: Explaining the differences between China and the West. *Journal of Business Venturing*, *18*(2), 233–259.

Bruton, G.D., Ahlstrom, D., & Singh, K. (2002). The impact of the institutional environment on the venture capital industry in Singapore. *Venture Capital: An International Journal of Entrepreneurial Finance*, *4*(3), 197–218.

Carter, R. B., & Van Auken, H. E. (2015). Effect of professional background on venture capital proposal evaluation. *Journal of Small Business Strategy*, *3*(1), 45–55.

Caselli, S., Gatti, S., & Perrini, F. (2009). Are venture capitalists a catalyst for innovation? *European Financial Management*, *15*(1), 92–111.

Cassar, G. (2004). The financing of business start-ups. *Journal of Business Venturing*, *19*(2), 261–283.

Cetindamar, D. (Ed.). (2003). *The growth of venture capital: A cross-cultural comparison*. Westport: Praeger.

Christensen, C. M., Raynor, M. E., & Anthony, S. D. (2003). Six keys to creating new-growth businesses. *Harvard Management Update*, *8*(1), 3–6.

Clarysse, B., Knocjaert, M., & Wright, M. (2009). *Benchmarking UK venture capital to the US and Israel: What lessons can be learned?*. London: British Venture Capital Association (BVCA).

Cowling, M., Liu, W., & Ledger, A. (2012). Small business financing in the UK before and during the current financial crisis. *International Small Business Journal*, *30*(7), 778–800.

Cumming, D. (2014). Public economics *gone wild*: Lessons from venture capital. *International Review of Financial Analysis, 36*(2), 251–260.
Cumming, D., & MacIntosh, J. (2006). Crowding out private equity: Canadian evidence. *Journal of Business Venturing, 21*(5), 569–609.
Da Rin, M., Nicodano, G., & Sembenelli, A. (2006). Public policy and creation of active venture capital markets. *Journal of Public Economics, 90*(8–9), 1699–1723.
Ding, X. D., & Li, J. (2015). *Incentives for innovation in China: Building an innovative economy*. London and New York: Routledge.
Engel, D., & Keilbach, B. (2007). Firm-level implications of early stage venture capital investment—An empirical investigation. *Journal of Empirical Finance, 14*(2), 150–167.
Fritsch, M., & Schilder, D. (2008). Does venture capital investment really require spatial proximity? An empirical investigation. *Environment and Planning A, 40*(9), 2114–2131.
Grilli, L., & Murtinu, S. (2014). New technology-based firms in Europe: Market penetration, public venture capital, and timing of investment. *Industrial and Corporate Change, 24*(5), 1109–1148.
Grilli, L., & Murtinu, S. (2015). New technology-based firms in Europe: market penetration, public venture capital, and timing of investment. *Industrial and Corporate Change, 24*(5), 1109–1148.
Hao, F. H., Sun, Y., Tian, W. Y., & Pan, Z. Y. (2015). Analysis on innovation incentive policy in China: *Proceedings of fifth international conference on education*. Amsterdam: Management, Information and Medicine. Atlantis Press. 574–578.
Harrison, R., Mason, C., & Robson, P. (2010). Determinants of long-distance investing by business angels in the UK. *Entrepreneurship and Regional Development, 22*(2), 113–137.
Harrison, R. T., & Mason, C. M. (2000). Editorial: The role of the public sector in the development of a regional venture capital industry. *Venture Capital, 2*(4), 243–253.
Hellmann, T., & Puri, M. (2000). The interaction between product market and financing strategy: The role of venture capital. *Review of Financial Studies, 13*(4), 959–984.
Hood, N. (2000). Public venture capital and economic development: The Scottish experience. *Venture Capital, 2*(4), 313–341.
House of Commons Public Accounts Committee (HCPAC), (2010). Department for business, innovation and skills: Venture capital support to small businesses: *Seventeenth report of session 2009–10*. London: The Stationery Office.
Hussain, J., Millman, C., & Matlay, H. (2006). SME financing in the UK and in China: A comparative perspective. *Journal of Small Business and Enterprise Development, 13*(4), 584–599.
Kortum, S., & Lerner, J. (2000). Assessing the contribution of venture capital to innovation. *The RAND Journal of Economics., 31*(4), 674–692.
Lahr, H., & Mina, A. (2012). *Coaching or selection? Venture capital and firms' patenting performance*. Cambridge: Centre for Business Research and UK~ IRC, University of Cambridge.
Lerner, J. (1999). The government as venture capitalist: The long-run impact of the SBIR program. *Journal of Business, 72*(3), 285–318.
Lerner, J. (2009). *Boulevard of broken dreams: Why public efforts to boost entrepreneurship and venture capital have failed and what to do about it*. Princeton, NJ: Princeton University Press.
Li, J. (2015). Bridging the equity funding gap in technological entrepreneurship: The case of government–backed venture capital in China. In J. G. Hussain & J. M. Scott (Eds.), *Research handbook on entrepreneurial finance* (pp. 185–205). Cheltenham: Edward Elgar.
Li, J., & Geng, S. (2012). Industrial clusters, shared resources, and firm performance. *Entrepreneurship and Regional Development, 24*(5–6), 357–382.
Li, J., & Wang, L. M. (Eds.). (2014). *China's economic dynamics: A Beijing consensus in the making?*. London and New York: Routledge.
Manigart, S., Baeyens, K., & Van Hyfte, W. (2002). The survival of venture capital backed companies. *Venture Capital: An International Journal of Entrepreneurial Finance, 4*(2), 103–124.

Marlow, S., & Patton, D. (2005). All credit to men? Entrepreneurship, finance, and gender. *Entrepreneurship Theory and Practice, 29*(6), 717–735.
Mason, C., Lynton, J., & Stephen, W. (2016). *The city's role in providing for the public equity financing needs of UK SMEs.* Strathclyde University Report. <http://strathprints.strath.ac.uk/id/eprint/28058> Accessed January 2016.
Mason, C., & Pierrakis, Y. (2013). Venture capital, the regions and public policy: The United Kingdom since the post–2000 technology crash. *Regional Studies, 47*(7), 1156–1171.
Murray, G. C. (2007). Venture capital and government policy. In H. Landstrom (Ed.), *Handbook of research on venture capital* (pp. 113–151). Cheltenham: Edward Elgar.
National Audit Office (NAO), (2009). *The department for business, innovation and skills: Venture capital support to small businesses.* London: NAO.
National Endowment for Science, Technology and the Arts (NESTA), (2009). *From funding gaps to thin markets: UK government support for early-stage venture capital.* London: Research Report, and September. NESTA.
Newman, A., Gunessee, S., & Hilton, B. (2011). Applicability of financial theories of capital structure to the Chinese cultural context: A study of privately owned SMEs. *International Small Business Journal, 30*(1), 65–83.
North, D., Baldock, R., & Ullah, U. (2013). Funding the growth of UK technology-based small firms since the financial crash: Are there breakages in the finance escalator? *Venture Capital: International Journal of Entrepreneurial Finance, 15*(3), 237–260.
Peltzman, S. (1976). Toward a more general theory of regulation. *Journal of Law and Economics, 19*(2), 211–240.
Pierrakis, Y., & Mason, C. (2008). *Shifting sands: The changing nature of the early stage venture capital market in the UK.* London: *Research Report.* NESTA.
Popov, A., & Roosenboom, P. (2012). Venture capital and patented innovation: Evidence from Europe. *Economic Policy, 27*(71), 447–482.
Porter, M. E. (1998). Cluster and the new economics of competition. *Harvard Business Review,* 77–90. November–December.
Pukthuanthong, K., & Walker, T. (2007). Venture capital in China: A culture shock for Western investors. *Management Decision, 45*(4), 708–731.
Rigby, J., & Ramlogan, R. (2013). *Access to finance: Impacts of publicly supported venture capital and loan guarantees.* London: NESTA Working Paper 13/02. NESTA.
Storey, D. J., & Westhead, P. (1997). Management training in small firms—A case of market failure? *Human Resource Management Journal,* 7(2), 61–71.
Ueda, M., & Hirukawa, M. (2008). *Venture capital and industrial 'innovation'.* <http://papers.ssrn.com/sol3/papers.cfm?abstract_id=1242693 > Accessed 13.03.16.
Wonglimpiyarat, J. (2015). *Technology financing and commercialization: Exploring the challenges and how nations can build innovative capacity.* Basingstoke: Palgrave Macmillan.
Xiao, L. (2011). Financing high-tech SMEs in China: A three-stage model of business development. *Entrepreneurship & Regional Development, 23*(3–4), 217–234.
Xiao, W. (2002). The new economy and venture capital in China. *Perspectives, 3*(6), 30.
Zhang, G., Peng, X., & Li, J. (2008). Technological entrepreneurship and policy environment: A case of China. *Journal of Small Business and Enterprise Development, 15*(4), 733–751.

CHAPTER 6

Assessing the Impact of the New Medical Reform on China's Pharmaceutical Supply Chain: The Case of Essential Medicines Distribution in Yuping, Luochan, and Minhang Regions

Zhao Guoqin[1], Sam Dzever[2] and Tang Renwu[3]
[1]Central University of Finance and Economics, Beijing, China
[2]Telecom Ecole de Management, Evry, France
[3]Beijing Normal University, Beijing, China; Zhejiang Normal University, Zhejiang, China

6.1 INTRODUCTION

Essential medicines are those that, according to the World Health Organization (WHO), satisfy priority healthcare needs of a population. Experience has shown that the strict selection of a limited number of essential medicines can improve healthcare quality and help to better administer medicines, including improvement of prescription drug quality and the application of health resources with comparative cost-effectiveness (WHO, 2009a, 2009b). Because essential medicines possess the most important, essential, and indispensable peculiarity to the healthcare needs of a population and, due to the significant role they play in developing countries, the availability and affordability of essential medicines have already been regarded as part of basic human rights (as well as health rights) of citizens. Extending the availability and affordability of essential medicines is one of the health-related Millennium Development Goals (MDG) that the international community has promised to achieve. In "Target 17" of the MDG, the United Nations (UN) has proposed that a collaborative effort between governments and pharmaceutical companies be put in place so as to make essential medicines more easily available to the population in developing countries (UN, 2000). The WHO and other leading international organizations have all actively advanced the

The China Business Model. DOI: http://dx.doi.org/10.1016/B978-0-08-100750-1.00006-1

importance of implementing an essential medicines policy in developing countries and the need to track the resulting effects of such policy (WHO, 2005a, 2006a, 2006b, 2007).

China has made great strides in the formulation of essential medicine list and the standard treatment guidelines of some diseases. There still exist relatively significant problems, however, in the accessibility of essential medicines for the low-income group (WHO, 2005b), especially in rural areas. Some scholars have investigated the availability of essential medicines in Shandong Province: the availability median of 39 investigated generic medicines in medical institutions and retail pharmacies is 0% and 5.0%, respectively, and only 54.0% of generic medicines can be found in the pharmacies of medical institutions (Sun, 2005). Some scholars have also carried out research on the availability of essential medicines in Shanghai City, and the results indicate that the availability median of 41 investigated generic medicines in medical institutions and retail pharmacies is 33.3% and 15.0%, respectively (Lu, 2006). The research on the availability of essential medicines in the rural regions of Xiaogan City, Hubei Province also indicates that in rural areas the availability of essential medicines needs further improvement and there still exists room for medicine price reduction (Yang et al., 2008).

WHO has proposed an eight-point procedure on how to improve the accessibility of essential medicines to developing countries in the Western Pacific region (WHO, 2005b). In addition some scholars (Shao et al., 2009; Wu, 2009) have proposed a procedure for improving the accessibility of essential medicines in China, through the establishment of a national institution under the framework of new medical reform in the country. These, and other scholars (Yang et al., 2009; Ye et al., 2008) have also indicated the reasons why the availability of essential medicines in China is kept low, thereafter putting forward countermeasures on improvement.

The Chinese government has already invested a great deal of financial resources and provided supporting policies to ensure the availability of essential medicines. Since 1982 the government has revised the list of essential medicines six times and devised a great number of practical measures related to this, including: insurance coverage, supervision of the supply chain, and so on—in order to explore measures which can be used to better promote the availability and affordability of these medicines in rural areas. The 17th National Congress of China's Communist Party put forward the goal of establishing a security system for the supply of medicines, which can cover both urban and rural areas as well as the creation of a national essential medicines institution in order to ensure the basic needs of essential medicines and food security in the country. In order to ensure the supply and quality of rural medicines and guarantee that people in rural areas can have ready access to convenient medicines at affordable prices the, Chinese government has simultaneously implemented a "Two Networks" solution, namely: the network of rural medicine supply and the network of rural medicine supervision. The "Two Networks" approach has significantly improved rural medicine supply and, at the same time, greatly improved the quality of these medicines. Research in 2007 related to the "Two Networks" solution—covering over 80% of the administrative villages in China as well as rural regions, found that the prices of common medicines had generally reduced to more than 20% (details on this is provided in "The Research and Evaluation Team of Constructing "Two networks" of Rural Medicines: The Exploration and Innovation of Constructing "Two networks" of Rural Medicines [R], 2008 (6)").

In April, 2009, the State Council of China issued the plan of the new healthcare system reform, which proposed that the construction of the "Two Networks" should aim at achieving a wide coverage of the concerned areas as well as demonstrating clear benefits to the citizens. At the same time, the plan suggested the establishment of a national supply chain for essential medicines The Chinese government will invite bids and then designate manufacturers to produce these medicines locally, or purchase them through a centralized system in the country. Grass-roots medical institutions, such as township hospitals and village clinics are all required to use essential medicines in order to ensure that people in the rural areas can have access to safe and effective medicines at reasonable prices. On August 18, 2009, the Chinese government issued the National Essential Drug List comprising some 307 medicines and started the construction of the National Institute for Essential Medicines.

Despite the positive effects of the above indicated measures, it should be added that both the medical reform and the ensuing National Institute for Essential Medicines are perhaps too directive. The promotion of easy access to essential medicines in rural China through the constructing of a new supply and security system for these still needs a lot of research for the simple reason that there are still a number of important questions to be clarified by the government.

6.2 PROBLEM DEFINITION

In terms of promoting the accessibility of essential medicines, WHO has proposed a "four action plan" identified as: reasonable choice and use of essential medicines, affordable price, sustainable financing system, and a reliable supply system (WHO, 2004). In rural areas of China it seems, however, that the target of policy designed for the constructing of a supply security system should focus on the availability and affordability of essential medicines. In light of this, whether the above-mentioned four action plan can be reasonably used is far from clear. Therefore, assessing the impact of the national medicines policy (NMP) in rural China's pharmaceutical supply chain should be carried out primarily through an investigation of the accessibility as seen from three perspectives: availability, affordability, and the rational use of medicines. This will provide a basis for better evaluating the impact of NMP on the elements and units of the whole pharmaceutical supply chain.

6.3 HYPOTHESIS

In accordance with calls directed at research and improvement of the pharmaceutical supply chain in rural China (Dong et al., 1999; Jiang et al., 2009; Tong et al., 2010) it is clear that the impact of the NMP needs to be focused specifically on the supply chain of essential medicines.

In this regard, it is expected that NMP can enhance the supply security of essential medicines through the contribution of distribution channels in rural areas, which will significantly stimulate the increased availability of these essential medicines. As a result the following hypotheses have been proposed for our research:

H1: The input brought by NMP will increase the availability of essential medicines in rural China.

H1a: NMP will enhance the contribution of supply channel of essential medicines in rural China which, in turn, would result to a higher level of availability of these medicines in rural areas.

H1b: NMP confirms the state as the main supplier of essential medicines thereby ensuring the high level of their availability in the rural areas.

Furthermore, a number of research findings (Li, 2010; Zhou & Yan, 2007; Zhou et al., 2006) indicate that public–private partnerships (PPP) would bring about an enhanced improvement in the existing public sector supply system which is also one of NMP's strategic orientations. It was therefore expected that NMP would bring about an enhanced competitive atmosphere, but also cooperation in the essential medicines supply chain in rural China thus leading to a significant reduction in price which, in turn, would lead to an increase in the affordability of these medicines. This leads us to Hypothesis 2, formulated as follows:

H2a: NMP contributes to enhanced competition between the private and the public sectors in the supply system for essential medicines in rural China. This, in turn, results to a significant reduction in the price of these medicines and a marked increase in their affordability among consumers.

H2b: As a result, it is expected that NMP would make a significant contribution to improving the prescription behavior of rural physicians which, in turn, would lead to a more rational consumption pattern for these medicines in the rural areas of China.

6.4 METHODOLOGY

6.4.1 Research Design

Based on the standard survey methodology developed by WHO and Health Action International (HAI) (WHO & HAI, 2003a, 2003b), and according to the requirements of the sample selection handbook of public medical institutions and retail pharmacies, the research team has taken, at random, a certain amount of materials about public medical institutions and retail pharmacies in Guizhou Province, Shaanxi Province, and Shanghai City in China. Random sampling method includes data on the level of availability of essential medicines in the indicated areas, dosage form, specification, as well as the wholesale and retail prices. The sampling method also included data on the influence of the NMP on rural pharmaceutical supply chain integrating qualitative and quantitative data.

6.4.2 Samples

This research selected three representative regions in China identified as: Yuping county from Guizhou Province (Southwest China), Luochuan County from Shaanxi province (Northwest China), and Minhang District from Shanghai (Eastern China).

Yuping County, with a population of 143,000 inhabitants, has jurisdiction over four towns and two townships. The average annual income in Yuping in 2008 was 2816 Yuan. Luochuan County has a population of 20 million inhabitants and jurisdiction over seven towns and nine townships. The average income of residents was 4500 Yuan in 2008. Minhang District has a population of 1,804,700 inhabitants and an average annual income in 2008 of 14,496 Yuan.

Table 6.1 The sources and composition of sample institutions

	Yuping County	Luochuan County	Minhang District
Public medical institutions	8	8	4
Retail pharmacies	4	8	6

In each region, a certain number of public medical institutions and retail pharmacies were chosen to be surveyed, as detailed in Table 6.1.

6.5 MEDICINES SURVEYED

Regarding the specific medicines to be included in the survey, the research team chose 30 essential medicines (see Table 6.2) recommended by WHO and HAI as the core list (Kirsten, 2008). According to the principle of rational drug use and the clinical diagnosis and treatment standards (WHO, 2009b; WHO Model Formulary (WMF), 2008), the complementary list is made up of 10 medicines which are used to treat a certain number of diseases that have relatively high morbidity in China's rural regions (according to the fourth National Health Survey),[1] as well as a certain number of diseases which have relatively high mortality rate at the county level, according to the health statistics summary (see Table 6.3). Most of the medicines chosen are contained in the reimbursement lists of the local new rural Cooperative Medical System (CMS) and all the medicines chosen are contained in the National Essential Drug List (2009 Edition).[2]

6.5.1 Method of Data Collection

Due to the multiplicity of the research objectives, two sets of questionnaires were designed for the survey. The first concerned quantitative data related to variables such as the availability and price of essential medicines in the public medical institutions and retail pharmacies, while the focus of the second was primarily the collection of qualitative information related to a number of variables at different levels of the distribution channels, including obstacles related to easy availability of the medicines.

Through field research, we collected data pertaining to how essential medicines were received at the central depots and further distributed

[1] Main results of this survey can be found at: http://www.moh.gov.cn/publicfiles/business/htmlfiles/mohbgt/s6690/200902/39201.htm.

[2] National Essential Medicines List (Part of healthy organization in grass-roots): http://www.gov.cn/gzdt/2009-08/18/content_1395524.htm.

Table 6.2 Core list

Drug name	Specification	Dosage form	Drug name	Specification	Dosage form
Aciclovir	200 mg	C/T	Fluconazole	200 mg	C/T
Amitriptyline	25 mg	C/T	Artesunate	100 mg	C/T
Amoxicillin	250 mg	C/T	Glibenclamide	5 mg	C/T
Atenolol	50 mg	C/T	Hydrochlorothiazide	25 mg	C/T
Captopril	25 mg	C/T	Metformin	500 mg	C/T
Carbamazepine	200 mg	C/T	Nifedipine retard	20 mg	C/T
Ceftriaxona	1 g	Inj	Omeprazole	20 mg	C/T
Ciprofloxacin	500 mg	C/T	Phenytoin	100 mg	C/T
Compound sulfamethoxazole	(8 + 40) $mg\,mL^{-1-1}$	PS	Ranitidine	150 mg	C/T
Diazepam	5 mg	C/T	Salbutamol	0.1 $mg\,mL^{-1}$	Inh
Diclofenac	25 mg	C/T	Beclomethasone	50 ìg dose	Inh
Fluoxetine	200 mg	C/T	Fluphenazine decanoate	25 $mg\,mL^{-1}$	Inj
Indinavir	400 mg	C/T	Lovastatin	20 mg	C/T
Pyrimethamine with sulfadoxine	(500 + 25) mg	C/T	Zidovudine	100 mg	C/T
Lovastan	50 mg	C/T	Nevirapine	200 mg	C/T

Source: Kirsten, M. (2008). The measurement of the availability and price of medicines. *China Licensed Pharmacist*, *9*, 47–49.

Table 6.3 Complementary list

Drug name	Specification	Dosage form	Drug name	Specification	Dosage form
Azithromycin	200 mg	C/T	Dexamethasone	5 mgmL^{-1}	Inj
Ofloxacin	200 mg	C/T	Ibuprofen	200 mg	C/T
Simvastatin	20 mg	C/T	Metronidazole	200 mg	C/T
Aminophylline	100 mg	C/T	Albendazole	200 mg	C/T
Chloramphenicol	250 mg	C/T	Clindamycin	300 mg	C/T

Source: World Health Organization. (2009b). *The model list of essential medicines*. Geneva; World Health Organization. (2008). *WHO Model Formulary*. Geneva.

downstream to the retail outlets, the operating conditions at different levels of the distribution network, and so on.

6.5.2 Method of Data Analysis

The availability of each medicine is summarized as the percentage of stock availability of the required medicines in the facilities, on the day of data collection (WHO & HAI, 2003a, 2003b). The following criteria were used to describe the availability of essential medicines:

- Low, < 30% of facilities;
- Relatively low, < 50% of facilities;
- Relatively high, > 50% of facilities.

6.5.2.1 Assessment of Affordability

The research team has adopted the WMF recommended by both WHO and HAI. The therapeutic process is based on the WHO Model List of Essential Medicines and British National Formulary (BNF). This is as presented in Table 6.4. The treatment period of acute infection is 7 days; the treatment period of adult chronic diseases is 30 days; the purchasing standards of medicines are represented by the minimum wage of the non-technicians working in the government. The survey targets are distributed in the Southwest, Northwest, and Eastern part of the country. So, on a 30-day month, the average daily wage of the three regions is 20, 16, and 32 Yuan, respectively.[3] The survey item of rational drug use will focus on the drug consumption as well as the abuse of injection and antibiotics.

[3]Since it is hard to define the minimum wage standard of the nontechnicians working in the government, the minimum wage of the investigated regions is defined according to the official minimum wage standards and their application scope. For instance, the minimum wage standard of Yuping County, Guizhou Province is 600 Yuan (Sources: http://gz.lss.gov.cn/gzldt/72345683297828864/20080107/4522.html), so according to the calculation of 30 days a month, the minimum daily wage of Yuping County is 20 Yuan.

Table 6.4 Examples of standard treatment guidelines

Disease	Drug name	Specification	Dosage form	Daily dose	Treatment period (day)	Total dose	References
Diabetes	Metformin	500 mg	C/T	2 tablets	30	60	BNF 43 (March 2002) Section 6.1.2.1
Hypertension	Hydrochlorothiazide	25 mg	C/T	1 tablet	30	30	BNF 43 (September 2001) Section 2.2.1
Adult respiratory infection	Amoxicillin	250 mg	C/T	3 tablets	7	21	BNF 43 (March 2002) Section 5.1.1.3
Depression	Amitriptyline	25 mg	C/T	3 tablets	30	90	BNF 43(March 2002) Section 4.3.1

According to the methodology recommended by WHO and HAI (2008), taking the pricing in *International drug price indicator guide (2008 Edition)* by Management Sciences for Health (MSH) as the international reference price, and determining the exchange rate on the basis of the Yuan central parity of 6.823 against the US dollar on July 31, 2009,[4] we can compare the prices of essential medicines in the rural areas of China with the international prices of the same medicines. Also, data for patient prices in the public and private sectors was included in the analysis where the medicines can be found in at least four facilities.

As the last, and perhaps one of the most important, circles in essential medicines supply chain, WHO has proposed a relatively feasible approach to measuring rationality in the prescription of drugs. Due to time constraints, however, we were not able to collect a sufficient amount of samples. Therefore, only an intuitive evaluation of the usage of antibiotics and injections in essential medicines prescription, the amount of the prescription, and prices will be attempted here.

6.6 REVIEW OF THE LITERATURE

Research into the accessibility of essential medicines in rural China has generated considerable interest in scholarly research during the past ten years. Some works have been concerned with a measurement of the affordability and availability of different parts of China based on the method given by WHO/HAI (Hao et al., 2010; Lu, 2006; Sun, 2005; Yang et al., 2008), while others are more concerned with an international comparative analysis, based on a number of secondary data sources (Camero et al., 2009; Shanthi et al., 2007). These measurements and comparison bring a very important reference to the present research, although, strictly speaking, rural and townships medicines distribution in China belong to a different medical security system. This is particularly the case due to the differences that exist in income levels in the rural and township regions, compared to urban areas in China. Furthermore, differences exist in the reimbursement mechanism between rural residents and township residents on the one hand, and between rural residents/township residents, and urban areas on the other. This fact has an important bearing on the selection of the reviewed literature in the present research.

[4]Data sources: http://www.pbc.gov.cn/huobizhengce/huobizhengcegongju/huilvzhengce/renminbihuilvjiaoyishoupanjia.asp?page=3&col=&fromyear=&frommonth=&fromday=&toyear=&tomonth=&today=.

As far as the supply chain of essential medicines in rural areas is concerned, a number of scholars have carried out research addressing these issues from different perspectives. Others (Chen, 2005; Li, 2010) have advocated the establishment of an integrated supply chain, and improving supply efficiency to reduce macro-level modern distribution systems' essential medicines expenditure. Still others have opined that institutional construction should be strengthened, and that the government should sufficiently improve the existing rural medical security system in order to better facilitate the reimbursement needs of rural residents (Tong, 2010). Previous research has also pointed out the problem of public service supply system for essential medicines in the rural areas of China (Tang et al., 2010). Through the analysis of policy reform of the distribution network, scholars (Sun et al., 2008) have proposed a new system for improving the supply chain of essential medicines in China's rural areas. The indicated literature provides some interesting methodological guidelines for future research concerned with this issue.

Based on the reviewed literature, the present assessment of the impact of the NMP on the country's pharmaceutical supply chain is expected to make a contribution as a useful complement to what is already available in terms of scholarly research. It is our hope that it can also provide possible future research threads for others.

6.7 EMPIRICAL DATA ANALYSIS

Regarding the availability of essential medicines in the indicated three regions, it is important to note that the position of public medical institutions is rather modest compared to the numerous private retail pharmacies. Furthermore, only a small number of medicines e.g., Amoxicillin and Omeprazole, can be easily found in the rural regions. Additionally, the availability of some essential medicines like Ranitidine and Fluoxetine hydrochloride is rather low, which, to some extent, reflects the deficiency of medicines used to treat mental illnesses in rural regions and the fact that grass-roots medical services attach only modest importance to the treatment of mental illnesses (see Table 6.5).

The reason for the low availability of these medicines can be explained from different perspectives. Research, however, indicates that the differences in dosage form and specification lead to the low availability of essential medicines in China's rural regions. Although certain essential medicines have been adopted by medical institutions, dosage forms for

Table 6.5 The availability of essential medicines in different rural medical institutions of the three regions

	Luochuan County		Yuping County		Minhang District	
	Public medical institution	Retail pharmacy	Public medical institution	Retail pharmacy	Public medical institution	Retail pharmacy
Availability median	37.5%	50%	25%	37.5%	25%	33.3%

these medicines are all administered by way of injection. Notable examples include medicines such as Acyclovir and Ciprofloxacin. On the other hand, Chinese patent medicines as well as traditional Chinese medicines are not included in the drug list of the present survey. In rural areas of many regions, quite a large number of rural doctors and peasants are more inclined to the consumption of Chinese patent medicines which, to some extent, contributes to the relatively low availability of essential medicines.

The underlying reason is, however, that the pursuit of profits in the supply chain of essential medicines has reduced the availability of medicines. The differences in dosage form and specification is directly attributable to the country's regulatory mechanism for the price of medicines. When a certain type of specific dosage form is under price regulation, unless the manufacturer and distribution company sees the potential for high profit margins it may not be interested in participating in the bidding process for new medicines. The result in cases like this would obviously be a continuation of the same medicines produced in different dosage forms.

Hypertension treatment can be used as an explanatory example for the low level of availability of some of the lower-priced essential medicines. The relatively cheap Hydrochlorothiazide has relatively high cost–benefit but, due to its low profit, manufacturers are unwilling to produce it and dealers are unwilling to sell it—contributing to a significant reduction in its availability on the market. A corresponding drug called Amlodipine is, on the other hand, readily available. It appears, however, that if the treating physicians suddenly exhibit a clear preference for this latter drug, which currently is readily available, it will result in a disproportionate increase in its price, thereby significantly reducing the level of its affordability. This reasoning can also be used to explain the availability gap between the drugs Amitriptyline and Fluoxetine hydrochloride, both of which are used in the treatment of depression.

In terms of the medicines' affordability, generally speaking, this still needs to be improved in the rural areas of China. The average medical expense for drugs used to treat Diabetes, Hypertension and Depression is 2.09–5.54 times higher than the minimum daily wage. Judging from the affordability of medicines used to treat diseases in Luochuan and Yuping Counties, the performance of public medical institutions can be said to be significantly lower in standard compared to private retail pharmacies. This is because retail pharmacies generally tend to be more market-oriented, choosing only the most cost-effective supply channels, whereas public medical institutions prefer drugs with high price due to various reasons, such as concern over Drug Addition Rate (DAR).

Following a detailed comparison of the survey data, our research discovered that, although the average minimum daily wage of Minhang District, Shanghai City was twice that of Luochuan County in Shanxi Province, the affordability of medicines used to treat certain diseases in Minhang District was lower than that in Luochuan County. This is because in both public medical institutions and retail pharmacies of Minhang District, innovator drugs and import drugs have a relatively high proportion of the medicines on sale, leading to a reduction in the relative degree of affordability of medicines.

As far as affordability is concerned, the relatively high setting of minimum wage standard has led to some misconception that the affordability of essential medicines in rural China is without a question. Our research chooses the official minimum wage standard for urban workers as the standard, but in there still exists a significant gap between the per capita income of peasants and the minimum wage standard for urban workers. On the other hand, if the present research were to choose per capita income of peasants as the standard then it is clear that the affordability problem of essential medicines will become much more serious (Table 6.6).

In comparing the international reference price, it can be easily discerned that among several essential medicines selected (with the exception of Captopril), the prices of the other four medicines are generally higher than the international reference prices and the comparative prices of certain medicines greatly exceed the bearable level of price differences (Table 6.7).

Through a careful check of prescription bills in outpatient clinics of a selected number of hospitals in the three regions surveyed, our research found that the number of drug variety is overwhelmingly related to prescriptions made by township hospitals (above 4). Through the method of *Expert Argumentation*, WHO has formulated the standard for rational drug

Table 6.6 Affordability (expressed in US$) of medicines used to treat certain types of diseases in rural areas of chosen three regions in China

Disease	Drug name	Luochuan County		Yuping County		Minhang District	
		Public medical institution	Retail pharmacies	Public medical institution	Retail pharmacies	Public medical institution	Retail pharmacies
Diabetes	Metformin	5.54	4.95	5.13	4.8	3.51	3.51
Hypertension	Hydrochlorothiazide	0.45	0.15	0.02	0.02	0.04	0.04
	Amlodipine	3.08	2.09	2.94	2.6	5.67	5.67
Adult respiratory infection	Amoxicillin	0.18	0.16	0.21	0.16	0.71	0.71
Depression	Amitriptyline	0.76	0.66	0.44	0.42	0.53	0.53
	Fluoxetine hydrochloride	4.32	3.96	3.67	3.53	2.21	2.21
Gastric ulcer	Ranitidine	0.6	0.48	0.3	0.25	0.35	0.35

Table 6.7 A comparison of international and local prices (expressed in Yuan) of certain types of medicines in rural areas of the three regions in China

Drug name	Luochuan County		Yuping County		Minhang District	International reference price
	Public medical institution	Retail pharmacy	Public medical institution	Retail pharmacy	Public medical institution/retail pharmacy	
Amoxicillin	0.1371	0.1219	0.2014	0.1523	1.0819	0.1651
Captopril	0.0376	0.0349	0.0274	0.0243	0.0734	0.0962
Nifedipine	0.5917	0.5573	0.6161	0.575	0.6521	0.1432
Omeprazole	0.6013	0.5786	0.5857	0.5429	3.4571	0.2231
Metformin	1.4473	1.32	1.7114	1.602	1.8721	0.1194

use in medical institutions' outpatient clinics in developing countries. According to WHO, the average number of prescription drug variety in a prescription bill should be 1.6–2.8. WHO further notes that in 11 Asian and African communities, the average number of prescription drugs used in a prescription bill is less than 2.2 (the smallest number being 1.6 and the largest 3.2). These findings seem to support the hypothesis that township doctors generally have a preference for excessive prescription of drugs (i.e., the so-called "Big Prescription" syndrome).

Generally speaking, it can be said that the excessive administration of prescriptive drugs by means of intravenous devices (i.e., "injection") is taken by WHO as the great hidden danger of irrational drug use. Although, to some extent, the effect of injection is said to be better compared to, e.g., oral administration, the level of safety of the former is much lower compared to the latter method. This is particularly the case in rural areas, where basic medical conditions are relatively poor, in addition to the fact that up-to-date information and proper guidance on these matters is not always easily available to the populace. Regarding treatment costs, administration by way of injection was found to be relatively higher, compared to oral method.

Besides injection, our research found the phenomenon of antibiotics consumption to be significant in the surveyed regions. By making a comparison of prescriptions collected through the use of Standard Formulary, our research found that the use of antibiotics is much higher in the target regions. This phenomenon appears to be an on-going problem across rural China.

6.8 DISCUSSION OF THE FINDINGS

Beside the above-mentioned factors, the impact of the supply security system of essential medicines on the availability and affordability of essential medicines in rural China is reflected in the following factors:

Firstly, it is clear that the NMP has not successfully accomplished the task of restructuring the essential medicines distribution network in a way that would enable a significant reduction of costs in the rural areas of China. High distribution costs for these medicines have led to a significant reduction in their availability in the rural areas of the country. China is a large, agricultural country with a large number of rural residents who are widely distributed in dispersed regions. As such, township hospitals, village clinics, and retail pharmacies—which should normally be able to satisfy the essential medicine needs of peasants, are dispersed in the vast rural areas. This, in turn, has led to a reduction in the availability of these medicines in such areas, as the distribution system is not able to cope with such geographic disparity. A good example of this problem is Bengshan County, which is located in a mountainous area with a narrow and long crescent-like landscape. There are 27 township hospitals and over 30 retail pharmacies, as well as 564 government village clinics, and a number of private ones found in Bengshan County. Numerous medical institutions are distributed in the extensive rural areas, but their average distance to the county seat is between 50 and 100 km away. The peculiarities of rural China combined with the dispersed geographical distribution of its medical institutions are important factors in the high costs associated with the distribution of essential medicines in these areas. Furthermore, the medicine needs of township hospitals and village clinics are relatively small, so, under the condition of restricting DAR, drug distribution companies cannot achieve higher price levels through scale operation, to make up for the relatively high distribution cost. There is little profit to be made in distributing medicines to remote regions of China. This, in turn, often means that drug distribution companies often have to absorb certain costs without any form of return on their investment (see Table 6.8). All this has led to a situation whereby wholesale drug companies are often forced to distribute medicines solely to township hospitals. The effect of this is the general shortage of such medicines right across the rural areas of the country.

Secondly, as the main body of essential medicines supply, the NMP has not ameliorated the basic distribution channels to a satisfactory level in the regions of our empirical research. The investment in constructing grassroots township hospitals and village clinics is seriously inadequate and the construction plan is irrational, which, in turn, has reduced the availability of essential medicines in these areas. Nationally, China has a large population in the rural regions, accounting for approximately 70% of the country's total population. Yet, sales of medicines in the rural regions account for a mere 15% of the total output in the country. Concerning the putting in place of necessary infrastructure for an efficient distribution network for medicines in the rural areas, it has been found that in 2008 there were a total of 39,080 township hospitals in the country. This accounted for an average of 1.14 township hospitals per town. Accordingly, up to 10.8% of the administrative villages in China have not yet set up village clinics. The number of drug sales outlets in the rural regions of the country is

Table 6.8 Medicine distribution cost (expressed in Yuan) of some villages in Yuping County of Guizhou Province

	Road condition	Location	Drug value	Distribution cost and times	Distribution profit (4–8%)
Clinic of Munong Village, Zhujia Chang	1/4 is country road	18 km from the county seat	800 Yuan	Once a month. Gas fee: 20 Yuan at a time; the cost of vehicle wear and labor are not included	32–64 Yuan
Drug chain store in Xiang Cha Village, Dalong Town	Mainly country road	12 km from the county seat	700 Yuan	Once a month. Gas fee: 20 Yuan at a time; the cost of vehicle wear and labor is not included	28–56 Yuan
Drug chain stores in Tianping Village, Tianping Town	Mainly high grade highway	40 km from the county seat	1500 Yuan	Once a month. Gas fee and highway toll: 66 Yuan at a time; the cost of vehicle wear and labor is not included	60–120 Yuan
Clinic of Guo Jia Wan, Yayu Town	High grade highway and country road	50 km from the county seat	600 Yuan	Once a month, Gas fee and highway toll: 86 Yuan at a time; the cost of vehicle wear and labor is not included	24–48 Yuan
Clinic of Zhangping Village, Tianping Town	High grade highway and country road	45 km from county seat	600 Yuan	Once a month, Gas fee and highway toll: 76 Yuan at a time; the cost of vehicle wear and labor is not included	24–48 Yuan

seriously insufficient. For example, approximately 7% of the administrative villages in Luochuan County do not have their own clinics, while ~8% of the administrative villages in Yuping County do not have their own. In the markets of the towns with relatively dense population and a relatively convenient transportation system, the distribution of drug sales outlets is relatively concentrated, while in the remote areas of rural regions the distribution of drug sales outlets is relatively dispersed so that it is extremely inconvenient for peasants to buy drugs.

The medicine variety of rural medical institutions and retail pharmacies is insufficient, which cannot satisfy the medicine needs in treating seasonal diseases, common diseases, and frequently occurring diseases for which people in rural regions are often afflicted—due to the specific nature of the environment and climatic conditions. With respect to the types of drug sales outlets, township hospitals and village clinics are still the main channel through which peasants can procure medicines they need. Our research indicates that 28% of the medicines used by the peasants of Luochuan County in the treatment of various diseases are from village clinics, 22% from township hospitals and only 12% and 7% are from rural retail pharmacies and county pharmacies, respectively. There are many reasons for this phenomenon and there is no doubt that the relatively insufficient medication knowledge of peasants accounts for this. A more important reason lies, however, in the inadequate number of retail pharmacies at the county level. Even though there are a few retail pharmacies in some villages, these retail pharmacies will be at a natural disadvantage in the competition with public medical institutions, unable to be absorbed into the reimbursement system of the new rural CMS.

Thirdly, under the weight of government intervention, the private sector has not played enough of an active role in the rural pharmaceutical supply chain. The benefit game of multiagents within the distribution system has led to the low levels of affordability of medicines today in rural China.

From the perspective of the purchasing power of the average consumer in rural China, it is very easy to see that the price of medicines (including essential medicines) is high. Using Luochuan County in Shanxi Province as an example: per capita annual consumption expenditure of rural residents in Shanxi Province was 2979.4 Yuan in 2008, while the result of our research in the region indicates that drug expenditure alone accounted for 28% of the peasants' total annual spend of between 400 and 800 Yuan and 10% above 800 Yuan.

The high price of medicines is another factor which accounts for this phenomenon. Since 1996, the National Development and Reform Commission of China (NDRC) has adjusted the drug price 24 times. Since May 2004 the price index of Chinese and Western medicines, and healthcare products has been sustainably increasing on the whole. This means that, for peasants, the burden of drug expense is far from being relieved. The main reason behind this phenomenon is that the fiscal expenditure that the government earmarks for rural healthcare is inadequate, which leads to the deviation of rural medical institutions' own positioning. Only by the measure of "healthcare supported by excessive drug sales" can they maintain the normal operational mode and the new rural CMS has further sharpened this problem.

The idea of "Pooling Funds for Serious Illnesses," which pays close attention to treatment instead of prevention, has stimulated the increase of drug income proportion. According to data from our survey of Luochuan County, in 2005 and 2006 the drug income of village clinics was respectively 76.59% and 78.01% of the whole medical income, while the drug income of township hospital was respectively 77.48% and 77.89% of the whole medical income.

Lastly, the NPM has failed to standardize the prescription behavior of rural physicians. The defects inherent in the prescription pattern of some rural physicians tend to distort their true behavior. The new rural CMS has intensified the increase of peasants' drug expenditure which is driven by "Physician-induced Demand," and has substantially reduced the affordability of medicines. Some scholars (e.g., Wang et al., 2004) are of the opinion that the new rural CMS has led to an increase in the overall medical expenditure of peasants. Although the present research did not address the issue of a long term, possible causal relationship between the new rural CMS policy and prescriptive medicines consumption patterns in the rural areas of China, it appears from the limited data we received, that such a pattern may exist. Likewise, on the premise of reimbursement of drugs expenses according to the total amount spent, the phenomenon of patients asking for more prescription drugs, and more drugs with relatively high price is particularly noteworthy. This has generally been referred to as "excessive consumption induced by demander." Meanwhile, alongside the phenomenon of "Big Prescription" and "High Price Drug," irrational drug use, such as the abuse of injection and antibiotics is still prevalent in rural regions (Wang et al., 2004).

6.9 IMPLICATIONS OF FINDINGS ON GOVERNMENT POLICY

China has already formed the explicit idea of macroscopically constructing the supply security system of essential medicines whereby the production of essential medicines adopts the method of procurement through inviting public bidding. Regarding price, the Chinese Central Government sets the retail reference price such that, within this reference price, provincial governments determine the centralized purchase price of their own province, according to tender bidding. Grass-roots healthcare institutions of urban and rural areas are all asked to procure and use essential medicines, and sell them by cost price. Within this system, essential medicines are all included in the drug reimbursement list of the basic healthcare security system and the reimbursement proportion of essential medicines is generally higher than that of nonessential medicines. After the analysis and discussion of the accessibility of essential medicines in rural regions, from the microcosmic perspective, the starting point of improving supply security of essential medicines can be explored in the following manner:

Firstly, realizing that the regulatory mechanism that can combine market competition with the government-oriented system is in need of the enrichment and activation of the rural drug circulation market. When the traditional, and rigid, top-down administrative power is replaced with a more market-oriented one, the government should pay more attention to the formation of the favorable environment, beneficial to the exertion of market mechanism. This includes, among others, the cultivation of real market mechanisms in a significant way. The past rural drug circulation market, coupled with the terrible institutional environment and low profit levels, constituted the two central thresholds that kept many enterprises away from the rural prescription medicines market. The activation of the rural drug circulation market can be considered from both internal and external perspectives. On one hand, the government should stick to the practice of a unified national market and, with appropriate policy orientation, encourage modernized logistics companies and other major actors in the distribution network to enter the rural prescription medicines market. Such an orientation should include the construction and maintenance of a fair and orderly competitive market environment. An orientation of this nature can also include fiscal measures, such as the reduction and exemption of taxes, and monetary approaches—credits and other forms of loan, to those operating in extremely remote areas of the country. The government can also consider offering governmental subsidies to enterprises, compared with direct governmental subsidies, which could lead to a certain degree of reproach from certain quarters. The government can, furthermore, subcontract a modern system of distribution and sales of drugs to enterprises through the method of governments purchasing services. Based on the idea of essential medicines being public goods, the government can consider sharing some resource allocation power with private businesses in the remote areas of the country. Based on the requirement of bringing real parity between public services and private companies, the government should make it possible to offer such services according to the principle of "universal service." Compared with direct governmental subsidies, these two methods are beneficial to restraining the propagation of power rent-seeking phenomenon.

Alternatively, the government should reduce the perennial nature of health departments, bringing in private capital and the prescription medicines distribution system in line with normal market mechanism. According to public choice theory, government departments often tend to utilize the maximum budgetary allocations. The resulting "internality" behavior often leads to a low level of efficiency inside the government departments which, in turn, leads to significant transaction cost. In the traditional supply mode of the new rural CMS, health departments are actually the policy makers, executors and supervisors of new CMS policy. As a result, health departments and public hospitals have become a benefit community, when there is a lack of restrictions from the outside—their objective being to maximize government subsidies, department scale and their own status. The state law relating to sale of prescription medicines and the distribution of same by private enterprises is much stricter than those of medical institutions. Under these circumstances, private capital often cannot survive. As a result, the government can consider offering the status of nonoperating and nonprofit public service organizations to private drug distribution companies, along the same principles as rural pharmacies, operated by peasants who have the necessary know-how and economic strength to lower the threshold for market entry, and to reduce (and be exempt from) certain related taxes. Further policy design can consider absorbing nonpublic drug distribution institutions, like rural retail pharmacies and private clinics, into the reimbursement list of the new rural CMS, in order to usher in competition mechanism and better activate the rural drug distribution market.

Secondly, the government should explore how to connect the new rural CMS with the national essential medicine institution, in order to improve medication status of peasants. Absorbing all essential medicines into the reimbursement list of the new rural CMS is undoubtedly the foundation for ensuring proper medication for peasants. In China there is presently no single, universally implemented or consulted medicine list under the new rural CMS system. In a small number of places, the medicine list of the new rural CMS has been united with the medicine list of the urban medical insurance schemes. In many places, however, the medicine list of the new rural CMS is separately compiled. Many provincial governments have compiled the unified medicine list of the new rural CMS for their own province and, in some places, the county governments have also compiled their own lists. This pattern of drug list compilation, largely devoid of specific reference standards, may be detrimental to maintaining a more rigorous and up-to-date list of essential medicines in various regions under the new rural CMS system. Meanwhile, in some places the renewal rate of the medicine list under the new rural CMS is relatively slow. The continuous emergence of new drugs, the changes in the disease spectrum and the ever-increasing drug resistance have, however, made the original drugs in the list unable to satisfy the drug needs of patients. So, absorbing the list of essential medicines into the medicine list of the new rural CMS is favorable for improving the medication status of peasants. Besides the connection of drug lists, the remarkable cost–benefit of essential medicines is also beneficial to reducing peasants' burden of medication expenditure, through enlarging the security ranges of the new rural CMS. In the past, because of high medical expenditure and long treatment cycles, many chronic diseases could not be absorbed into the reimbursement range of the new rural CMS. Through the introduction of essential medicines, the medical expenditure can now be reduced on the whole, which perhaps makes the treatment cost come within the commitment range of the new rural CMS and, consequently, absorbed into its reimbursement range. In the end, the government should rationally determine the reimbursement proportion relationship between nonessential medicines in the medicine list of the new rural CMS, and essential medicines. If there is little difference in the reimbursement proportion, it will perhaps be nothing else but the excessive restraint of demands. Once the reimbursement proportion of essential medicines is much larger than that of nonessential medicines, it will not be good for the consumption of nonessential medicines, which may even trace back upstream through the industry chain, having a negative influence on the R&D and innovation of the pharmaceutical industry.

Lastly, according to National Essential Drugs Clinical Guide, the government should set standards for rural doctors' use of drugs and consider guiding the rational use of essential medicines through the coordination of the multisupervisory mechanism design. At present in China, 78% of drug expenditure is made through doctors' prescription (Hu, 2009). As a result, the question of whether doctors can sufficiently use medicines is a key part of the success of an essential medicine institution. When the nonmarket financing, such as government input and social insurance, is inadequate and medical institutions need to charge patients in order to compensate for the inadequate financing, the strong position of doctors as professional agents will not be changed short term. The government can, however, standardize and guide the behavior of rural doctors through the related mechanism.

Other irrational drug use behaviors such as "Big Prescription" are likely caused by lack of professional quality and vocational morality, besides the share drive of the distorted institution. This kind of defect can be corrected in the training of front-end behavior and the supervision of back-end behavior. Pertaining to supervision and administration, in the past, health departments in rural areas universally adopted the management and control methods like prescription structure control and prescription cost control, but there was generally a lack of universal, rational, and specific operational standards and methods. Alongside the penetrating implementation of the national essential medicine institution policy the issue and implementation of National Essential Drugs Clinical Guide and Chinese National Formulary can provide supervisory methods, with strong manipulability for the use of essential medicines. In terms of exercising supervisory rights, aside from Central Government departments and other appropriate authorities, the government can include trade associations—professional physician associations, and organize the supervisory force among villages, in order to provide guidance on rational drug use behavior of rural doctors through multisupervisory mechanism.

6.10 AVENUES FOR FUTURE RESEARCH

The result of our research suggests that the effects of policy will become easily discernible only with the passage of time. The procedure of policy-making is also the procedure of a constant improvement of policy. The fact that the short-term effects of policy are not always visible does not mean there is policy failure. So, future research can be based on this point and proceed with long-term observations and measurement, in order to find the necessary amendments to the basic rural medicines supply chain.

Other than the above, it is also worth noting here that most of the research addressing specifically the issue of PPP in the Chinese health sector has not been incorporated into the present paper. A modern distribution system built on PPP is the core principle and key approach to solving the problem of essential medicines supply in rural China. Future research could explore more ways to optimize the pharmaceutical supply chain in China and on the improvement of efficiency under the framework of PPP.

REFERENCES

BNF, *The British National Formulary*. Learn from <http://www.bnf.vhn.net/home>.

Camero, A., et al. (2009). Medicine prices, availability, and affordability in 36 developing and middle-income countries: A secondary analysis. *The Lancet*, *373*, 240–249.

Chen, W. (2005). Orderly promote the reform of the pharmaceutical circulation system. *International Medicine & Health Guidance News*(3), 106–107.

Dong, H., et al. (1999). Drug policy in China: Pharmaceutical distribution in rural areas. *Social Science & Medicine*, *28*, 777–786.

Hao, Y., et al. (2010). Prices, availability and affordability of essential medicines in rural areas of Hubei Province, China. *Healthy Policy and Planning*, *25*, 219–229.

Hu, S. L. (2009). Analysis on the difficulties of essential medicine policy. *Chinese Journal of Health Policy*, *4*, 1–3.

Junhao, J., et al. (2009). Thinking on developing the optimum mechanism of drug circulation under the background of new medical reform. *The Chinese Health Service Management*, *9*, 609–614.

Kirsten, M. (2008). The measurement of the availability and price of medicines. *China Licensed Pharmacist*, *2008*(9), 47–49.

Li, X. (2010). Research on the integration of pharmaceutical supply chain. *Management World*, *2010*(5), 176–177.

Lu, Y. (2006). A survey of medicine prices, availability and affordability in Shanghai, China using the WHO/HAI Methodology. *HAI*.

MSH. *International drug price indicator guide*. <http://erc.msh.org/dmpguide/pdf/DrugPriceGuide_2008_en.pdf>.

Shanthi, M., et al. (2007). The availability and affordability of selected essential medicines for chronic diseases in six low-and middle-income countries. *Bulletin of the World Health Organization*, *85*(4), 279–288.

Shao, R. Q., et al. (2009). Discussion on construction of national essential drug policy under the circumstances of new health reform. *Chinese Pharmaceutical Affairs*, *2009*(2), 139–143.

Sun, Q. (2005). *A survey of medicine prices, availability, affordability and price components in Shandong province*. China: HAI.

Sun, Q., et al. (2008). Pharmaceutical policy in China. *Health Affairs*, *27*(4), 1042–1050.

Tang, R., et al. (2010). Research on the accessibility of the essential medicines in rural area under the background of new medical reform. *Expanding Horizons*, *1*, 18–20.

The Academic Group of the Research and Evaluation Team of Constructing "Two networks" of Rural Medicines. (2008). *The exploration and innovation of constructing "two networks" of rural medicines*. 6.

Tong, D., et al. (2010). Thoughts and suggestions for the distribution of essential drugs under the background of new medical reform. *China Pharmacy, 16*, 1467–1468.
UN. (2000). *Millennium development goal*. <http://www.un.org/millenniumgoals/>.
Wang, J., et al. (2004). Effect of basic drugs and rational drug use policies on rural drug use. *Medicine and Society, 2*, 63–66.
World Health Organization, (2004). *Equitable access to essential medicines: A framework for collective action*. Geneva: WHO.
World Health Organization, (2005a). *Regional strategy for improving access to essential medicines in the Western Pacific Region, 2005-2010*. Geneva: WHO.
World Health Organization. (2005b). *Essential medicines annual report 2004*. <http://www.who.int/medicines/publications/AnnualReport2004EN.pdf>.
World Health Organization. (2006a). *Essential medicines annual report 2005*. <http://www.who.int/medicines/publications/AnnualReport05En.pdf>.
World Health Organization. (2006b). *Injection safety*. <http://www.who.int/mediacentre/factsheets/fs231/en/>.
World Health Organization. (2007). *The pharmaceutical scene in 2006*. <http://www.who.int/medicines/publications/WHO_pharma_annual_report_En.pdf>.
World Health Organization. (2008). *WHO Model Formulary*. Geneva.
World Health Organization. (2009a). *Essential medicine*. <http://www.who.int/topics/essentialmedicines/en/>.
World Health Organization. (2009b). *The model list of essential medicines*. Geneva.
World Health Organization and Health Action International Medicine Prices, (2003a). *A new approach to measurement working draft for field testing and rescission*. Geneva: WHO.75–79.
World Health Organization and Health Action International Medicine Prices, (2003b). *A new approach to measurement working draft for field testing and rescission*. Geneva: WHO.98–103.
Wu, S. Q. (2009). Discussion on the defects of national essential drug system in our country and its improvement. *Chinese Pharmaceutical Affairs, 2009*(1), 43–55.
Yang, H., et al. (2008). Research on the ability to essential medicines in rural area of Hubei Xiaogan rural area. *China Pharmacy, 29*, 2242–2247.
Yang, H., et al. (2009). An analysis of the low affordability of medicines and drugs in China. *Medicine and Society, 2009*(2), 22–24.
Ye, L., et al. (2008). The problems and causes of essential drug production, distribution and use. *Chinese Health Resources, 3*, 51–53.
Zhou, C., & Yan, S. (2007). Preliminary discussion on the introducing the mechanism of the public-private partnerships into medical system reform of China. *Chinese Health Economics, 6*, 25–27.
Zhou, C., et al. (2006). *The application of the public-private partnership in the health field*. Chinese Health Economics 2006-05.73–75.

CHAPTER 7

Exploring Manager-Employee-Heterophily (MEH) in US-Owned and Managed Plants in Taiwan

Kirk Chang[1,2], Julie Taylor[3] and Kuo-Tai Cheng[4]
[1]HC HRM Consultancy Ltd, Manchester, United Kingdom
[2]University of Salford, Manchester, United Kingdom
[3]University of Cumbria, Carlisle, United Kingdom
[4]National Hsinchu University of Education, Hsinchu City, Taiwan

7.1 INTRODUCTION

Starting from the position of a low-cost manufacturing provider, Taiwan has transformed itself into a major player in international business. The fast-growing markets in Taiwan, enabled by business-friendly regulations and a plentiful workforce, have created opportunities for overseas investors and organizations to set up companies in Taiwan (Chang & Smale, 2014; Zhou, Gao, Yang, & Zhou, 2005). These opportunities have resulted in a situation referred to as Manager-Employee-Heterophily (MEH). MEH refers to a position whereby the owners and/or senior managers of a business are from different ethnic and cultural backgrounds to those they employ, i.e., managers are often expatriates from overseas parent-companies, while the general workforce typically comprises individuals with permanent Taiwanese re sidency.

Evidence is emerging to suggest that the relationship between American managers and local Taiwanese workers is not always harmonious; with reports of increases in the number of worksite disputes and conflicts (Lee & Jin, 2001; Mannix & Neale, 2005). An increase in discord has been observed and reported by the Taiwanese media, but has attracted little research attention to date—with the exception of Zhou et al. (2005). Given the potential impact of such disharmony on organizational performance, it is concerning that research investigating the impact of MEH and strategies to ameliorate its' impact have not been forthcoming.

The current research aims to: (1) clarify MEH's influence on facets of organizational culture; and, (2) use the research findings to support HR practitioners in their management of MEH. MEH is on the increase across

The China Business Model. DOI: http://dx.doi.org/10.1016/B978-0-08-100750-1.00007-3

Asian countries (OECD, 2013), e.g., Carrefour in South Korea, Walmart in Japan, and Siemens in Taiwan, which means that the findings from the current investigation may have applicability beyond Taiwan.

7.2 LITERATURE REVIEW

7.2.1 MEH in Taiwan

The rapid economic market growth in Taiwan has created opportunities for overseas investors and enterprises to expand their business and set up companies in Taiwan (Chang & Smale, 2014; Zhou et al., 2005). One positive consequence is the growth of Taiwan's economy, averaging 7.8% in 2009–12 and predicted to continue at this pace for some time to come (Du, 2011; OECD, 2013). Nevertheless, this level of prosperity is tempered by a growing concern that the relationship between overseas managers and local Taiwanese workers is discordant. Understanding how MEH may impact on the workforce is important for a number of reasons; one of the main advantages of developing our understanding is that it would enable HRM (Human Resource Managers) in developing and implementing strategies to temper any negative effects, and harness positive opportunities.

Based on the extensive work of Hofstede, Hofstede, and Minkov (2010), we intend to examine the particular relationship between expatriate managers from the US and Taiwanese employees. Hofstede et al. (2010) described six culturally salient dimensions within their organizational cultural model, these are: *Power Distance Index (PDI); Individualism versus Collectivism (IDV); Masculinity versus Femininity (MAS); Uncertainty Avoidance Index (UAI); Long Term Orientation versus Short Term Normative Orientation (LTO); Indulgence versus Restraint (IND).* The US and Taiwanese cultures are proposed to differ quite markedly on Individualism versus Collectivism and Long Term Orientation versus Short Term Normative Orientation. Where Taiwanese culture has been observed to display high degrees of interdependence between societal members—long term goal setting and a concomitant respect for tradition, the American culture is typically seem as valuing independence and working on relatively short term goals. The former, it has been argued, foster collaboration whilst the latter competition (Hofstede et al., 2010). If the managers of a workforce subscribe to one set of values and the employees another, then leadership styles that are not sensitive to value-based differences may generate tension.

Zhou et al. (2005) reported that many foreign managers may not be aware of the disparity between Western and Chinese work ethics, e.g., political communication style, hierarchical personnel system, and work overtime culture. This may appear superficially innocuous in a world where difference is celebrated, but these differences could strike at the heart of a central value system, and may become significant sources of pressure at work (Mannix & Neale, 2005; Robinson & Dechant, 1997). Empirical research by Chang and Lu (2007) indicated that a failure to become familiar with the Taiwanese work ethic may result in foreign managers being too eager to solicit feedback, something which may lead to feelings of discomfort among a Taiwanese workforce. Similarly, Chang and Parker (2004) observed that US managers tend to employ conflict resolution strategies such as working to resolve difficulties (or problems) in groups, which may generate feelings of unease among their Taiwanese employees. Unlike US managers, Taiwanese managers are more likely to adopt palliative and nonconfrontational approach when dealing with difficulties and problems. Taiwanese management is typically underpinned by a goal of enabling employees to manage difficulties and problems as they arise (Yang & Kuo, 1991). Empirical research to date does indicate some support for the argument that differences on cultural dimensions within the workplace, particularly in the form MEH, may affect the employer–employee relationship (Chang & Smale, 2014).

In order to explore the potential impact of MEH further, the concepts of homophily and heterophily warrant consideration. Homophily generally describes the tendency of individuals to bond with similar others. Homophily is often expressed in the adage "birds of a feather flock together". Heterophily, in contrast, refers to "a tie in which the two individuals manifest substantial differences on relevant dimensions" (Lord, Lee, & Choong, 2001). In the workplace, homophily refers to the tendency for employees to associate with the colleagues who are similar to themselves in terms of attributes and values (Lazarsfeld & Merton, 1954). It is often seen as a basic organizing principle that limits people's social worlds in ways that can impact all aspects of their social functioning. It may also determine, for instance, the types of interactions experienced; the attitudes that are formed; and the information that is available to them (McPherson, Smith-Lovin, & Cook, 2001). Lazarsfeld and Merton (1954) further hypothesized two types of homophily: *status homophily*, in which similarity is based on formal/ascribed status, and *value homophily*—based on values, attitudes, and beliefs. Using this dichotomy of homophily, Lazarsfeld and Merton sought to explain why managers are likely to be closer with other managers from other departments, rather than their subordinates in the same department.

At the individual level, people in homophilic relationships may share common characteristics such as: job beliefs, worksite values, work ethics, and the educational background that make communication and relationship formation easier (Lazarsfeld & Merton, 1954). To a certain degree, the concept of homophily has explained the occurrence of homogamy, e.g., popularity of collaboration between business enterprises with similar marketing strategies, and unions between new members with the same ethics and beliefs (McPherson et al., 2001; Mollica, Gray, & Trevino, 2003). Several empirical studies have addressed the phenomenon of homophily at work and the evidence demonstrates that it has a significant role to play in organizational success (Burt, 2000), workforce dynamics (Ibarra & Smith-Lovin, 1997), and task accomplishment (Aldrich, Elam, & Reese, 1996). The aforementioned studies of homophily may have different research aims and objectives, but their findings convey a clear message: *similarity breeds connection*. It seems that homophily acts like a social glue linking individuals who share similar characteristics (McPherson et al., 2001).

At the organizational level, homophily may become a salient factor in management, especially when managers and their employees (subordinates) are from different ethnic backgrounds. According to Gerstner and Day (1994), managers in traditional societies, e.g., Greece and India, tend to prefer autocratic management styles with passive subordinates, whereas managers in technologically-developed societies, like Germany, the United States, and Canada, prefer subordinates who are active and participatory. Ralston, Gustafson, Elsass, and Cheung (1992) found that American managers are more concerned with worker productivity, using a task-oriented management style, whilst Chinese managers are more concerned with maintaining a harmonious work environment, using a relation-oriented management style. Taken together, these findings provide preliminary support for the proposition that MEH may affect the employer–employee relationship in American-owned enterprises in Taiwan. In particular that cultural differences on a number of Hofstede et al. (2010) organizational dimensions may present workplace challenges that are particularly evident where senior managers are predominantly from one culture and the workforce predominantly from another i.e., where MEH is evident.

However, it is important not to ignore the possibility that heterophily may have a potentially useful role to play in the workplace. Where homophilious relationships may be harmonious and enable collaboration, heterophilious ones may promote the dissonance required to generate paradigm shifts and innovation (Lord et al., 2001). This study intends to explore whether MEH does impact on manager–employee relationships, perceived workplace stress, and hypothesized moderating factors with a view to consider how the findings may be used to inform the development of appropriate HRM strategies.

7.2.2 The Influence of MEH in the Workplace

A potential concern arising from heterophily of a hierarchical nature, such as MEH, might be workplace stress emerging from a perceived lack of person-organization fit. Person Organization (P-O) fit is a concept that has been used to describe the congruence between the individual's goals and the goals of the organization (Cheng, 2015; Parkes, Bochner, & Schneider, 2001). Managers have been found to play a key role in the misfit perceptions (Cooper-Thomas & Wright, 2013) and so understanding this process is extremely relevant in contemporary organizations where MEH exists. If management and organizational goals are distinct or in conflict with those of the employee, then that perceived fit between the two might be incongruent and experienced as stressful. The majority of work-related stress theories have been established on the basis of Western values and norms. The interpretation of stress-related behaviors may also reflect Western ideology and cultural imperatives that emphasize the individual's need for generic control of their work environment (Chang & Lu, 2007). Scholars generally agree on three assumptions: (1) occupational stress arises from an individual's subjective perception of their work; (2) controllability equates with a feeling of being able to control environmental/working conditions; and (3) a lack of control can result in occupational stress. In their Demand-Control Model, Karasek and Theorel (1979) proposed that the *quantity of demands placed on an employee* and *their decision latitude* are two key factors in the formation of stress at work; problems with either quantity or quality of demands can trigger occupational stress.

Evidence suggests that culture influences both what is experienced as stressful and how people respond to stress (Liu, Spector, & Shi, 2007). Therefore, in organizations in which those charged with managing come from a different culture to the majority of those they manage, understanding workplace stress would be of particular importance. In Taiwan, e.g., personal control has been found to be a less-significant factor in stress formation than in western culture. In Taiwanese culture, more emphasis is placed on obedience and conformity to the organizational environment, with these behaviors and attitudes typically considered to be virtues (Yang & Kuo, 1991). Power distance i.e., the extent to which a culture accepts power differentials among citizens (Hofstede, 1980) is just one example of how a management structure dominated by one culture may generate stress in employees from another if understanding is not reached. In the case of US and Taiwanese culture this difference may be exacerbated by the Taiwanese moral principle that dictates respect for older, senior, or those with higher status (Chang & Parker, 2004). Employees thus generally believe that they should not express personal opinions if their social status (e.g., if they are younger, less experienced, of a lower position, or more recently employed) does not qualify them to do so. In short, Taiwanese organizations are typified by a traditional authoritarian and/or paternalistic culture rather than a democratic, egalitarian one (Lu, Tseng, & Cooper, 1999), which encourages people to become involved in decision making (Li, Lee, Lee, Chen, & Chi, 2001). American managers, however, may not recognize these subtle differences in values and beliefs, so may inadvertently create tension and stress in a predominately Taiwanese workforce.

Two hypotheses were developed to examine these propositions:

H1: Taiwanese employee manager preference ratings will be higher for Taiwanese managers than American managers.

H2: Working for American managers will be rated as more stressful than working for Taiwanese managers.

7.2.3 Proposed Moderators to the MEH-Related Stress

The review of empirical studies suggests that MEH may affect the employer–employee relationship in American-owned enterprises in Taiwan. Identifying stress as a potential consequence of MEH is important, but only the first stage in the process from an HR intervention perspective; the second stage is to identify possible moderating factors. Research pertaining to MEH-related stress and manager preference is still in its infancy, but a number of recent studies have suggested that any negative effects resulting from non-Taiwanese management styles may have less of an impact on employees who possess certain characteristics, or who, by virtue of their employment term, have acclimatized to the ways of their managers and organizations (Chang & Lu, 2007, 2009; Hayes, Strosahl, & Wilson, 2004). On the basis of the findings from these studies, two potential moderators emerge:

Psychological acceptance at work. The term psychological acceptance denotes a willingness to experience unpleasant psychological events without changing, avoiding, or otherwise controlling them (Hayes et al., 2004). "Unpleasant events" at work may include negative thoughts about colleagues, unsatisfactory feelings/sensations about the job, or an uncomfortable organizational culture that could harm employees' mental well-being and work performance (Chang & Lu, 2007). Acceptance-based theories of psychopathology claim that if people are willing to accept unpleasant events and the concomitant negative feelings, they can prevent or alleviate emotional problems such as strain, depression and anxiety (Hayes, Jacobson, Follette, & Dougher, 1994). That is, employees who have higher levels of psychological acceptance at work will be less impacted by MEH-related stress. Bond and Bunce (2003) claimed that psychological acceptance is positively correlated with enhanced job performance, asserting that such acceptance helps people cope with the challenges of the workplace. Research has also shown that employees feel more self-assured and capable the more willing they are to accept negative feelings at work. They also respond to these experiences in a more objective and constructive manner (Yeung, 2006). On the basis of these findings, it seems reasonable to propose that psychological acceptance is a promising moderator to MEH-related stress. These findings led to the proposition of a third hypothesis:

H3: Psychological acceptance at work will moderate the stress perceived by employees.

That is, employees with higher psychological acceptance will feel less stressed, compared to the employees with lower psychological acceptance.

Job tenure. Prior studies have investigated the extent to which job tenure can moderate stress at work, and there are grounds for predicting that stress may vary over the duration of an employee's employment. Frese and Zapf (1988) described two plausible patterns of change; an employee's perception of stress may have little initial impact and may begin to cause problems after an extended period of exposure (a relationship Frese and Zapf called the "sleeper effect" model). Alternatively, stress perception may increase steadily with exposure early in an employee's career, but stabilize at some ceiling afterwards (the "accumulation" model). Employees with longer tenure will, e.g., be more familiar with their company policy, ethics, and worksite (i.e., they are more experienced). Therefore, when problems arise they are more likely to know where to find possible solutions—knowledge that may help to reduce stress accumulation (Chang & Lu, 2009). More experienced employees may also develop strategies to manage workplace stressors; this would account for higher levels of perceived stress during the early employment phase with a gradual reduction as tenure continues (the "adjustment" model; Frese & Zapf, 1988). This model may see employees building up a repertoire of practical, social, and/or psychological resources to manage non-Taiwanese management styles, such as support from spouses, task variety, or access to training (Demerouti,

Bakker, Nachreiner, & Schaufeli, 2001). While the process of adaption is unlikely to be uniform (with some employees leaving the organization or "drifting" into other jobs), *selection attrition* is likely to be observed, which means that those who "suffer least stay the longest" (Bradley, 2007; Zapf, Dormann, & Frese, 1996). Very likely, the net result of these adaption and selection effects is: the impact of non-Taiwanese management style is likely to be greater earlier—rather than later—in an employee's job tenure. Thus, our final hypothesis proposes:

H4: Job tenure will moderate ratings of perceived stress.

That is, employees with longer job tenure will feel less stressed, compared to the employees with shorter job tenure.

7.2.4 Conceptual Framework

To consolidate the research hypotheses and clarify the associations between the research variables, an integrative framework has been developed (see Fig. 7.1). This framework is informative in several ways: (1) management style preference is correlated with stress at work (i.e., positive and negative); (2) the relationship between management style preference and stress at work is moderated by psychological acceptance and job tenure; and, (3) employees with higher psychological acceptance and longer job tenure feel less stressed, compared to employees with lower psychological acceptance and shorter job tenure.

7.3 METHOD

7.3.1 Sample and Procedure

This research focused on the employees from three US-owned and run plants (pharmacy, food, cosmetics) in X (blinded for the review purposes),

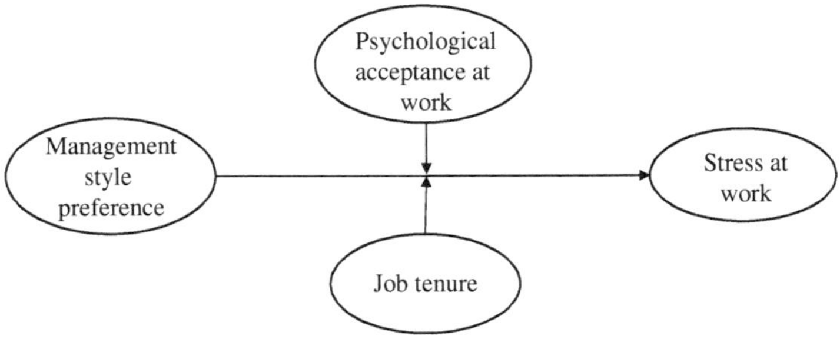

Figure 7.1 Conceptual framework.

as per the research grant criteria. Participants were contacted via the personnel managers or secretaries of each company and questionnaires were distributed in booklet form (via corporate email), with a cover-letter assuring anonymity and explaining the voluntary nature of participation. A reminder email was sent out 7 days after the initial invitation with the aim of boosting the response rate. The completed questionnaires were then returned via email to the researchers. Of the 700 copies of questionnaires initially distributed, 515 were returned, of which 474 are useable (response rate = 67.71%). More respondents were received from employees at the pharmacy plant (n_1 = 189) and the food plant (n_2 = 181), than from the cosmetics plant (n_3 = 104). No between-group differences were detected in terms of gender (χ^2 (2) = 2.78, p = .35) or age (χ^2 (2) = 1.50, p = .66). The mean age of participants was 33.0 years old (SD = 6.22). Mean job tenure was 8.4 years (SD = 5.39). Educational levels were stratified with high school education representing 14% of the sample, college graduates 81% and 5% held postgraduate awards. The sample comprised 37% male respondents and 63% female. The participant's organizational status was distributed as follows: junior posts (2%), mid-level posts (57%), senior positions (31%), and upper management positions (10%).

7.3.2 Measures

Three standardized scales were adopted for the measurement:

Management style preference was measured by the management style preference scale (Chang, 2002; 5 items; α = 0.75), which assesses whether Taiwanese managers are more preferable (favorably perceived) by Taiwanese employees. All items are preceded by the stem: *Please rate the truth of each statement as it applies to you in your workplace.* These items are: (1) *Compared to American managers, Taiwanese managers are more suitable to Taiwanese employees*; (2) *Compared to Taiwanese managers, American mangers more focus on the final output and hence lead to more pressure at work*; (3) *Compared to American managers, Taiwanese managers better understand our expectation and needs at work*; (4) *Compared to American managers, Taiwanese managers are more communicable and considerate in organizational policies*; and, (5) *The workplace is more harmonious when managed by Taiwanese managers.* Responses are measured on a 7-point Likert scale (*1 = Not true at all, 7 = Very true*). Higher scores indicate a view that, compared to American managers, Taiwanese managers are rated as more suitable/preferable for Taiwanese employees.

Psychological acceptance at work was measured by the acceptance and action questionnaire (Hayes et al., 2004; 9 items; α = 0.80), designed to assess experiential avoidance, experiential control, psychological acceptance, and actions taken despite the experience of negative private events. All items are preceded by the stem: *Please rate the truth of each statement as it applies to you at work*. Samples items are: (1) *I am able to take action on a problem even if I am uncertain what the best action is*; (2) *I am not afraid to face my own feelings*; and (3) *When I evaluate something negatively, I usually recognize that this is just a reaction, not an objective fact*. Responses are measured on a 7-point Likert scale (*1 = Completely disagree, 7 = Completely agree*). Higher scores indicate that individuals are more willing to accept negative events in their workplace, i.e., higher levels of psychological acceptance.

Perceived stress at work was measured by the perceived stress scale (Cohen, Kamarck, & Mermelstein, 1983; 10 items; $\alpha = 0.85$), which assesses the degree to which situations in one's life are appraised as stressful. All items are preceded by the stem: *In the last month, how often have you………at work*. Sample items are: (1) *Been upset because of something that happened unexpectedly*; (2) *Felt nervous and under tons of pressure*; and (3) *Felt that you could not cope with all the things that you had to do*. Responses are measured on a 7-point Likert scale (*1 = Never, 7 = Always*). Higher scores indicate higher levels of perceived stress at work.

Both second and third scales are originally validated in English, so the questions (scale items) were translated into Traditional-Chinese for the purpose of this survey, a back-translation procedure was used to ensure language equivalence and appropriateness. Two bilingual experts in management studies were invited to examine the validity and clarity of scale items, and further revisions were made accordingly.

7.4 RESULTS

Descriptive statistics, correlations, and reliability coefficients of variables are shown in Table 7.1. These reveal that management style preference is negatively correlated with perceived stress at work ($r = 0.16$, $p < .01$) and positively correlated with job tenure ($r = 0.13$, $p < .01$). Psychological acceptance at work is negatively correlated with perceived stress at work ($r = -0.53$, $p < .001$). Job tenure is also negatively correlated with perceived stress at work ($r = -0.22$, $p < .01$). Jointly, these statistical figures have shown significant inter-relations between the research variables.

Table 7.1 Descriptive statistics of the research variables (N=474)

	Mean	SD	α	1	2	3
1. Management style preference	5.64	1.03	0.75			
2. Psychological acceptance at work	4.06	0.55	0.80	0.05		
3. Perceived stress at work	3.86	0.78	0.85	0.16**	−0.53***	
4. Job tenure*	8.36	5.34	–	0.13**	−0.02	−0.22**

Note: *Job tenure is measured by a single item and hence no α (*** $p < .001$; ** $p < .01$).

7.4.1 Common Method Variance (CMV)

Due to the cross-sectional research design, the likelihood of common method variance (CMV) bias increases (Podsakoff, MacKenzie, Lee, & Podsakoff, 2003). One strategy to combat CMV bias was to adopt a temporal separation strategy, collecting data relating to different variables at different times. This strategy was rejected by the HR managers from the three plants because of the implications repeated data collection would have on their workloads. An alternative strategy to combat CMV-bias was required. Reynolds (1982) proposed the inclusion of a social desirability scale to act as a marker or surrogate variable (Reynolds, 1982; Podsakoff et al., 2003). The proposition is that the surrogate variable would enable the researcher to partial out a social desirability score from each measure and correlate it against the constructs of interest, both with its inclusion, and without it. The purpose of which is to examine whether the surrogate for common method variance (social desirability) explains the variance in the observed relationships. If it does, then CMV has impacted on the findings, if not them the impact of CMV may be within tolerable limits.

Having applied the *Pearson's* formula to examine the correlation coefficients between the marker/surrogate variable and all other variables, the results showed that the correlation coefficients (r): acceptance and action questionnaire (0.21), perceived stress scale (0.16), and management style preference (0.30), were small. None of the coefficients were close to or higher than 0.07, suggesting that CMV bias was not impacting on the relationships in a significant way (Podsakoff et al., 2003).

We also adopted Harman's single factor test to examine the potential bias caused by CMV (Podsakoff et al., 2003). All research variables were first merged into one factor, and the results showed poor fit—suggesting that one single factor of merging all variable was inappropriate for data analysis (χ^2 (350) = 6330.78, $p < .001$, RMSEA = 0.243, NFI = 0.66, CFI = 0.68, IFI = 0.68, SRMR = 0.198). We then adopted an unmeasured latent construct method in order to measure the potential influence of CMV, as recommended by Podsakoff et al. (2003). The Chi-square difference test was not statistically significant ($\Delta\chi^2$ (1) = 3.64, $p > .05$) and results were consistent with the findings of Harman's single factor test. To simplify: the influence of CMV was very slim, thus the research dataset should be accepted for further data analysis.

7.4.2 Analysis of the Measurement Model

Confirmatory factor analyses (CFAs) were undertaken on all research variables. The hypothetic model (4-factor) was then compared with alternative models, including one 3-factor model, one 2-factor model, and a 1-factor model (see Table 7.2). CFAs revealed that the hypothetic model provided a sound fit to the data; specifically, the 4-factor model had a significantly better fit than the first 3-factor model ($\Delta\chi^2 = 614.54$, $p < .001$), the 2-factor model ($\Delta\chi^2 = 3029.35$, $p < .001$) and the 1-factor model ($\Delta\chi^2 = 5157.30$, $p < .001$). Taken together, the hypothetic model represented the best fit to the data ($\Delta\chi^2$ (344) = 1173.48, $p < .001$, RMSEA = 0.07, NFI = 0.90, CFI = 0.93, IFI = 0.93, SRMR = 0.06).

7.4.3 Hypotheses Testing

Management style preference was operationalized to assume that Taiwanese managers (rather than US managers) would be more-favorably perceived—thus deemed more suitable—by Taiwanese employees. Scores significantly higher than the mid-point would indicate a preference for a Taiwanese management style. Statistical analysis revealed that the mean score (management style preference; $M = 5.64$, SD = 1.03) was significantly higher than the scale mid-point of 3.50 ($MDiff = 2.14$, $p < .001$), indicating that Taiwanese employees generally reported a preference for a Taiwanese management style. Hence, the first hypothesis is supported.

This research is keen to understand the relationship between a preference for Taiwanese managers in an environment where the management style was not Taiwanese and the perception of workplace stress, i.e., to explore whether working for American managers was perceived to be more stressful (compared to Taiwanese managers). Congruent with expectations, statistical analyses confirmed a positive correlation (r = 0.16, $p < .01$) between management style preference and perceived stress at work. That is, employees who indicated a preference for a Taiwanese

Table 7.2 Comparison of the model fitness: hypothetic model and three alternative models

Model	Factors	$\div^2$	*df*	$\Delta \div^2$	RMSEA	NFI	CFI	IFI	SRMR
Hypothetic model	Four-factor model: management style preference, psychological acceptance at work, perceived stress at work, and job tenure	1173.48	344		0.07	0.90	0.93	0.93	0.06
Model 1	Three-factor model: management style preference and psychological acceptance at work are merged. Perceived stress at work, and job tenure stand alone	1788.02	347	614.54	0.12	0.85	0.88	0.88	0.09
Model 2	Two-factor model: management style preference, psychological acceptance at work, and perceived stress at work are merged. Job tenure stands alone	4202.83	349	3029.35	0.19	0.75	0.78	0.78	0.15
Model 3	One-factor model: dispositional envy, positive- and negative-gossip engagement and employee cynicism are all merged	6330.78	350	5157.30	0.24	0.66	0.68	0.68	0.19

management style would report perceiving greater levels of stress in a US-owned company; whilst employees who do not indicate a preference for Taiwanese management may report feeling comparatively less stressed at work. In addition, it is important to note that employees did typically agree with the statement that compared with Taiwanese managers, American mangers place greater emphasis on the final output which was observed to add more pressure at work ($M = 4.41$, SD = 1.12). The mean score was higher than the scale mid-point of 3.50 (*MDiff* = 0.91, $p < .05$). Taken together, these findings suggest that working for American managers was perceived to be more stressful than working for Taiwanese managers, lending support to the second hypothesis.

Table 7.3 Summary of moderating analysis

(Models)	**Perceived stress at work**			
	M1	**M2**	**M3**	**M4**
Control variables				
Age	−0.18**	−0.19**	−0.18**	−0.17**
Rank of position	−0.02	−0.02	−0.01	−0.01
Educational levels	0.03	0.03	0.03	0.02
Gender	0.03	0.02	0.02	0.03
(ΔR^2)	(0.05*)			
Research moderators				
Psychological acceptance at work		−0.54***		−0.45***
Job tenure		−0.18**		−0.16**
(ΔR^2)		(0.31***)		
Independent variables				
Management style preference			0.17**	0.12*
(ΔR^2)			(0.05*)	
Moderating effect				
Psychological acceptance at work × management style preference				−0.24***
Job tenure × management style preference				−0.34***
(ΔR^2)				(0.11**)
R^2	0.55	0.53	0.44	0.50
Adjusted R^2	0.52	0.51	0.43	0.49
F value	30.15***	30.11***	26.44***	29.93***
df	4470	6468	5469	9465

Note: *** $p< .001$; ** $p< .01$; * $p< .05$.

Further hypothesis testing, using regression analyses, was undertaken to examine the moderating effect of two proposed moderators (see Table 7.3 for detailed statistics). To closely observe the impact of aforementioned interactions, two line charts are presented to further explain the moderating effect (see Figs. 7.2 and 7.3). As it is shown in Table 7.3, psychological acceptance at work ($\beta = -.54$, $p < .001$), job tenure ($\beta = -18$, $p < .01$), and management style preference ($\beta = 17$, $p < .01$) all significantly predicted perceived stress at work, although with different predicting directions. These findings are largely consistent with the research expectations. To be specific, as it is shown in Fig. 7.2, employees with more belief in management style preference (i.e., people who believe that Taiwanese managers are more suitable to Taiwanese employees) reported feeling more stressed at work, compared to those who with less belief. Yet, employees with lower level of psychological acceptance at work reported

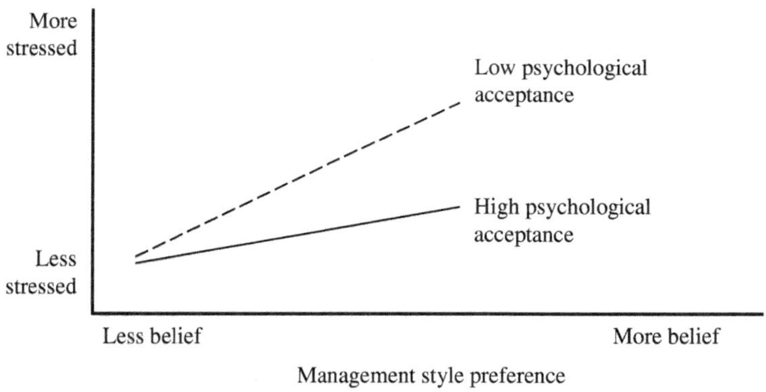

Figure 7.2 Moderating effect of psychological acceptance.

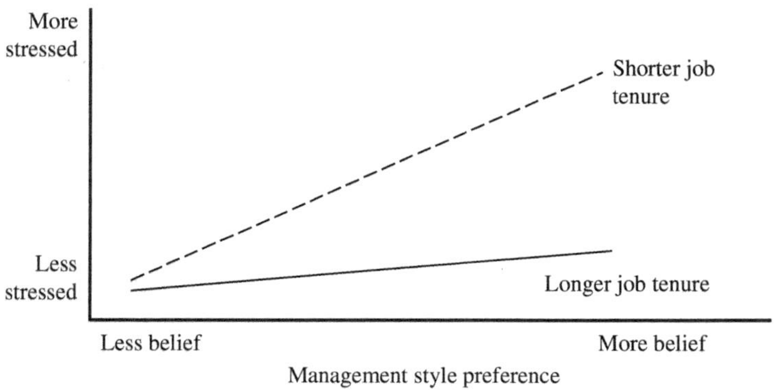

Figure 7.3 Moderating effect of job tenure.

feeling even more stressed at work, compared to those with a higher level of psychological acceptance. On the other hand, as it is shown in Fig. 7.3, employees with more belief in management style preference (i.e., people who believe that Taiwanese managers are more suitable to Taiwanese employees) reported feeling more stressed at work, compared to those who with less belief. Yet, employees with shorter job tenure reported feeling even more stressed at work, compared to those with longer job tenure. Hence, based on these findings, we are of the view that the third and fourth hypotheses should be supported.

7.5 DISCUSSION

As MEH has become a popular phenomenon in workforce across Asian countries (OECD, 2013), our research is keen to examine the concept of MEH and understand its influence in the workplace. Specific hypotheses were developed and supported by the research data. Specifically, Taiwanese employees have indicated a preference for Taiwanese management styles, a relationship was discovered between this preference and stress perception at work, and the two factors identified as possibly moderating the effect of the discrepancy between American and Taiwanese management styles did have the predicted effect. The research findings concur with previous research by Hayes et al. (2004) and Lazarsfeld and Merton (1954). Their analysis suggested that the stress experience may result from a perception of a poor fit between the values of the workforce and those of the senior management. The level of stress experienced may be reduced over time, as employees adjust and adapt to their job role. Furthermore, those who rated high on psychological acceptance were less likely to score highly on workplace stress perception.

Previous studies have explored the impact of management style on employees (Gerstner & Day, 1994; Ralston et al., 1992) and described the disharmony between non-Taiwanese managers and Chinese employees (Zhou et al., 2005). Our findings compliment and extend these in several meaningful ways: they affirm that the majority of Taiwanese employees do feel that Taiwanese managers are more suitable for them across a wide range of industries and diverse work contexts (e.g., participants are recruited from US-owned and run pharmacy, food, cosmetics plants in Taiwan). This preference may be predicted in terms of *value homophily* theory. The participants reported a number of motivations for manager ethnicity preference. These included: (1) Taiwanese employees feel that

American managers place too much emphasis on operational procedure and outcomes, which is demanding and stressful; (2) companies with Taiwanese managers enjoy a more-harmonious and less-competitive work climate; (3) Taiwanese managers are seen as having a better understanding of their subordinates' needs and expectations. These reasons concur with the organizational values discussed earlier in the chapter, e.g., whereby the harmony and collectivistic values associated with Taiwanese employees are not evidenced in the competitive, individualistic environment encouraged by American management styles. The power distance expectation may also be compromised in an American-led organization, where employees need to know their place but are simultaneously expected to make contributions to decision making. Uncertainty avoidance may be higher in this situation because a clear access to career pathways is obscured and inaccessible—as a consequence of little opportunity for either *status* or *value homophily* (Brass, 1995).

Our research has identified important individual moderators that can alter the relationship between a preferred management style and workplace stress. Specifically, we have found that employees with a higher psychological acceptance to negative events are better protected from feeling stressed and this finding partially corroborates results from prior studies. For instance, proactive and nonaversive attitudes are found to help individuals re-evaluate stressors and devise effective coping strategies (Bond & Bunce, 2003). Our research findings have provided preliminary support for the view that psychological acceptance may help people to regulate emotions and respond to stressors in a more adaptive manner, thus coping better with stress (Hayes et al., 1994), and that psychological acceptance may also result in improved job performance. Although, more research is necessary toward psychological acceptance and the nature of work performance (Hayes et al., 2004).

Our research has also found that employees with longer job tenure feel less stressed. Experience does appear to help, as more-seasoned Taiwanese employees can better appreciate different management styles, whereas those with shorter tenure may be unfamiliar or uncomfortable with an American management style. Conclusions here are tentatively drawn, however, because studies have shown that other factors such as age, experience, gender and level of education could act as cultural amplifiers, and, if this were the case, then job tenure alone may only provide part of the moderation narrative. It could be, e.g., that those who have had experience of Taiwanese managers and then moved to organizations with

American managers may have found this adjustment more difficult than those new to the workplace and who have little or no previous history of being managed in an employment context. Alternatively, new recruits straight from education may require a different induction program to that offered experienced workers from Taiwanese owned-and-run companies. Moreover, those with considerable experience within the American-run companies might make excellent mentors and assist in the induction process. In other words: although job tenure clearly moderates the relationship between management style preference and stress, it is an area that warrants further investigation.

7.5.1 Implication of the Research Findings

Our research does not seek to emphasize difference in order to be pessimistic; the purpose is to explore the phenomenon of MEH and analyze its potential influence in the workplace. Moreover, our research has presented an opportunity to discuss the extent to which ethnic homophily might be observed, even when the potential for homophily is additionally compromised by status. The final, and possibly most important, goal is to use the findings to develop ways of working that may alleviate the impact of discord generated by a poor fit between manager and employee values, both in the immediate and longer term.

We found that, among Taiwanese employees, stress may arise from divergent values in the two systems; employee values may be shared amongst the majority of the workforce but not by senior managers, so increasing uncertainty and a lack of role clarity. In the immediate term we would suggest that, as a minimum, tailor-made induction programmes should be arranged for foreign managers and new employees. New managers can be inducted into the values of the workforce and can also be made aware of the potentially negative effects of certain management styles. The employees would benefit from an induction into the organization which explained the differences, identifies progression routes within the organization and assigns mentors with long service (and possibly high levels of psychological acceptance).

Globalization brings the promise of significant wealth and prosperity to Taiwan, so we propose that a longer-term and further-reaching policy measure would see the Taiwanese education system include a focus on management styles rooted in non-Taiwanese cultures. This could be introduced as part of the wider curricular or through vocational workshops, but the purpose would be to familiarize students with diverse foreign management styles and prepare them for today's culturally diverse workplaces. These workshops can also potentially help students establish a cognitive buffer—alleviating the impact of a foreign management style on stress formation.

7.5.2 Research Limitations and Recommendations

In this research, participants were only recruited from American owned-and-run enterprises in Taiwan, as per the research grant criteria. It would be ideal for more companies i.e., owned and run by managers from other cultures, to be compared and differences examined. These diversity factors may generate a more nuanced interpretation of MEH. There might be a lot to learn by examining differential effects on the manager–employee relationship, and exploring potential moderating factors by adopting a wider lens. Moreover, for the purpose of research, all American managers are seen as operating a similar management style, which is of course an artificial simplification. The similarities assumed are those that Hofstede et al. (2010) refer to as broad cultural norms, so are regularly applied in this manner. Despite the regularity of the application, it remains a limitation and is subject to criticism, as one may claim that such categorization (American vs Taiwanese managers) does not account for sample heterogeneity. Moreover, individual differences between managers cannot be scrutinized. Despite this, our research aimed to explore a relatively new workforce phenomenon in Asian countries, so a macro perspective and country-wide approach was an appropriate place to start.

The MEH phenomenon has been found in American owned-and-run enterprises in Taiwan. It would be ideal if a reverse-setting research could be conducted, i.e., to examine whether the MEH phenomenon exists in Taiwanese-owned and run enterprises in the United States. Furthermore, self-assessed data are mainly based on individual subjective experiences, which may reflect the reality an individual observes rather than any underpinning reality (Podsakoff et al., 2003). In our research, stress levels were measured by self-report; respondents were asked to isolate their perception of workplace stress independently of other sources of stress—this is difficult and artificial and so may have implications for data interpretation. Further research may offer alternative explanations for the associations discovered. Finally, the interactions between variables, e.g., job tenure, management style preference, should be interpreted with caution, as the cross-sectional design cannot explain the direction of interactions. Future studies may adopt an experimental approach with a counter-analysis procedure, so that the interaction of variables can be better clarified (Liakhovitski, Stone-Romero, & Jaccard, 2008). Finally, throughout the paper there have been allusions to the possibility that MEH may have positive implications for organizations. There is a lack of research in this area but this author believes it is worthy of future investigation; surrounding oneself with likeminded individuals may be comfortable and lead to harmonious environments, but may ultimately stifle innovation and organizational transformation.

REFERENCES

Aldrich, H. E., Elam, A., & Reese, P. R. (1996). Strong ties, weak ties and strangers. In S. Birley & I. MacMillan (Eds.), *Entrepreneurship in a Global Context* (pp. 1–25). London: Rutledge.

Bond, F. W., & Bunce, D. (2003). The role of acceptance and job control in mental health, job satisfaction, and work performance. *Journal of Applied Psychology*, *88*, 1057–1067.

Bradley, G. (2007). Job tenure as a moderator of stressor-strain relations: A comparison of experienced and new-start teachers. *Work & Stress*, *20*(1), 48–64.

Brass, D. J. (1995). Men's and women's networks: A study of interaction patterns and influence in an organization. *Journal of Academic Management*, *28*, 327–343.

Burt, R. S. (2000). Decay function. *Social Networks*, *22*, 1–28.

Chang, K. (2002). Managerial difference and employee performance in Taiwan. In: K. Chang. & L. Lu. (Eds.), Characteristics of organizational culture, stressors and well-being—The case of Taiwanese organizations. Journal of Managerial Psychology, 22(6), 549–568.

Chang, K., & Lu, L. (2007). Characteristics of organizational culture, stressors and well-being—The case of Taiwanese organizations. *Journal of Managerial Psychology*, *22*(6), 549–568.

Chang, K., & Lu, L. (2009). The influence of occupation on stressors and work behaviours. *International Journal of Human Resource Management*, *20*(3), 591–605.

Chang, K., & Parker, D. (March 10, 2004). Efficacy and applications of stress coping strategies: *Paper presented at the Occupational Psychology Symposium*. Taiwan: Chang-Hua University of Education.

Chang, Y., & Smale, A. (2014). The transfer of Taiwanese management practices to British subsidiaries: A diachronic perspective. *Asia Pacific Journal of Human Resources*, *52*(2), 234–254.

Cheng, K. T. (2015). Doing good in public schools: Examining organisational citizenship behaviour in primary school teachers. *Journal of Management & Organization* Available on CJO 2015. http://dx.doi.org/10.1017/jmo.2015.47.

Cohen, S., Kamarck, T., & Mermelstein, R. (1983). A global measure of perceived stress. *Journal of Health and Social Behavior*, *24*, 386–396.

Cooper-Thomas, H. D., & Wright, S. (2013). Person-environment misfit: The neglected role of social context. *Journal of Managerial Psychology*, *28*(1), 21–37.

Demerouti, E., Bakker, A. B., Nachreiner, F., & Schaufeli, W. B. (2001). The job demands-resources model of burnout. *Journal of Applied Psychology*, *86*, 499–512.

Du, M. S. (2011). *Taiwan's economical development and performance*. Taipei, Taiwan: Council for Economic Planning and Development, The Central Government Bureau.

Frese, M., & Zapf, D. (1988). Methodological issues in the study of work stress: Objective versus subjective measurement of work stress and the questions of longitudinal studies.

In C. L. Cooper & R. Payne (Eds.), *Causes, coping and consequences of stress at work* (pp. 375–411). Chichester: Wiley.
Gerstner, C., & Day, D. V. (1994). Cross-cultural comparison of leadership prototypes. *Leadership Quarterly, 5*, 121–134.
Györkös, C., Becker, J., Massoudi, K., de Bruin, G. P., & Rossier, J. (2012). The impact of personality and culture on the job demands-control model of job stress. *Swiss Journal of Psychology, 71*(1), 21.
Hayes, S. C., Jacobson, N. S., Follette, V. M., & Dougher, M. J. (Eds.), (1994). *Acceptance and change: Content and context in psychotherapy*. Reno, NV: Context Press.
Hayes, S. C., Strosahl, K. D., & Wilson, K. G. (2004). Measuring experiential avoidance: A preliminary test of a working model. *The Psychological Record, 54*, 553–578.
Hofstede, G., Hofstede, G. J., & Minkov, M. (2010). *). Cultures and organizations: Software of the mind* (Revised and Expanded 3rd ed.). New York, NY: McGraw-Hill.
Hofstede, G. J. (1980). Culture and organizations. *International Studies of Management & Organization, 10*, 15–41.
Ibarra, H., & Smith-Lovin, L. (1997). Alternative routes: A social network perspective on gender and careers. In C. Cooper & S. Jackson (Eds.), *Creating tomorrow's organizations* (pp. 359–384). New York, NY: Wiley.
Karasek, R., & Theorel, L. (1979). Job demands, job decision latitude, and mental strain: Implications for job redesign. *Administration Science Quarterly, 24*, 285–308.
Lazarsfeld, P. F., & Merton, R. K. (1954). Friendship as a social process: A substantive and methodological analysis. In M. Berger (Ed.), *Freedom and control in modern society* (pp. 18–66). New York, NY: Van Nostrand.
Lee, C. H., & Jin, S. N. (2001). *Labor rights and dispute management*. Beijing: China Democracy.
Li, T. C., Lee, Y. D., Lee, Y. Y., Chen, C. C., & Chi, C. H. (2001). Validation of the Chinese-version MPSS-R for occupational stress among emergency nurses. *Journal of Psychosomatic Research, 51*, 379–385.
Liakhovitski, D., Stone-Romero, E. F., & Jaccard, J. J. (2008). Strategies for detecting joint dichotomous moderators in HRM research. *Human Resource Management Review, 18*, 164–179.
Liu, C., Spector, P. E., & Shi, L. (2007). Cross-national job stress: A quantitative and qualitative study. *Journal of Organizational Behavior, 28*, 209–239.
Lord, K. R., Lee, M. S., & Choong, P. (2001). Differences in normative and informational social influence. *Advances in Consumer Research, 28*, 280–285.
Lu, L., Tseng, H. J., & Cooper, C. L. (1999). Managerial stress, job satisfaction and health in Taiwan. *Stress Medicine, 15*, 53–64.
Mannix, E., & Neale, M. A. (2005). What differences make a difference? The promise and reality of diverse teams in organizations. *Psychological Science in the Public Interest, 5*(2), 31–55.
McPherson, M., Smith-Lovin, L., & Cook, J. M. (2001). Birds of a feather: Homophily in social networks. *Annual Review of Sociology, 27*, 415–444.
Mollica, K. A., Gray, B., & Trevino, L. K. (2003). Racial homophily and its persistence in newcomers' social networks. *Organization Science, 14*(2), 123–136.
OECD, (2013). *Organization for economic cooperation and development*. Taipei: Department of Finance and Planning, Central Administration Bureau.
Parkes, L., Bochner, S., & Schneider, S. (2001). Person–organization fit across cultures: An empirical investigation of individualism and collectivism. *Applied Psychology: An International Review, 50*, 81–108.
Podsakoff, P. M., MacKenzie, S. B., Lee, J. Y., & Podsakoff, N. P. (2003). Common method biases in behavioural research: A critical review of the literature and recommended remedies. *Journal of Applied Psychology, 88*(5), 879–903.

Ralston, D., Gustafson, D., Elsass, P., & Cheung, F. (1992). Eastern values: A comparison of managers in the US, Hong Kong, and China. *Journal of Applied Psychology*, *77*, 664–671.
Reynolds, W. M. (1982). Development of reliable and valid short forms of the Marlowe-Crowne social desirability scale. *Journal of Clinical Psychology*, *38*, 119–125.
Robinson, G., & Dechant, K. (1997). Building a case for diversity. *Academy of Management Executive*, *21*(3), 21–31.
Yang, C. F., & Kuo, S. Z. (1991). *Chinese people and Chinese thought*. Taipei: Yuan-Liou.
Yeung, R. (2006). *The rules of EQ*. New York, NY: Cyan Book & Marsha.
Zapf, D., Dormann, C., & Frese, M. (1996). Longitudinal studies in organizational stress research: A review of literature with reference to methodological issues. *Journal of Occupational Psychology*, *1*, 145–169.
Zhou, K. Z., Gao, G. Y., Yang, Z., & Zhou, N. (2005). Developing strategic orientation in China: Antecedents, consequences of market and innovation orientations. *Journal of Business Research*, *58*(8), 1049–1058.

PART III

Finance and Investment

CHAPTER 8

Folk Lending and P2P: Monitoring Maturation in Chinese Financial Contracting

Travis Selmier II
Indiana University, Bloomington, IN, United States

8.1 INTRODUCTION: DEVELOPMENT OF PRIVATE MONITORING IN CHINESE FINANCIAL CONTRACTING

Between the 1949 Revolution and the introduction of the Four Modernizations program in 1978, China suffered from too few financial institutions, too little financial capital and weak informational capital (Eckstein, 1977; Lardy, 1998). The Four Modernizations program made brief explicit mention of finance intermediation (de Wulf, 1985) although implicitly—through promoting a comprehensive economic program—set the stage for considerable broadening and deepening of Chinese banking and finance. Over the four decades since, China has matured from a capital-starved, mono-bank-centric financial system to a capital-rich system with great variety of financial intermediation (Cousin, 2007; Lardy, 1998, pp. 60–61; Tanaka & Molnar, 2008). Although the sophistication of Chinese banking and financial contracting has increased dramatically over those years, further progress is needed in delegated monitoring functions in banking and finance.

Delegated monitoring is a costly, delegated role, defined as one in which a financial intermediary (extended, in this paper, to investors acting in financial contracting roles) gathers and uses information ex post and ex ante to structure and renegotiate a financial contract.[1] Monitoring

[1] This chapter implicitly relies on Krasa and Villamil's (1992) model of a finite number of monitors (financial intermediaries). This reliance is due to three reasons: (1) the Chinese government has attempted to limit the number of financial intermediaries through many policies; (2) this limitation has served to increase informal financial intermediation, resulting in (3) increasing inefficiency in Chinese financial contracting due, in part, to inefficient, ineffective, or corrupted monitoring.

The China Business Model. DOI: http://dx.doi.org/10.1016/B978-0-08-100750-1.00008-5

is costly, because information collection and analysis requires expertise, time, and money; it is delegated in that societies have given over to financial intermediaries this role to improve efficiency in banking (Diamond, 1984; Krasa & Villamil, 1992) and in traded financial markets (Allen & Santomero, 1997). Delegated monitoring provides information, discipline, risk management, and managerial improvement in intermediated financial markets. These benefits ripple through an economy. As banks embrace social and business responsibilities in order to monitor financial contracts (Diamond, 1984; Schumpeter, 1939), covenants are constructed and enforced around this monitoring function (Krasa & Villamil, 1992; Rajan & Winton, 1995). Through these mechanisms, financial intermediaries overcome financial market inefficiencies by acting as information conduits (Allen, 2001; Allen & Santomero, 1997; Rajan & Winton, 1995).

We can examine monitoring in Chinese financial contracting by flipping the title of this chapter around. First, this chapter monitors maturation of banking and financial contracting in China to examine how and why monitoring remains the last major step in Chinese financial modernization. The formal and informal challenges faced by Chinese banks and other financial intermediaries in performing this monitoring function have eased since 1978, but still remain. Discomfort with uncontrolled information flows has retarded development of monitoring in China. As monitoring provides both a governance component as well as a social responsibility component, Chinese government officials have been uncomfortable with delegating governance authority to private actors (see, for instance, Selmier, 2016a; Yang, 2014).

Secondly, this chapter examines maturation of monitors themselves by focusing on the informal sectors in Chinese financial contracting. In this, I look at how informal finance channels credit to small- and medium-sized enterprises (SMEs), mostly through examining Wenzhou, a smaller city in southern Zhejiang Province which, for a quarter century, was the fastest-growing municipality in China's fastest-growing province. SMEs in Wenzhou, as elsewhere in China, became dependent on so-called "folk-lending"—loans and investment funds channeled through friends, or friends of friends. Wenzhou has also recently become a pan-China center for peer-to-peer online lending. These sources of capital were absolutely critical to SME growth as large state-owned banks would not lend to them (Bailey, Huang, & Yang, 2011; Lin & Chen, 2012; Zhang, 2002), while smaller banks focused on specific sectors and better-heeled clients (Tanaka & Molnar, 2008; Zhang, Xu, & Qin, 2013). Tsai (2009, p. 80) calculated in 2007 "only 1.3% of the loans extended by state banks went to private enterprises." Yet SMEs provide an important, fast-growing share of the Chinese economy, recently accounting for "60% of the country's gross domestic product (GDP) and over 75% of urban job opportunities" according to Cunningham and Rowley (2010, p. 125).

In effect, monitoring the maturation shows the impressive development of Chinese banking and financial intermediation. But the maturation of the monitors is still lagging. To examine changes in SME financing, the financial intermediation chains servicing SMEs, and the governance challenges that arise, this chapter employs a mixed-methods approach: Integrating macroeconomic data gathered through online and published government sources, extant papers (primarily in Chinese and mostly anecdotal), and 18 face-to-face semi-structured interviews conducted with local and national bankers, government officials, and financial academics in Wenzhou, Hangzhou, and Beijing in 2014 and 2015.

Section 8.2 monitors maturation in financial intermediation in China by focusing on six key developmental steps where Chinese financial intermediation broadened and deepened, but did not much progress in monitoring. In effect, the Chinese government did not delegate authority to financial intermediaries to monitor. Section 8.3 looks at transactional and relationship banking theory and examines the challenges faced by Multinational Enterprises (MNEs) in obtaining financing. Section 8.4 examines the challenges of monitoring in Wenzhou SME finance by discussing two channels of informal lending: folk-lending and peer-to-peer online lending platforms. Section 8.5 gives final thoughts as to the intimate linkages between delegated monitoring and the soft budget constraint.

8.2 MONITORING LAGS IN DEVELOPMENT OF FINANCIAL INTERMEDIATION IN MODERN CHINA

Over the four decades since 1978, China has matured from a mono-bank-centric system to a that with great variety of financial intermediation since the late-1970s (Cousin, 2007; Lardy, 1998, pp. 60–61; Tanaka & Molnar, 2008). Sometimes change was gradual: a bankruptcy law which would allow arms-length restructuring required nearly two decades to implement (Tanner, 1999, pp. 135–166). Sometimes change was rapid, revolutionizing the nature of banking and financial intermediation in China, as in the mid-1990s when state-owned Chinese banks were dramatically altered from redistribution mechanisms for regional development and put on the path to modern commercial banks (Brandt & Zhu, 2007).

Yet, great hurdles remain. The specter of financially weak state-owned enterprises (SOEs) being kept on life support continues to haunt China's state-owned Chinese banks to this day (Steinfeld, 1998; Tan, 2013). Equity markets retain their casino-like nature, rather than developing into a more-efficient capital allocation mechanism (Allen, Qian, & Qian, 2005; Branstetter, 2007)—partly due to informal financial intermediaries providing capital to speculators (Hess, 2015; Interviews in Wenzhou and Beijing, 2014, 2015a). Real estate remains a highly speculative investment class. And SMEs continue to be capital-deprived and more dependent on informal financing (Shi & Ye, 2001; Tanaka & Molnar, 2008; Zhang et al., 2013). All these hurdles are partly due to underdeveloped, inefficient or even stymied monitoring functions in Chinese financial intermediation.

Banking theory posits that banks and other financial intermediaries embrace a social responsibility to monitor financial contracts (Diamond, 1984) and that covenants are constructed around this monitoring function (Rajan & Winton, 1995). Through monitoring, financial intermediaries overcome financial market inefficiencies by acting as information conduits (Allen, 2001; Rajan & Winton, 1995). Chinese banks and other financial intermediaries lag in fulfilling this social responsibility. To understand this lag we need to understand better how far Chinese banking and financial intermediation has progressed. Six key steps have already been taken in this process of development. Each of these steps might have catalyzed monitoring improvement, but fell short. The steps are: (1) splitting the system into separate banks and financial services firms in the early 1980s; (2) the slow establishment of a bankruptcy law between 1985 and the late 1990s; (3) the establishment and growth of equity and bond markets since the late 1980s; (4) major reform of banks between 1994 and 1999; (5) the slow internationalization of Chinese financial over the last decade; and (6) a second round of bank reform which began in the 2000s and continues until this day.

Although nominally a banking system with three banks in 1978, China was effectively a one-bank system in which the Peoples Bank of China (PBoC) controlled the Bank of China while the China Construction Bank acted as a captive capital distribution wing of the Ministry of Finance (Branstetter, 2007, pp. 28–30). Splitting the system up in the early 1980s established the four large state-owned banks—the Big Four—and began establishing smaller, often specialized financial intermediaries focused on investments and regional development, while carving out a modern central banking role for the PBoC beginning in 1984 (Lardy, 1998, pp. 61–64, 66–76). This institutionalized a government role in monitoring banks and the financial system, but monitoring through private institutions and individuals was left underdeveloped (Table 8.1).

Table 8.1 Six key steps in modernization of Chinese financial intermediation

Time period	Key step	Effect on monitoring	Notes
Early 1980s	Splitting the system up into separate banks and financial services firms	Only addressed capital allocation aspects, not governance through monitoring	Just the beginning of an ongoing sophistication process in financial intermediation
1985–mid-1990s	Slow establishment of a bankruptcy law	Might have given banks "teeth" in pursuing assets of SOEs	Still considered quite underused by legal scholars
1980s until present	Establishment and growth of equity and bond markets	Did not link corporate governance to corporate ownership	Firms rely mostly on internal financing and bank loans
1994–99	Major bank reform	Began separation of regional, national, and party interests in bank governance	Concurrent with SOE reform
1999 until present	Slow internationalization of Chinese financial firms	MNE effect: 1. overseas listing 2. reporting requirements through M&A 3. foreign banks monitoring Chinese MNEs RMB internationalization requires PBoC to manage economy Little direct effect yet on Chinese banks	Beginning with WTO, more prominent after second round of bank reform
2000s until present	Second round of bank reform, including considerable information systems upgrading	Big Four have become more oriented toward delegated monitoring Better linkage between lending and client performance for big banks Little effect on smaller banks Effect through bankruptcy, Big Four lending to SMEs not yet noticeable	Financial intermediaries still restrained by government; considerable informal intermediation

Two crucial steps were started in the mid-1980s which may have enhanced private sector monitoring: passing of a bankruptcy law, and the establishment of equity markets. That neither has fulfilled their promise indicates deeply entrenched political influence over financial intermediation. The slow establishment of a bankruptcy law beginning in 1980 required significant policy entrepreneurship (Tanner, 1999) and, to this day, has not had much impact in *de jure* outcomes (the legal capacity to follow through to liquidation of a company's assets, see Jiang, 2014) or *de facto* outcomes (i.e., informational content sent to economic participants through monitoring actions of a financial intermediary filing a bankruptcy action against that company). The 1986 law required 6 years of negotiation and was a very tentative move forward in dialogue about bankruptcy; updated in 2007, it is still rarely invoked (Bufford, 2015). Branstetter noted in 2007 (p. 58) "as China's banks and asset management companies have discovered, the *de jure* legal right to force a debtor into bankruptcy does not translate into a *de facto* right to acquire control over the debtor's assets,". Recent bankruptcy filings by state-owned shipbuilders like Wuzhou Ship Repairing & Building and Sainty Marine (Bao, 2015), and the related asset filings by these firms' banks, will test whether this is changing; if so, this would represent progress toward private sector monitoring, particularly steps taken by the Big Four.

Establishment of equity and bond markets required a similarly long gestation period. Discussions around the governance benefits of equity ownership began in policy circles shortly after the Four Modernizations began (Steinfeld, 1998, pp. 130–137). These discussions resulted in a lightning-rod editorial published in the top economics newspaper, *Jingji Ribao* [经济日报] in 1985. The young economists who wrote this piece ascribed lofty ideals to investors:

> *The main purpose of risk capital is not to profit, but for future development; not to accelerate business [and profits], but rather to accelerate innovation.*[2]

The authors were purposefully controversial, invoking Adolf Berle's paean to corporate protection of property rights and corporate social responsibility, *The 20th Century Capitalist Revolution.*[3] An important part of

[2]"风险资本主要目的不是为了眼前利润，而是为了未来发展；不是为了促进企 业，而是为了促进创新。" translation by this author.

[3]Jiang (2009, pp. 27–30) notes the disjoint between "traditional culture concept" in which "personal moral objectives" held sway and the present market economy in China result in a "culture lag" which has affected informal finance, an idea which could be extended to formal finance in China and beyond. While Wu's (1985) essay may appear naive now, but a strong belief in moral economics provided a powerful argument in post-Cultural Revolution China.

their argument was the monitoring capacity of equity markets. But what Branstetter (2007, p. 54) noted a decade ago is still true today: "... equity prices were meant to serve as a summary statistic of the performance of the firm, guiding capital to the most productive, best managed enterprises. Equity prices do not... play this critical signaling role..." The main equity markets in Shenzhen and Shanghai were established a quarter century ago, yet China remains a bank-intermediated financial system. Furthermore, while joint stock banks were founded in the 1980s, only one bank was listed by the end of the 1990s (Lardy, 1998, p. 65). Li, Makaew, and Winton (2014) find, however, that Chinese equity markets may have begun to provide more monitoring.

The end of the 1990s saw China's admission to the WTO after a half-decade of major banking and SOE reform. One important component of this reform was to remove the responsibility of banks to redistribute capital as a social function, divorced from business concerns. A PBoC report from early 1980s laid out a policy of using the Big Four to finance local development (Shih, 2008, pp. 32–36). These banks were required to lend locally and, combined with the appointment of local government-linked bank managers by local officials, greatly increased political influence over local funding. The Big Four were also used to shift funds from capital-rich to capital-poor Chinese regions (Brandt & Zhu, 2007, pp. 98–103; Cao, Qian, & Weingast, 1999; Hsu, Arner, Wan, & Wang, 2005, pp. 45–46). Combined with SOE reform—which also sought to separate social burdens such as housing, education, and healthcare, and retain under state control only the larger SOEs (Steinfeld, 1998; Zheng & Chen, 2009),[4] the possibilities of enhanced monitoring and higher bank profits grew dramatically. In profit terms, the Big Four showed considerable profit and efficiency improvement since China's accession to the WTO in 1998, even as Chinese banking was opening up to more competition (Yin, Yang, & Mehran, 2013). Although monitoring again lagged behind, as monitoring confers political as well as economic power upon financial intermediaries. "Since the financial system... is the last remaining powerful instrument through which the state and party directly influence resource allocation, they are naturally reluctant to give up this power" noted Lardy (1998, p. 221).

The run-up to WTO membership catalyzed the gradual internationalization of Chinese financial institutions, as well as broader aspects of

[4] Summed up as "grasping the large and letting the small go" [抓大放小], the idea was to dramatically shrink the state-owned portion of the economy through downsizing, sell-off of firms, and corporatization, including equity listing and official recognition of all linked companies and interests.

Chinese finance. Three internationalization processes were tightly linked, financially and politically: globalization of nonfinancial Chinese MNEs, international network expansion of Chinese banks and financial firms (Tokuchi, 2013), and the internationalization of the RMB (Subramanian, 2011). Former Chairman of CITIC Securities International, Ted Tokuchi, summarized this interlinkage in 2013:

> *A key part of their [the Big Four's] plans at present is to grow their international banking business through footprints of China's development strategy and that means by focusing on Africa and Latin America in particular.*
>
> **Quoted in Selmier (2013, p. 747).**

Each of the three processes provided opportunities to enhance monitoring in domestic Chinese financial intermediation, yet each has yet to fully deliver. Globalization of Chinese MNEs is the most impactful of the three in furthering monitoring. Monitoring is increased through listing overseas and thereby disclosing information, acquiring non-Chinese firms, so reporting to non-Chinese regulators, and using services of foreign banks that monitor Chinese MNEs activities and loan covenants. The internationalization of the RMB exerts a powerful, although indirect, set of effects. The PBoC implicitly committed itself to manage the Chinese macroeconomy and its banks, through comments such as PBoC Vice Chairman Xiaolian Hu's (2009, p. 7) that "the Fed seemed to have a let-it-be attitude… until the burst of asset bubbles [in the latest global financial crisis]." The PBoC is also committed through the costs of the RMB becoming a reserve currency, as outlined by Subramanian (2011, pp. 6–8): likelihood of additional currency appreciation through foreign demand; leverage over domestic financial policy obtained through extensive foreign holdings of the RMB; embedded responsibility commensurate with being a lead currency; and the requirement for an open currency. Such Chinese bank internationalization has not yet had a large impact on monitoring simply because, as Chairman Jiang Jianqing of China's most international bank, ICBC, sadly mused "We are now just an international bank, not yet a real global bank" (quoted in Yang, 2014). Without a large foreign presence, state-owned Chinese banks will not become more scrutinized or pressured toward monitoring by non-Chinese financial intermediaries and governments.

Lardy (1998) estimated that nonperforming loans in the Chinese banking system were roughly 35% and were concentrated more in state-owned banks. While contentious when his book was published, the late 1990s recapitalization of banks proved insufficient, and a second round of reform began in the early 2000s (Brandt & Zhu, 2007; Hsu et al., 2005). Again, this provided opportunities to enhance the delegated monitoring roles of financial intermediaries, and the probability of this opportunity improved as the Big Four considerably upgraded their information systems and credit scoring (Hansakul, 2006). Perhaps underappreciated, the Big Four may be more advanced in delegated monitoring than smaller banks and certainly the informal sector. For instance, Chen, Liu, and Su (2013) find that the Big Four are more likely to allocate loans based on better performance while smaller banks may be swayed through bribery. Increasingly strict loan covenants and even bankruptcy suits by the Big Four are also unusual in Chinese banking. And expansion into SME lending by the Big Four is not only a sign of increased interest in this sector but also that banks with government ownership will participate in banking to smaller private firms.

Importantly, in 2003 the China Banking and Regulatory Commission (CBRC) was established, creating an independent, professional regulatory body. Despite this, a significant part of Chinese financial intermediation is still not transparent, and transparency is required for delegated monitoring to work effectively. Jianjun Li estimated in 2005 that informal lending was roughly 28% of amount of formal institutions' total lending (cited in Tsai, 2009, fn.8, p. 85). Informal lending and smaller banks still dominate SME financing, and here monitoring is especially weak. To understand why this is so, we first turn to banking theory, and then apply this to financial intermediation in Wenzhou.

8.3 SME LENDING IN THE CHINESE CONTEXT

Monitoring is conditioned by the two archetypal banking types: transactional banking and relationship banking (Allen, 2001; Boot, 2000; Boot & Marinč, 2008). Transactional banking is defined, in part, by that which is not relationship banking: a focus on the hard data-oriented, transaction core of banking—pushing to arms-length the relationship which may develop between banker and client. Transactional banking's essential strategy is to increase the number and efficiency of transactions and so drive down costs, achieving a comparative advantage through speed, volume, and efficiency (see Boot on securitization, 2000: 11–12, also Allen & Santomero, 1997). Information availability is essential to properly function as a bank or financial intermediary whether a transactional- or relationship-oriented strategy is pursued. Relationship bankers attempt to capture information that is more difficult to quantify, gathered through numerous meetings between banker and client over a long period, resulting in the banker judging the risk and return based on her knowledge of the client. This tacit knowledge, collected through the social network of the banker, is then infused throughout her bank. In practice, the relationship banker typically also gathers harder data, which she culls from client financial records and other sources. Transactional banking does not, or perhaps more accurately cannot, effectively collect, manage and employ this tacit knowledge and so relies on hard data.

Whether the bank is operating in developed or less-developed, capitalist, communist, or mixed-model economies, theory argues that banks ameliorate economic inefficiencies by acting as information conduits (Diamond, 1984; Rajan & Winton, 1995; Tanaka & Molnar, 2008). Substantial information search costs, as well as the costs associated with information capture, storage, usage, and transmission, are the reason for their respective reliance on different kinds of information. The investment required to conduct relationship banking is considered both large and asset-specific to the banking relationship (Berger & Udell, 1992, 2006; Tanaka & Molnar, 2008).

Smaller banks and other financial intermediaries have an advantage in controlling such costs and overseeing their employees, while maximizing returns when engaged in SME lending—termed the "small bank advantage" (Berger & Udell, 1992, 2006; Boot & Marinč, 2008, pp. 1190–1191; Zhang, 2002). The "small bank advantage" is viewed as the classic example of successful relationship banking when the bank's oversight restrains a banker from becoming too close to her client and over-extending credit, mitigating any soft budget constraints. Soft budget constraints "exist when the strict relationship between expenditure and earnings has been relaxed" (Kornai, 1986). Sometimes the banker does not correlate lending discipline to the actual financial condition of the firm, and may continue to extend loans (Qian, 1994). The bank may be unaware of this action, or may encourage it (Bailey et al., 2011; Selmier, 2016a, 2016b). In China, this is often called "lending new to repay old"[5] (Cousin, 2007, p. 88), a problem which has long been linked to SOE lending.

Banking theory holds that smaller banks lend to SMEs because smaller banks' size enable them to more-efficiently gather "soft data" and better monitor their bankers' tendencies to over-lend. China leans toward the relationship banking pole by nature of the structure of China's *guanxi*-based, social-network, banking system, and stage of financial development (Bailey et al., 2011; Zhang, 2002). SMEs are also dependent on smaller

[5]"借新还旧"—Jie xin hai jiu.

banks and informal finance (Allen et al., 2005; Guo & Liu, 2002). Chinese SMEs face the same obstacles facing SMEs elsewhere in obtaining capital from banks, plus additional challenges, which push Chinese SMEs to look outside the formal banking channels to what Tsai (2002) refers to as "back-alley banking." Table 8.2 outlines these obstacles.

First, SMEs' size and shorter histories often translate into fluctuating demand for capital and lack of banking ties to larger banks. This significantly increases the rates they must pay (Berger & Udell, 1992, 2006; Cousin, 2007; Zhang, 2002). Second, additional upward pressure on rates is seen because of SMEs' lack of professionally audited accounting records or credit history, partly due to a lack of collateral and elevated firm failure rates (Lin & Chen, 2012; Tanaka & Molnar, 2008; Zhang, 2002). Third, larger banks' formal loan approval processes sometimes cannot adjust to SMEs' seasonal, and often very short term, demand for capital. This pushes Chinese SMEs' in particular toward fast solutions with less credit scoring, such as folk-lending (Bailey et al., 2011; Fu & Bao, 2011; Guo & Liu, 2002).

Fourth, from a capital supply perspective, larger banks consider these higher risk factors, the lack of incentives to take on risks and small loan sizes, and so have tended to ignore SMEs (Bailey et al., 2011; Cousin, 2007; Zhang, 2002).[6] Fifth, the structure of Chinese banking requires smaller, local financial intermediaries' to request funds and approval through their supervising banks, further delaying businesses opportunities requiring rapid investment (Lin & Chen 2012, p. 9; also Tanaka & Molnar, 2008). Sixth, after onset of the 2007–08 Global Financial Crisis, China's central government raised interest rates (Ding, 2012) whilst setting a ceiling on rates that could be charged (PBoC, 2012). Structuring this interest rate "corridor" dampened informal financial contracting; this, combined with concerns about SMEs' overseas markets and better returns available through other investments, caused a decline in folk-lending.

These obstacles were compounded in Wenzhou by two additional, related obstacles (labeled 7 and 8 in Table 8.2): seventh, Wenzhou has perpetually been in capital-deficit and dependent on significant capital flows from the rest of China (Tsai, 2009; Zhang et al., 2013); Eighth, this is partially due to the unbridled nature of Wenzhou-style business and Wenzhou's long history as an independent-minded part of China, resulting in the now famous "Wenzhou Model" (Liu, 1992; Sonobe, Hu, & Otsuka, 2004; finance-specific, see Tsai, 2009, pp. 88–92).

[6] However some large banks such as Bank of China have recently established SME Departments to pursue this business, as noted earlier.

Table 8.2 Obstacles to obtaining finance for Chinese SMEs

	Number	Obstacle	Notes
Obstacle seen globally by SMEs	1	Size and shorter histories	Leads to lack of banking ties, fluctuating demand for capital, and higher rates paid
	2	Lack of professionally audited accounting records	Also lack longer credit histories, collateral, and high failure rates
	3	Very short-term requirements	Pushes SMEs to informal, fast lenders
	4	Supply-side constraints	Bankers lack incentives and do not wish to face higher risks
China-wide obstacle for SMEs	5	Smaller banks must obtain approval from supervising banks	Structure of Chinese banking
	6	Post-2008 interest rate channel	Interest rate "corridor" curtailed informal financing
Wenzhou-specific SMEs	7	Perpetually in capital-deficit	Dependent on significant capital inflows, Wenzhou has paid highest rates in China
	8	Fallout from the "Wenzhou Model"	High-debt, high-growth, informal finance, SME and non-SOE regional economy

Culled from: Bailey, W., Huang, W., & Yang, Z. S. (2011). Bank loans with Chinese characteristics: Some evidence on inside debt in a state-controlled banking system. The Journal of Financial and Quantitative Analysis, *46*(6), 1795–1830; Berger, A. N., & Udell, G. F. (1992). Some empirical evidence on the empirical significance of credit rationing. Journal of Political Economy, *100*, 1047–1077; Berger, A. N. & Udell, G. F. (2006). A more complete conceptual framework for SME finance. Journal of Banking & Finance, *30*(11), 2945–2966; Cousin, V. (2007). Banking in China. Basingstoke, England; New York: Palgrave Macmillan; Ding, Qi. [丁琪]. (2012). Resolution on folk lending in Wenzhou [解析温州民间借贷]. *Technological Development of Enterprise, 31* (4,7) [企业技术开发], 165–166; Fu, X. L., & Bao, Q. H. [付晓亮 & 包清华]. (2011). Theoretical research on application of relationship banking loans in China. [关系型银行贷款理论及其在我国的应用研究]. *Operations and Management, 16*《经营管理者: 16期》; Guo, B., & Liu, M.-L. [郭斌 & 刘曼路]. (2002). Private finance and small & medium sized enterprises development: Empirical evidence from Wenzhou Region [民间金融与中小企业发展： 对温州的实证分析]. *Economic Study, 21*(31), No. 4, 7 [经济研究] 10, 40–46; Lin, G., & Chen, T. [林贵 & 陈婷]. (2012). Risk and prevention of establishing private banks in Wenzhou [温州建立与发展民营银行的风险与防范]. *Journal of Wenzhou Vocational &Technical College, 12*(1) [温州职业技术学院学报], 8–23; Liu, A. P. L. (1992). The "Wenzhou Model" of development and China's modernization. Asian Survey, *32*(8), 696–711; Selmier, W. T. (2016a). Netizens and private monitoring in Chinese banking. In J. C. Choi, M. R. Powers, & X. T. Zhang (Eds.), *Political economy of Chinese finance*, Vol. 17 of International Finance Review. Bingley: Emerald Group Publishing Limited; Selmier, W. T. (2016b). *Social capital and folk-lending in China's hottest financial market.* Working paper; Tanaka, K., & Molnar, M. (2008). What is different about informal finance? Financing of Private Firms in China. Revue économique, *59*(6), 1131–1143; Tsai, K. S. (2009). Beyond banks: The local logic of informal finance and private sector development in China. In J.-J. Li, & S. Hsu (Eds.), Informal *finance* in China: American and Chinese *perspectives* (pp. 80–103). Oxford: Oxford University Press; Zhang, J. [张捷]. (2002). Relationship lending to small and medium enterprises and the organizational structure of banks [中小企业的关系型借贷与银行组织结构.]. *Economic Research* [经济研究], 6.

8.4 INFORMAL FINANCE IN WENZHOU PRESENTS UNIQUE MONITORING PROBLEMS

8.4.1 Folk-Lending and Related Monitoring Complexities

The Wenzhou model was particularly dependent on informal types of financing for a number of reasons. Firstly, Wenzhou was considered geographically undesirable due to its proximity to Taiwan (Tsai, 2009), and a history of regional independence which made Wenzhou seem less easy to govern (Liu, 1992; interviews). Both factors, combined with limited arable land and few natural resources—aside from the Ou River and its trade flows, meant that Wenzhou was capital-deprived, with the national government reticent to site SOEs in Wenzhou (Liu, 1992; Tsai, 2009). Wenzhou people, however, were a natural resource in, and of, themselves, renowned for three characteristics: their much-mentioned reputation for being extremely hard-working (interviews, Wenzhou and Beijing)[7]; their extremely high risk tolerance (Lin & Chen, 2012; Liu, 1992; Shi & Ye, 2001)[8]; and, in the words of a senior local banker, "Wenzhou people love debt."[9]

Employing the resources at hand, Wenzhou SMEs and individuals began pooling capital in the 1980s within small networks, which lent at high interest to local businesses. Wenzhou's reputation for successful SME and regional growth outweighed successive scams and collapses (Shi & Ye, 2001; Tsai, 2009) that dented, but did not destroy, the emerging brand name of the Wenzhou Model. By the 1990s Wenzhou's multitiered financial network structure had become an important component of the Wenzhou model (Sonobe et al., 2004; Interviews, 2015b).

If Wenzhou SMEs relied solely on smaller banks in which relationship banking was practiced, one might expect some buffering of economic downturns, as suggested in the model proposed by Bolton, Freixas, Gambacorta, and Mistrulli (2013). Economic downturns since the 1980s were, however, often more severe in Wenzhou than in other parts of China, and more severe than these economists might predict. In fact, the higher interest rates charged through informal channels make loan repayment more difficult, often resulting in violent conflicts between the

[7]"温州人很勤劳" is a constantly-heard phrase, mentioned in interviews with academics, regulators, and bankers.

[8]Mentioned in interviews with two local and two national bankers, several financial academics and a regulator.

[9]This banker said "温州人爱贷款."Seven other interviewees told me this in very similar terms.

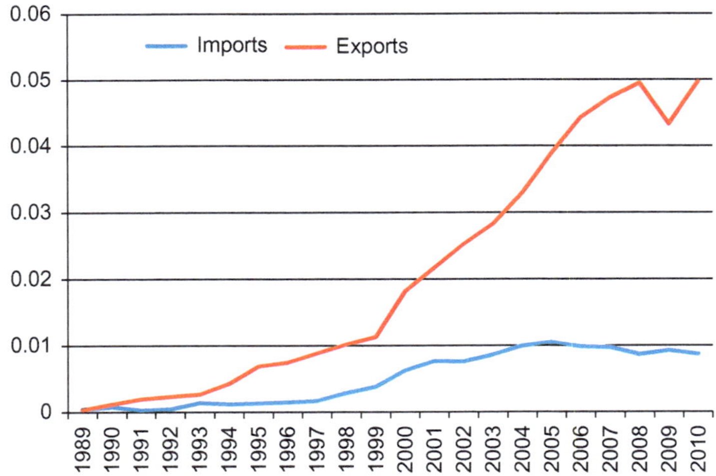

Figure 8.1 Imports and exports' portion of Wenzhou real GDP (sized to 1). *Data is calculated from Wenzhou Statistical Yearbook.*

lenders and SME owners (Lin & Chen, 2012). Consequently, the impacts from the global economic downturn beginning in 2007–08 immediately blunted Wenzhou exports as shown in Fig. 8.1 and, by 2011, a recession hit the entire Wenzhou regional economy with a vengeance.

The credit contraction in Wenzhou was so profound that the municipal and central governments felt compelled to implement China's first, and thus far only, "complete financial reform" [jinrong zonghe gaige—金融综合改革] (PBoC, 2012). In the process of reform, a number of financial intermediaries and holding companies were established and more extensive links established between local financial intermediaries and national financial authorities—including the PBoC and the CBRC (Selmier, 2016a). A Local Financial Management Bureau [difang jinrong guanliju—地方金融管理局] was established to provide on-the-ground oversight. This ongoing profound contraction is largely an outcome of weak monitoring. Examining the structure of informal financial intermediation in Wenzhou helps explain how and why delegated monitoring functions are still weak in China.

Wenzhou's history of financial innovation is famous for its sophistication in "folk-lending," an informal form of financing which translates directly from Chinese as "loans between people" [minjian jiedai—民间借贷]. Folk-lending arrangements are usually structured

Table 8.3 Six monitoring problems arising under folk-lending [minjian jiedai—民间借贷]

Number	Monitoring problem	Reason for problem
1	Capital in loan channel unknown	Informality and quasi-legal status make tracking and registration impossible. Wenzhou has created a Center to register minjian jiedai, but reporting is voluntary
2	Imminently callable or nonrollable	Intermediaries have little capital and may call loans as they must pay, or simply not roll the loan
3	No hard constraints	Monitoring without teeth is weak or nonexistent monitoring
4	Exit or find another to bail out position rather than monitor	As the borrower/capital-requirer cannot be compelled to pay or change covenants, better moves for the capital-provider are to remain quiet and act on privileged information
5	Low bar to entry into lending channel	Not clear that many lenders/capital-providers have the skill set to properly monitor
6	Unstable network	All above-mentioned monitoring problems contribute to this problem

Source: Author's conception.

between geographically close borrowers and lenders who have a long-established personal relationship and are usually more risk-tolerant, compared with formal banks' lending channels (Ding, 2012; Guo & Liu, 2002; Lin & Chen, 2012). This very informality, however, caused six monitoring problems, as outlined in Table 8.3.

(1) There was no way to know precisely how much capital was involved in the Wenzhou folk-lending market because, until the Wenzhou Private Lending Registration Service Center was established in 2011, there simply was no record of extant lending. (2) The speed at which such loans could be called, or simply not rolled over, was extremely disruptive to SMEs' ongoing working capital needs. For example, after the export downturn started in 2009, many lenders/capital-providers in the folk-lending channel simply shifted their capital to other profitable investments in coalmining, real estate or elsewhere outside Wenzhou (Yu, 2013), causing a precipitous decline in available capital within Wenzhou.

(3) There was little in the way of hard constraints to bind a borrower/capital-requirer, so instead of incented to monitor a financial contract for

society's benefits, capital-providers were motivated to monopolize information rather than divulge it. Jiang (2009, p. 29) notes:

> *Most informal financing activities are based only on an oral agreement and lack collateral, while even those having a written contract are weakly protected by the legal system since informal finance is still an underground activity. Therefore, one often finds that moral constraints are the only type of constraint that prevails.*

(4) This weak constraint provides an incentive for lenders/capital-providers to not simply hide information, but to exit positions before anyone finds out. Consider the situation wherein no penalty exists for acting on nonpublic information. If a counterparty is in trouble, the lender/capital-provider's rational response is either to exit the position or attempt to arrange additional loans with other, unknowing, lenders/capital-providers in order to bail herself out.

(5) There is a low bar to becoming a financial intermediary in such informal circumstances. A potential entrant requires only contacts or a bit of capital. Jiang (2009, p. 22) cites an example of an informal intermediary whose very name connotes this potential problem of lack of expertise: the Old Lady Bank in Wenzhou, whose banking network members are "middle aged women up to 60 years of age, who have little education." Here, a prospective borrower/capital-requirer simply contacted one of the older women in this multivillage network and explained his need. The network would look for available capital to lend. Schumpeter (1939, p. 117) summed up this situation well when he wrote:

> *... bankers may, at some times and in some countries, fail to be up to the mark corporatively: that is to say, tradition and standards may be absent to such a degree that practically anyone, however lacking in aptitude and training, can drift into the banking business, find customers, and deal with them according to his own ideas. In such countries or times,* wildcat banking *develops.*[10]

(6) These first five monitoring problems engender a systemic problem made more severe through weak monitoring—considerable network risk in Wenzhou. Financial contracting under folk-lending involves a guarantor who either supplies capital and provides assurance for debt payment, or simply provides assurance to the lender/capital-supplier in a separate contract. This is known as "carrying guarantee" [担保—*danbao*]. One senior banker told me "*danbao* is a China-wide phenomenon, [but] in Wenzhou

[10] Emphasis added. Note that part of this quote also cited in Diamond (1984).

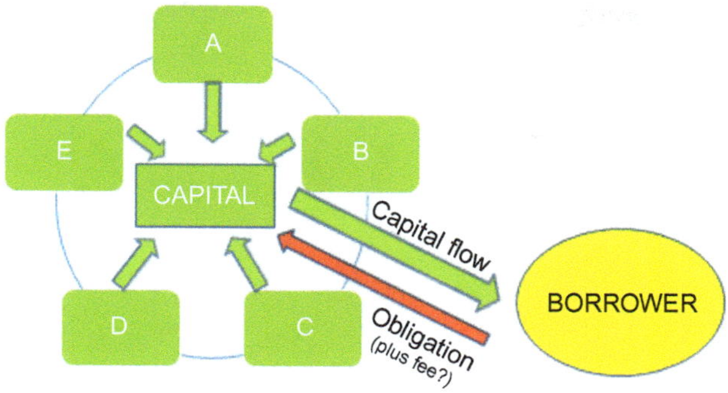

Figure 8.2 Guarantor group [保团—*baotuan*]. *From Selmier, W. T. (2016). Social capital and folk-lending in China's hottest financial market.*

it is very advanced". *Danbao* came to be seen as a separable financial good which could be purchased, lessening or even removing the moral constraint which came through interpersonal relationship (Selmier, 2016b).

Financial innovation in Wenzhou created more complex, more networked syndication arrangements such as *baotuan* [保团], where a group of individuals pools capital to lend through informal syndication arrangement (see Fig. 8.2). The borrower may pay an origination fee and/or a guarantor fee to the *baotuan*, to one if its members, or to a facilitator who introduces the borrower to the *baotuan*. *Baotuan* syndicates enabled financiers to take on investments in large projects in Wenzhou and elsewhere; one finance academic revealed that some Wenzhou-based *baotuan* "swooped down" and bought out whole floors or buildings in Shanghai and Beijing.

Network risk also existed in the long chains of folk-lending arrangements called *lianbao* [连保], in which a guarantor to one borrower is a borrower from another, and these arrangements become organically tied together. Selmier (2016b) describes the systemic risk resulting from these complex linkages as "countless spider webs in an old barn, interlinked and difficult to pull apart without destroying all the webs." Fig. 8.3 shows why those lender/capital-providers tied together in this structure are highly unlikely to know the others. In fact, "no one knew where the risk was in the system" because folk-lending had few public records and no registry of any kind.[11]

[11]This was mentioned in interviews with two financial academics, two government officials, and two bankers.

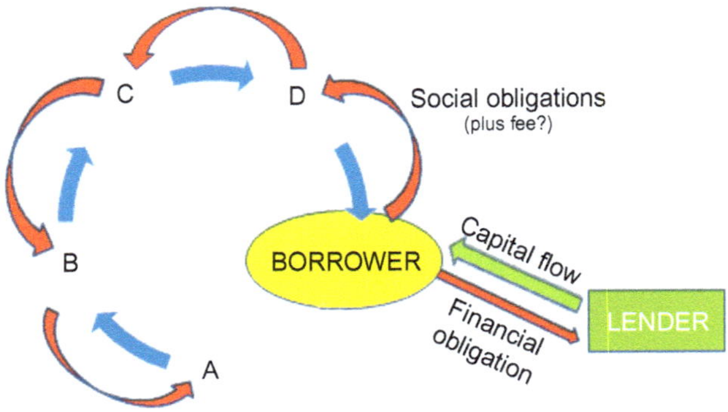

Figure 8.3 Guarantor circle [连保—*lianbao*]. *From Selmier, W. T. (2016). Social capital and folk-lending in China's hottest financial market.*

8.4.2 Wildcat Banking in Wenzhou: The Rise of "P2P" and a New Set of Monitoring Issues

Even after the financial crisis hit Wenzhou and folk-lending contracted, the channel still accounted for roughly 20% of total loans disbursed in Wenzhou (PBoC, 2012; Interview with Wenzhou Private Lending Registration Service Center, 2015b). But folk-lending is being eclipsed by a new type of financial intermediary. Part of the credit transmitted through folk-lending channels has now shifted to peer-to-peer online lending platforms [P2P ping tai (P2P平台), or simply P2P]. Growth in the P2P channel exploded in China since 2011, and Wenzhou is one of China's main P2P centers (Caijing, 2014: numerous interviews, 2014: 2015). Of the roughly 3000 P2Ps known to have existed in China in April 2015, more than 100 were based in Wenzhou (interviews with Local Financial Management Bureau and others). China's largest P2P, Wenzhou Dai, started in Wenzhou, and several of the larger, and more-successful, P2Ps are based in Wenzhou. "The P2P model fits better to Wenzhou's culture" according to a senior local banker (interviewed in April, 2015).

While folk-lending arrangements might be characterized as geographically close between those with personal relationships, P2P platforms bring together geographically distant actors without personal relationships. In banking's simplest terms, folk-lending is more akin to relationship banking while P2P is closer to transactional banking. Another six monitoring problems have arisen with P2P. Some are similar to the previously outlined problems encountered under folk-lending, but others are not.

Table 8.4 Six monitoring problems arising under peer-to-peer online lending platforms (P2P platforms (P2P ping tai, 平台), or simply P2P)

Number	Monitoring problem	Reason for problem
1	Gates on removal of capital mean dependence of P2P for monitoring	P2P platforms may choose to not monitor, monitor but provide only positive information, or release flowery descriptions of borrowers/capital-requirers' positions
2	Independent verification of monitored information difficult	Geographically distant lenders/capital-providers cannot verify projects by looking at them
3	Even weaker moral constraints	Geographically distant P2Ps
4	Systemic weakness due to immaturity, information asymmetry, and "runaways"	Lenders/capital-providers engage in herd behavior while P2P bosses absconding with capital are now commonplace
5	Low bar to entry into lending channel	Not clear that many lenders/capital-providers have the skill set to properly monitor
6	P2Ps act like real banks	Chinese P2Ps are taking in capital, then allocating to of borrowers/capital-requirers

Source: Author's conception.

(1) While the possibility of a loan being suddenly called by the investor/capital-provider is lessened, the financial intermediary now has wide discretion over how to monitor the borrower/capital-requirer, how much to report, and the accuracy of such reporting. (2) Independently verifying the information provided through monitoring is now more difficult for the lenders/capital-providers who are now usually geographically distant and so cannot verify projects by looking at them (note Agarwal, Li, Liu, & Zhang, 2015, find that establishing personal guarantee on a loan may help to lessen this problem). (3) The removal of this geographic proximity removes the disciplining nature on P2P to which intermediaries and borrower/capital-requirers under folk-lending may be subject. That is to say, the "moral constraints" Jiang mentions are even weaker (Table 8.4).

(4) These weakening moral constraints have led to systemic-level issues under P2P lending, which increase monitoring difficulties. One related problem is what Chen, Hu, Lou, and Yong (2015) analyze as herding behavior, in which lenders/capital-providers invest capital by following others.

They attribute this to two possible reasons: immaturity of loan market due to information asymmetry, and a closely linked reason: inexperience on the part of lenders/capital-providers. This is has led to a certain ennui on the part of the investing public: "Runaway P2P bosses are no longer newsworthy," as the Economist (2016) quoted from a *Jinling Evening News* article.[12]

(5) P2Ps also have very low bars to entry, just as with folk-lending. The skill set required to clear this low bar is different, though. Whereas the potential entrant in folk-lending requires only contacts or a bit of capital, the potential P2P entrant only requires skill in coding an elegant website. Once up and running, the physical location of the P2P is sometime difficult to uncover, leading to confusion as to which government agency is tasked with that P2P's regulatory responsibility (interviews with Local Finance Management Bureau officials).

(6) Many Chinese P2Ps are acting like real banks. That is, they are taking in capital, then allocating to borrowers/capital-requirers rather than merely acting as transparent conduits connecting investor/lender and borrower/capital-requirer, as American P2P platforms do. However, if Chinese P2Ps were actually banks they should be licensed and regulated by the CBRC and subject to capital requirements set by the PBoC. Yet, a CBRC official told me in April 2015: "Since we have not issued bank licenses to any P2P platforms, they cannot be banks." But the Senior Director of one of Wenzhou's largest and most profitable P2Ps countered in another interview, "Yes of course we are a bank. Chinese P2P are not like American P2P [in acting as capital conduits]."

Wenzhou P2P are involved in a full range of financing, including to individuals, SMEs, crowd-sourced projects, and recapitalization, and workout restructurings of bankrupt businesses (interviews). Yet, regulatory responsibilities for Wenzhou-based P2Ps had been pushed onto the Local Financial Management Bureau, which was not sufficiently staffed to handle so many P2Ps and their very rapid growth. Interviewees from banking, regulation, and academia all stated that they believed P2Ps were indeed banks; many argued that P2Ps were funding stock market speculators and so partially responsible for the spike in equity prices from late-2014 until summer 2015. P2Ps were not, however, pulled under regulatory jurisdiction of the CBRC in summer of 2015, and this regulatory transition remains a work-in-progress. Over the last four decades, financial intermediation in China has grown increasingly sophisticated, with impressive

[12] One of China's top newspapers, based in Nanjing.

development in "fin tech" (financial technology) channels such as P2P, but with all this sophistication, it is difficult to see delegated monitoring progress if public monitoring of China's fastest-growing lending channel (Caijing, 2014) is inadequate and poorly coordinated.

8.5 FINAL THOUGHTS: MONITORING AND THE SOFT BUDGET CONSTRAINT

Throughout Chinese SMEs' rapid growth, questions and problems arose as to informational asymmetry and transparency surrounding their financial state and resulting misunderstanding of their debt obligations. The financial health of weak SMEs was often not known until an SME collapsed. At that point, there would usually be a struggle over what entity was actually responsible for the debts incurred. Sometimes local governments would be the final guarantor, sometimes entrepreneurs and firm owners were held responsible, other times, financial intermediaries were left with the accumulated debts. Nearly always, the SME's workers suffered sudden loss of income, and occasionally loss of ownership shares.

These issues could be partially addressed through enhancing monitoring in financial intermediation. Delegated monitoring confers governance, influence, and responsibility upon a financial intermediary. That responsibility comes with a price that many delegatees may not wish to pay. Delegating this responsibility for monitoring may make formal financial institutions the targets of additional blame for financial crises, would likely limit margins and increase taxes for informal financial institutions and capital-providing individuals, and bring into view the operations of borrowers/capital-requirers who may prefer to keep their financial operations out of view. There has been little motivation on the part of Chinese governments, whether local or national, to give over some governance power to financial intermediaries.

Delegated monitoring is not the mirror image of the soft budget constraint, but their converses are intimately related. We can compare across monitoring, soft budget constraints and the present state of informal finance channels by examining the inherent options of *exit*, *voice*, and *loyalty* available to financial intermediaries. A lender/capital-provider suffering under a soft budget constraint is only allowed *loyalty*. Any financial counsel given is spoken *sotto voce*, as making public a borrower/capital-requirer's weakened position is not an option. *Exit* is also not an option, as the lender/capital-provider is locked into a position as a near-captive capital supplier. Monitoring gives *voice* to the lender/capital-provider, through both her ex post and ex ante actions regarding the borrower/capital-requirer. She may also show *loyalty*, through sound financial counsel, or *exit* the position. Both of these actions actually give *voice* as well, as observers see the action of the lender/capital-provider, anticipate the implicit signals in her monitoring, and then react. Financial intermediaries in informal financing channels have two options, *loyalty* or *exit*. Monitoring—i.e., using *voice*—is not required and little is gained from voluntary monitoring. *Loyalty* may be given in situations where a lender/capital-provider knows the counterparty quite well and is willing to increase her risk exposure. When the risk exposure seems too large and private information gives an advantage, *exit* is sometimes an available option.

A debate now rages as to whether government organizations should play an intermediate role in financial contracting, including directing state-owned banks to provide direct financing to SMEs (Ding, 2012; Shi & Ye, 2001), or establishing innovative financial organizations that serve SMEs (Guo & Liu, 2002; Lin & Chen, 2012). Additional government intervention will not strengthen Chinese banking and financial markets, nor would it necessarily benefit society. The next major step in Chinese financial intermediation is to empower financial intermediaries to use their asymmetric information advantages by delegating monitoring to them, then hold them to the set of responsibilities which come with that empowerment. This will not only improve financial information flows, but also bind Chinese financial intermediaries into more robust and resilience financial governance.

REFERENCES

Agarwal, S., Li, Y., Liu, C.-L., & Zhang, J. (2015). *Personal guarantee and peer-to-peer lending: Evidence from China*. Downloaded on November 11, 2015 at <http://dx.doi.org/10.2139/ssrn.2638546>.

Allen, F. (2001). Presidential address: Do financial institutions matter? *Journal of Finance*, *56*, 1165–1175.

Allen, F., Qian, J., & Qian, M. (2005). Law, finance, and economic growth in China. *Journal of Financial Economics*, 77, 57–115.

Allen, F., & Santomero, A. M. (1997). The Theory of Financial Intermediation. *Journal of Banking and Finance*, *21*, 1461–1486.

Bailey, W., Huang, W., & Yang, Z. S. (2011). Bank loans with Chinese characteristics: Some evidence on inside debt in a state-controlled banking system. *The Journal of Financial and Quantitative Analysis*, *46*(6), 1795–1830.

Bao, Z. (2015). *State-owned shipbuilder goes bankrupt as industry slows*. Caixin Online 12.31.2015. Downloaded on January 25, 2016 from <http://english.caixin.com/2015-12-31/100895039.html>.

Berger, A. N., & Udell, G. F. (1992). Some empirical evidence on the empirical significance of credit rationing. *Journal of Political Economy*, *100*, 1047–1077.

Berger, A. N., & Udell, G. F. (2006). A more complete conceptual framework for SME finance. *Journal of Banking & Finance, 30*(11), 2945–2966.

Bolton, P., Freixas, X., Gambacorta, L., & Mistrulli, P. E. (2013). *Relationship and transaction lending in a crisis*. NBER Working Paper No. 19467.

Boot, A. W. A. (2000). Relationship banking: What do we know? *Journal of Financial Intermediation, 9*, 7–25.

Boot, A. W. A., & Marinč, M. (2008). The evolving landscape of banking. *Industrial and Corporate Change, 17*(6), 1173–1203.

Brandt, L., & Zhu, X. -D. (2007). China's banking sector and economic growth. In C. Calomaris (Ed.), *Chinese finance at the cross-roads* (pp. 86–136). New York, NY: Columbia University Press.

Branstetter, L. (2007). China's financial markets: An overview. In C. Calomaris (Ed.), *Chinese finance at the cross-roads* (pp. 23–78). New York, NY: Columbia University Press.

Bufford, S. (2015). *Supreme people's court interpretations of China's Bankruptcy Law: Translations and commentary. Penn State Law* Research Paper No. 9. Available at SSRN or <http://dx.doi.org/10.2139/ssrn.2663508>.

Caijing [财经] (2014). *Turnover of 2013 P2P tops 100 billion: Wenzhou Dai is the top, Lu Jinsuo is triumphant*. [2013年P2P成交量上千亿：温州贷占鳌头，陆金所高歌猛进.] *Caijing Wang [财经网]*. Downloaded on February 15, 2015 from <http://stock.caijing.com.cn/2014-01-14/113811762.html>.

Cao, Y. -Z., Qian, Y. -Y., & Weingast, B. R. (1999). From federalism, Chinese style to privatization, Chinese style. *Economics of Transition*, 7(1), 103–131.

Chen, D. -Y., Hu, H. -L., Lou, H., & Yong, W. (2015). Herding behavior in online microloan markets: Evidence from China. *WHICEB 2015 Proceedings, Paper 84* Available at <http://aisel.aisnet.org/whiceb2015/84>.

Chen, Y. -L., Liu, M., & Su, J. (2013). Greasing the wheels of bank lending: Evidence from private firms in China. *Journal of Banking & Finance, 37*(7), 2533–2545.

Cousin, V. (2007). *Banking in China*. Basingstoke, England; New York: Palgrave Macmillan.

Cunningham, L. X., & Rowley, C. (2010). The changing face of small and medium-sized enterprise management in China. In C. Rowley & F. L. Cooke (Eds.), *The changing face of management in China* (pp. 125–148). London: Routledge.

de Wulf, L. (1985). Economic reform in China. *Finance and Development, 22*(1), 8–12.

Diamond, P. W. (1984). Financial intermediation and delegated monitoring. *Review of Economic Studies, 51*, 393–414.

Ding, Qi. [丁琪]. (2012). Resolution on folk lending in Wenzhou [解析温州民间借贷]. *Technological Development of Enterprise, 31* (4,7) [企业技术开发], 165–166.

Eckstein, A. (1977). *China's economic revolution*. Cambridge: Cambridge University Press.

Economist. 2016. *China's P2P lending boom—Taking flight*. January 23, 2016.

Fu, X. L., & Bao, Q. H. [付晓亮 & 包清华]. (2011). Theoretical research on application of relationship banking loans in China. [关系型银行贷款理论及其在我国的应用研究]. *Operations and Management, 16*《经营管理者: 16期》.

Guo, B., & Liu, M.-L. [郭斌 & 刘曼路]. (2002). Private finance and small & medium sized enterprises development: Empirical evidence from Wenzhou Region [民间金融与中小企业发展： 对温州的实证分析]. *Economic Study, 21*(31), No. 4, 7 [经济研究] *10*, 40–46.

Hansakul, S. (2006). Chinjua's banking sector: Ripe for the next stage? *Deutsche Bank Research* December 7, 2006. Accessed January 28, 2016 at <http://www.dbresearch.ru/PROD/DBR_INTERNET_EN-PROD/PROD0000000000204417.PDF>.

Hess, P. (2015). How likely is a financial crisis in China? *The Diplomat* November 17, 2015. Accessed January 8, 2016 at <http://thediplomat.com/2015/11/how-likely-is-a-financial-crisis-in-china/>.

Hsu, B., F. -C., Arner, D., Wan, Q., & Wang, W. (2005). Banking liberalization and restructuring in post-WTO China. *Banking & Finance Law Review, 21*, 23–59.

Hu, X. L. (2009). *On the roots of the current financial crisis*. Interdepartmental Group of Twenty Four Reseach Papers. <http://173.254.126.101/~gtwofouo/wp-content/uploads/2014/03/Hu-1.pdf>. Accessed 04.01.15.

Interviews, face-to-face semi-structured (2014). Hangzhou.

Interviews, face-to-face semi-structured (April 2015a). Beijing.

Interviews, face-to-face semi-structured (April and December 2015b). Wenzhou.

Jiang, S. -X. (2009). The evolution of informal finance in China and its prospects. In J. -J. Li & S. Hsu (Eds.), *Informal Finance in China: American and Chinese Perspectives* (pp. 12–38). Oxford: Oxford University Press.

Jiang, Y. J. (2014). The curious case of inactive bankruptcy practice in China: A comparative study of U.S. and Chinese bankruptcy law. *Northwestern Journal of International Law & Business*, *34*, 559–582.

Kornai, J. (1986). The soft budget constraint. *Kyklos*, *39*, 3–30.

Krasa, S., & Villamil, A. P. (1992). Monitoring the monitor: An incentive structure for a financial intermediary. *Journal of Economic Theory*, *57*, 197–221.

Lardy, N. R. (1998). *China's unfinished economic revolution*. Washington, DC: Brookings Institution Press.

Li, M.-W., Makaew, T., & Winton, A. (2014). *Cheating in China: Corporate fraud and the roles of financial markets*. Retrieved from <http://ssrn.com/abstract=2521151>.

Lin, G., & Chen, T. [林贵 & 陈婷]. (2012). Risk and prevention of establishing private banks in Wenzhou [温州建立与发展民营银行的风险与防范]. *Journal of Wenzhou Vocational & Technical College*, *12*(1) [温州职业技术学院学报], 8–23.

Liu, A. P. L. (1992). The "Wenzhou Model" of development and China's modernization. *Asian Survey*, *32*(8), 696–711.

PBoC (People's Bank of China). (2012). *Report on the Wenzhou folk-lending market* 《温州民间借贷市场报告》2012年7月21日.

Qian, Y. (1994). A theory of shortage in socialist economies based on the 'soft budget constraint'. *American Economic Review*, *84*(1), 145–156.

Rajan, R. G., & Winton, A. (1995). Covenants and collateral as incentives to monitor. *Journal of Finance*, *50*, 1113–1146.

Schumpeter, J. (1939). *Business cycles*. New York, NY: McGraw-Hill. Abridged version downloaded from http://classiques.uqac.ca/classiques/Schumpeter_joseph/business_cycles/schumpeter_business_cycles.pdf.

Selmier, W. T., II (2013). Political resistance in Chinese mergers and acquisitions: An interview with Ted Tokuchi. *Business Horizons*, *56*(6), 743–748.

Selmier, W. T. (2016a). Netizens and private monitoring in Chinese banking. In J. C. Choi, M. R. Powers, & X. T. Zhang (Eds.), *Political economy of Chinese finance* (Vol. 17 of International Finance Review). Bingley: Emerald Group Publishing Limited.

Selmier, W. T. (2016b). *Social capital and folk-lending in China's hottest financial market*. Working paper.

Shi, J.-C., & Ye, M. [史晋川&叶敏]. (2001). Financial arrangement in unusual institutional environment: The Case of Wenzhou [制度扭曲环境中的金融安排：温州案例]. *Economic Theory and Management*, *1* [经济理论与经济管理], 63–68.

Shih, V. C. (2008). *Factions and finance in China: Elite conflict and inflation*. New York, NY: Cambridge University Press.

Sonobe, T., Hu, D., & Otsuka, K. (2004). From inferior to superior products: An inquiry into the Wenzhou model of industrial development in China. *Journal of Comparative Economics*, *32*, 542–563.

Steinfeld, E. (1998). *Forging reform in China: The fate of state-owned industry*. Cambridge: Cambridge University Press.

Subramanian, A. (2011). Renminbi rules: The conditional imminence of the reserve currency transition. Peterson Institute for International Economics Working Paper 11–14.

Tan, M. N. T. (2013). *Corporate governance and banking in China*. New York: Routledge.

Tanaka, K., & Molnar, M. (2008). What is different about informal finance? Financing of private firms in China. *Revue économique*, *59*(6), 1131–1143.

Tanner, M. S. (1999). *The politics of lawmaking in post-Mao China*. Oxford: Clarendon Press.

Tokuchi, T. [德地立人]. (2013). The path towards a world-class investment bank [走向国际一流投行的路径.]. *Caijing Magazine Forecasting and Strategy*, [财经预测与战略*2013*], 80–83.

Tsai, K. S. (2002). *Back-alley banking: Private entrepreneurs in China*. Ithaca, NY: Cornell University Press.

Tsai, K. S. (2009). Beyond banks: The local logic of informal finance and private sector development in China. In J. -J. Li & S. Hsu (Eds.), *Informal finance in China: American and Chinese perspectives* (pp. 80–103). Oxford: Oxford University Press.

Wu, J.-X. [吴稼祥]. (1985). Equitization: Ideas to advance reform [股份化：进一步改革的思路.]. *Economics Daily* [经济日报.], 1985年8月3日第1版.

Yang, G. B. (2014). Internet activism & the party-state in China. *Daedalus*, *143*(2), 110–123.

Yang, L. (2014). *How can China's largest commercial bank grow into a real multinational?* Forbes Asia 2/24/2014. Downloaded on May 30, 2015 at <http://www.forbes.com/sites/linyang/2014/02/24/how-can-chinas-largest-commercial-bank-grow-into-a-real-multinational/>.

Yin, H. -Y., Yang, J. -W., & Mehran, J. (2013). An empirical study of bank efficiency in China after WTO accession. *Global Finance Journal*, *24*, 153–170.

Yu, R. (2013). Filling the gap in Wenzhou's finance market. *China Daily*. Downloaded on February 15, 2015 from <http://europe.chinadaily.com.cn/business/2013-01/24/content_16168791_2.htm>.

Zhang, J. [张捷]. (2002). Relationship lending to small and medium enterprises and the organizational structure of banks [中小企业的关系型借贷与银行组织结构.]. *Economic Research* [经济研究], 6.

Zhang, X.-C., Xu, Z., & Qin, D. [张雪春，　徐忠, & 秦朵]. (2013). The outlet of folk lending interest rates and folk capital: The case of Wenzhou [民间借贷利率与民间资本的出路：温州案例]. *Journal of Financial Research*, *393* [金融研究], 1–14.

Zheng, Y. -N., & Chen, M. -J. (2009). China's state-owned enterprise reform and its discontents. *Problems of Post-Communism*, *56*(2), 36–42.

CHAPTER 9

A New FDI Framework in the Chinese Services Industry

Ivana Beveridge[1], Johannes Kadura[2] and Andreas Stratemeyer[3]
[1]Université Panthéon-Assas Paris 2-Sorbonne Universités, LARGEPA, Paris, France
[2]Peking University, Beijing, China
[3]California State University, Fresno, CA, United States

9.1 INTRODUCTION: CONTEXT CHANGE IN THE CHINESE MARKET

This chapter suggests a new internationalization strategy for transnational entrepreneurs (TEs) in the relatively unexplored Chinese service segment. Our research question was: what is a suitable internationalization strategy for TEs in the Chinese services segment? We acknowledge the context change in the Chinese market, where the service sector is becoming an important driver of the economy, accounting for 48.2% of China's economic output in 2014 (KPMG, 2015). This shift from the traditional manufacturing base creates new opportunities in the Chinese services market, fueled by the growing middle class and the pace of urbanization. Our starting assumption was that this unparalleled shift in the Chinese market requires a paradigm change for crafting successful internationalization strategies.

The rise of Chinese entrepreneurial stars, such as Alibaba Group's founder Jack Ma, has generated keen global interest, portraying China as an emerging entrepreneurial hotspot. China ranks rather high amongst a number of other nations on dimensions such as fear of failures and entrepreneurial intentions (Global Entrepreneurship Monitor, 2010). Furthermore, China's homegrown startups are amongst the most successful in the world: in 2014, Alibaba Group had the largest US IPO ever at $25 billion (Forbes, 2014). Although small and medium-sized enterprises are estimated to account for about 60% of China's industrial output, China's economic success is seldom associated with entrepreneurship (IFC – World Bank, 2012).

The Chinese entrepreneurship has attracted research interest in the recent years; however little has been said about specific opportunities and challenges for a growing number of TEs in China. Although a substantial

The China Business Model. DOI: http://dx.doi.org/10.1016/B978-0-08-100750-1.00009-7

body of academic research focuses on opportunities and challenges for multinational companies in China, the opportunities they present in the entrepreneurial sector remain relatively unexplored. Entrepreneurship is not sufficiently studied in emerging and developing economies—the issue of access to information and social networks requires further attention (Child & Hsieh, 2014).

An aftermath of the global economic crisis coupled with rapid globalization saw the emergence of TEs, as a new breed of entrepreneurs from developed countries starting businesses in developing countries. In the last decade Transnational Entrepreneurship was established as an independent field of study between International Entrepreneurship and Ethnic Entrepreneurship. Today, transnational entrepreneurship is a growing phenomenon, with an increasing number of Western professionals deciding to utilize opportunities in the fast-developing, dynamic emerging markets that offer a large commercial scale and fast return on investment. Owing to their agility and a unique transnational cultural repertoire, TEs may be in a better position to elaborate, adapt, or modify the rules to novel circumstances (Drori, Honig, & Wright, 2009), internationalize directly (Terjesen & Elam, 2009), and use customer service as a key source of their competitive advantage. TEs are especially well-suited to learning and adapting to the specific cultural and economic characteristics of the host country as opposed to multinational corporations. Thereby, TEs with their unique ability to understand and blend in with the local economy might be able to profit from China's shift toward a consumption-based economy and set up successful service businesses in China.

As a result of empirical research on a pool of 200 TEs and 150 service clients, we propose a new internationalization strategy specifically suited for the Chinese services segment. Our Transfer-Adapt-Scale (TAS) framework is tailored toward TEs operating in the fast-growing and a relatively unexplored Chinese service market. We suggest this three-step framework for TEs in order to succeed in the Chinese market and utilize the current economic change, unparalleled in Chinese history. Consequently, TEs must initially identify successful business models in their home countries. Rather than copying these service models, TEs need to adapt them to the specific Chinese market segments. Once TEs have successfully adapted their service business to the Chinese market, the next step is to scale up, in order to take advantage of China's growing middle class as a prospective customer base.

We focus on the adaptation stage of our suggested framework. This is where most TEs' creativity and management skills are needed. Using a Chinese dialectical logic as a departure from prevalent binary models for cultural analysis, we shed light on important cultural parameters that exert strong influence on the adaptation of Western services in the Chinese market.

9.2 THEORETICAL UNDERPINNINGS

TEs are defined as "social actors who enact networks, ideas, information, and practices for purpose of seeking business opportunities or maintaining businesses within dual social fields, which in turn force them to engage in varied strategies of action to promote their entrepreneurial activities" (Drori et al., 2009, p. 1001). They are seen as "social actors capable of bearing risks and taking strategic initiatives to establish, integrate, and sustain foreign operations" (Yeung, 2002, p. 37). TEs are rapidly emerging across the world and they form an important aspect of international business expansion. Academic research on this topic, however, is limited: it lacks rigor and focuses primarily on concept definition rather than empirical studies and applications (Connelly, 2010; Drori, Honig, & Ginsberg, 2006).

Horizontal Foreign Direct Investment (HFDI) has been the most prevalent Foreign Direct Investment (FDI) model; yet, there is also evidence of a surge of vertical Foreign Direct Investment (VFDI) (Hanson, Mataloni, & Slaughter, 2001; Navaretti & Venables, 2004). The OLI paradigm proposed by Dunning (1977) remains one of the prevalent conceptual frameworks for internationalization. This "eclectic paradigm" suggests a three-tiered framework to determine whether FDI is beneficial in a foreign country. It suggests advantages of ownership (comparative advantage of the company seeking to engage in FDI), location (attractiveness of the selected location and whether a company derives greater benefit through a foreign establishment) and internationalization (advantages by own production rather than through partnership) as necessary conditions for successful FDI (Dunning, 1977).

Cultural analysis is essential for crafting successful strategy, considering that socio-cultural values are a major aspect of a firm's environment (Mooij & Hofstede, 2010). The ability to exercise influence in culturally mixed interpersonal networks has a strong impact on global management effectiveness (Fu et al., 2004). Cultural factors are particularly important, given that ethnocentric predisposition and cultural imperialism are amongst the key reasons for failure in a multicultural context (Chaney & Martin, 2010).

The change of values within China are apparent in the last three decades, and they come as a consequence of "*proactively invited collisions* with foreign systems, foreign values, and foreign lifestyles" (Fang, 2011). Although a number of studies have been conducted on Chinese cultural factors exerting influence on international business, there is an apparent over-reliance on a small number of frameworks to interpret Chinese and Western cultural differences, notably Hofstede's (1980) cultural dimensions model. Validity and applicability of this model has been questioned by Chinese and international researchers alike, highlighting its static, binary nature. Very few other categorizations of culture have been applied in cross-cultural research; conflicting findings and inconsistencies appeared in the studies using this approach (Briley & Aaker, 2006; Fang, 2003, 2011, 2014; Faure & Fang, 2008; Heine, Lehman, Kaipeng, & Greenholtz, 2002; Hong & Mallorie, 2004; McSweeney, 2002; Tung & Verbeke, 2010; Zhang, Beatty, & Walsh, 2008).

Chen (2011) suggested that dichotomizing culture is a common problem in academic research. Static, polarized, "either/or" and noncontradictory approaches classifying cultures along a fixed scale provide general methodological advantages for cultural analysis, however they carry a risk of missing diversity within culture (Fang & Faure, 2011). As the market matures in China, it is necessary to move beyond normative assumptions and to recognize that diverse, context-specific factors beyond bipolar dimensions prevail in the process of attitude formation (Chu, Hsu, & Li, 2008). There is a need to extend the existing binary methodology for the analysis of the Chinese cultural values in order to capture the complexity and changes in today's Chinese society (Fang & Faure, 2011).

Confucian philosophy has held a dominant position in the Chinese history and it still exerts great influence on the Chinese business dynamics, forming the framework for business practices today. The concept of "rule by man" was advocated throughout the Chinese history by Confucian scholars, versus the "rule by law" suggested by the followers of the legalist school (Fung, 1966). Jacobs, Gao, and Herbig (1995) point at the historic origin of this concept, revealing the differences from the Western world where a combination of contractual relations used for the serf system, and church support exercised control over behavior and served as a disciplinary mechanism. Ancient China had neither contractual relations nor religion, and it remained without a code of civil law similar to the Roman law, with only the criminal law and imperial decrees (Hendryx, 1986).

9.3 METHODOLOGY

We applied a mixed research methodology. We first collected data using qualitative observations on a group of 200 TEs, currently representing active members of the "China Entrepreneur Net" platform. This Beijing-based nonprofit organization caters to a growing pool of TEs in China. At the time this chapter is written, it has 850 members in China and abroad. Observations were held over a period of the 2 years since its inception in January 2014, with a view of understanding which internationalization strategies are used by successful TEs in the Chinese service sector. This was combined with a quantitative survey of 47 TEs in the Chinese service industry who are also the members of the platform. The survey focused on understanding their main business challenges and factors of success in the Chinese service market. In order to understand specific factors for successful adaptation of the TAS model, we applied an ethnographic research method to study one transnational service startup. Ethnographic research was operationalized through participatory observations held over 18 months on a total population sample of 150 Chinese service customers, and in-depth semi-structured interviews in Chinese with 49 respondents from this group were conducted. We used stratified random sampling in both cases. The advantage of this method is the ability to representatively sample even the smallest and most inaccessible subgroups, inclusive of the rare extremes in the given population. Moreover, it has a high statistical precision, thereby requiring a small sample size that saves time and effort (Särndal, Swensson, & Wretman, 2003).

In order to move beyond the prevalent binary models for cultural analysis, we used the prism of paradox theories previously mentioned as a valuable approach to reveal other possibilities in any theories constructed on clear-cut distinctions (O'Driscoll, 2008; Ybema, 1996). Fang (2011, p. 45) suggested that, although China management research has been a subject of much interested in recent years, "business journals have had the propensity to unquestioningly adopt 'established' Western approaches without penetrating beneath their underlying assumptions." To avoid the traps of using a Western-centric approach to study Chinese service consumers, we applied a dialectical approach to cultural analysis through the inherent Chinese symbolism of *Yin* and *Yang*. Fang (2011, p. 27) also suggests that there is a potential to incorporate *Yin Yang* dialectical thinking in cross-cultural research as "more embracive and holistic in nature than the current cultural models." The *Yin Yang* perspective for understanding cultures is suggested as a valuable prism for cultural analysis because potential paradoxical values coexist in any culture. This approach embraces opposite traits of any cultural dimension, and presents an alternative to the static cultural dimension model (Fang, 2011). The ability to manage paradoxes is proposed as China's most important cultural characteristic. From a Chinese perspective, everything embraces opposite properties; Chinese worldview is essentially "both-and" instead of "either/or" (Fang, 2003).

This dialectical approach to cultural analysis was operationalized through the framework of "eight pairs of paradoxical values" suggested by Faure and Fang (2008): (1) *Guanxi* vs Professionalism; (2) Importance of face vs Self-expression and directness; (3) Thrift vs Materialism and ostentatious consumption; (4) Family and group orientation vs Individuation; (5) Aversion to law vs Respect for legal practices; (6) Respect for etiquette, age and hierarchy vs Respect for simplicity, creativity and competence; (7) Long-term orientation vs Short-term orientation; and (8) Traditional creeds vs Modern approaches.

9.4 DISCUSSION

9.4.1 Transfer-Adapt-Scale Framework

The Chinese society is experiencing an unparalleled change of context, undergoing a transformation from a production-based society to a consumer-and-service society. We suggest that TEs are in a unique position to take advantage of the transformation process in China and use this potential to tap into a vast services market with a substantial, emerging middle class. Today, China has approximately 52% urban population. This is expected to increase to 63% in 2022 when China's middle class could number 630 million, or 76% of urban Chinese households and 45% of the entire population. The upper-middle class currently accounts for 20% of China's urban private consumption and is expected to comprise 56% of urban private consumption by 2022 (McKinsey & Company, 2014). This large consumer group is picking up Western consumption patterns and integrating them within their own cultural milieu.

This societal change is unparalleled in the Chinese history and necessitates a paradigm shift for crafting successful internationalization strategies.

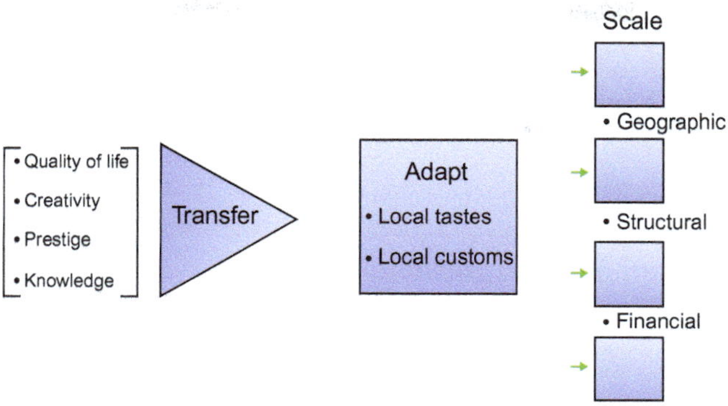

Figure 9.1 Transfer-Adapt-Scale framework.

To that end, we propose a new internalization strategy for TEs in the Chinese services industry visualized in the TAS framework presented in the Fig. 9.1.

TAS is a threefold framework that involves the following steps: a transfer of successful Western service models in the specific industry segments where opportunities for TEs arise from contextual circumstances; their adaptation to suit the local consumption needs and tastes; and scaling up to utilize the commercial scale of the emerging Chinese services market. Our research indicates that there are four main areas of interest for the Chinese service consumer, including: quality of life, creativity, prestige, and knowledge-related services. These are also the services where TEs have a potential to obtain competitive advantage *vis-à-vis* large multinationals. Adaptation involves customizing the service offering to suit the local market needs, including the finding and managing the Chinese partner who becomes a potential buyer if a TE decides to exit by selling to the same partner, or through other types of mergers or acquisitions. Commercial scale could be achieved through organic growth or through partnerships. The scaling process applies relevant to geography, structure and capital, and expansion into second-, third- and fourth-tier cities in China.

TAS is specifically tailored toward the services industry in China. It makes use of context and takes advantage of the transformation process that China is going through. Its approach is market-led, and is based on matching the very specific Chinese market needs to what Western economies have to offer in terms of services. As such, TAS encompasses the market process, allowing TEs to contribute to the current transformation in China. While adjusting to the market conditions, TEs simultaneously have the potential to shape the market and influence its trends. TAS framework considers added benefits of partnerships in certain segments, in order to scale within the Chinese services market—characterized by volume and vast differences between the regions.

Finally, the TAS framework incorporates macro factors by looking at industry-level developments at a regional level. It matches the most prospective industries in a single market to regional developments, as to pave the way for future regional expansion. All of the prospective service areas identified by the TAS framework present strong potential for further development in Asia for the TEs expanding from their China base.

9.4.2 Main Challenges for TEs in the Chinese Service Market

In this section, we demonstrate findings from the quantitative survey of 47 TEs in the Chinese service segment. As shown in the Fig. 9.2, cultural challenges—namely lack of understanding of Chinese cultural values—present the single biggest business issue for 34% of TEs. Partnership issues resulting from cultural challenges emerged as the second biggest issue for TEs in the Chinese service domain (25.5%), therefore showing that 59.5% of business challenges for TEs in this sector have a strong correlation to cultural factors.

As shown in Fig. 9.3, lack of information about the market (23.4%) and unclear procedures (31.9%) jointly account for 55.3% of the main issues regarding doing business in China. We suggest there is a clear correlation between cultural factors and a lack of information about the market and its procedures, as shown in the Fig. 9.2.

Fig. 9.4 shows the most attractive industries for TEs in China, demonstrating the aforementioned change in the maturing service market.

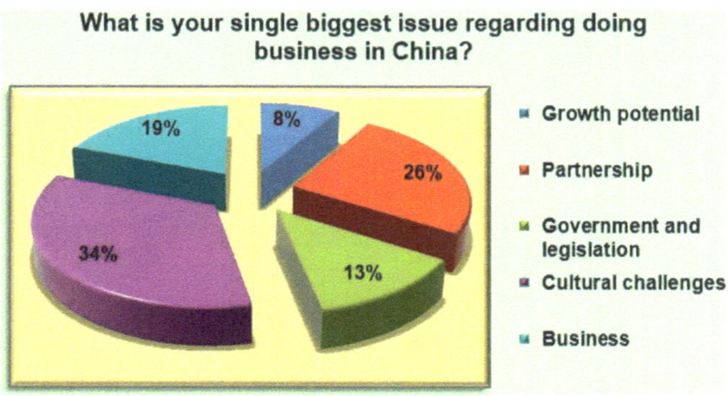

Figure 9.2 Single biggest issue regarding doing business in China.

Consulting takes up 27.7%, leading traditional sectors, such as trade and manufacturing, which jointly represent 25.5%.

Rising interest in private education in China further testifies to the market change. This relatively unexplored segment is ranked as one of the most prospective industries for development over the next 10 years (McKinsey & Company, 2014). Asian students represent 52% of foreign students enrolled worldwide, and they are set to account for 70% of the global demand for international higher education by 2025. The number of Chinese students overseas more than tripled between 2003 and 2013 and 92 % of them are self-funded (ICEF Monitor, 2015). This trend has lead to a rapidly raising demand for undergraduate education across Asia using English to teach academic subjects and life skills to prepare children for studying abroad. English language international schooling has developed

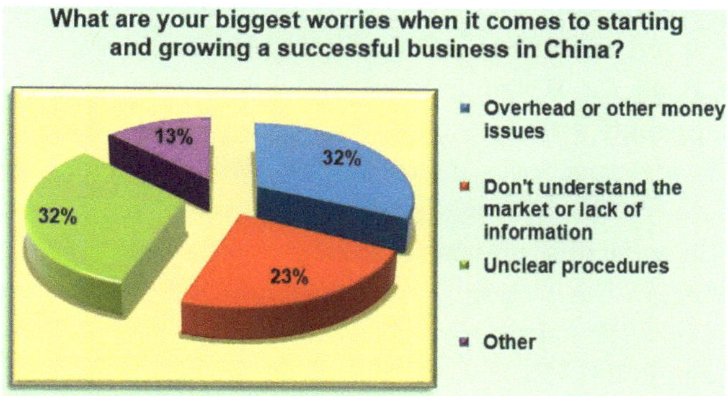

Figure 9.3 Biggest worries when it comes to starting and growing a successful business in China.

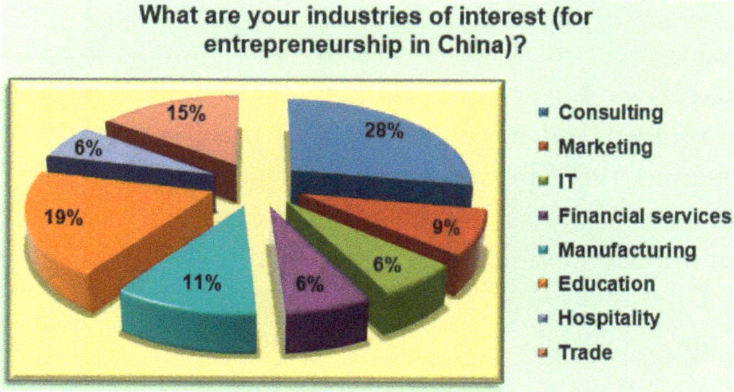

Figure 9.4 Industries of interest (for entrepreneurship in China).

exponentially in the first decade of this century, and the number of students attending English-speaking international schools grew globally by 140% (International School Consultancy Group, 2014). This process is accompanied with the shift from a traditional nonprofit to a for-profit model, the proliferation of private educational companies, and a growing army of "edupreneurs" (Bunnell, 2014). Demand outstrips supply in a counter-cyclical Chinese private education market, offering a substantial commercial scale (Morgan Stanley, 2011). If the potential for international schooling is realized in China, "it is likely to dwarf growth in any other country" (ICEF Monitor, 2014).

9.5 PARAMETERS FOR WESTERN SERVICE ADAPTATION IN CHINA

In many transition countries, firms innovate primarily by adopting existing products and technologies and adapting them to local circumstances (European Bank for Reconstruction and Development, 2014). Thereby, adaptation presents a unique opportunity for TEs to innovate and gain competitive advantage over multinationals. We focused on cultural factors serving as parameters for the adaptation stage of the TAS framework. Likewise, these factors present a source of competitive advantage for TEs in China. In this section, we present findings from the ethnographic research of one TE startup, combined with qualitative observations performed amongst 200 TEs.

Ethnographic research was performed on one successful TE startup in the educational domain. This company manages a full-time preschool and a part-time tutoring school in Beijing, and uses English to teach academic subjects and life skills. It has achieved high market growth (30%) and client retention (over 80%).

All company clients were subjects of observations and interviews as Chinese parents or buyers of education whose children are aged 3–15. They have middle- and upper-middle class income and they were born between the mid-1960s to mid-1980s. This "generation X" received traditional Chinese education and they are now experiencing a very different China from the one in which they were born.

We used the dialectical *Yin Yan* approach to cultural analysis, operationalized through "eight pairs of paradoxical values." Our research has empirically demonstrated that a tendency to reconcile between paradoxical values is the key driver of consumer attitudes in this Chinese services segment. Paradoxes that appear binary from the perspective of Western formal logic are complimentary in the eyes of the Chinese consumers. Thereby, the opposites are not seen as a win-lose proposition or a dilemma as a predicament of choice. Instead of "either/or," the "both-and" (Fang, 2003) approach prevails in their behavior.

This is shown on the example of parental perception of differences between Western and Chinese educational systems. Figs. 9.5 and 9.6 show how respondents perceive differences between the two educational systems. As shown in Fig. 9.5, only 36.7% of the respondents believe that there are essential methodological differences between the two educational systems, while 55.1% consider that there are "some differences." In both cases, Western education is not seen as superior to the Chinese in order to justify high tuition fees charged by the Western learning centers. In particular, preschool fees in first and second Chinese cities are on par with or higher than many prestigious US schools. This indicates that Chinese consumers in this segment are significantly different from their counterparts in other non-Western countries where English language education is considered superior to the national public education. The rising middle class, especially in Asia, is increasingly turning to international schooling as a better alternative to the national education offered in public schools (Hayden & Thompson, 2011).

Conversely, 77.6% of respondents believe that there are essential structural differences between the two educational systems, as shown in Fig. 9.6.

Dialectical prism for cultural analysis enabled us to see the "both-and" cultural trait clearly on this example: structural differences are not seen as an indicator of superiority/inferiority of the Western/Chinese systems.

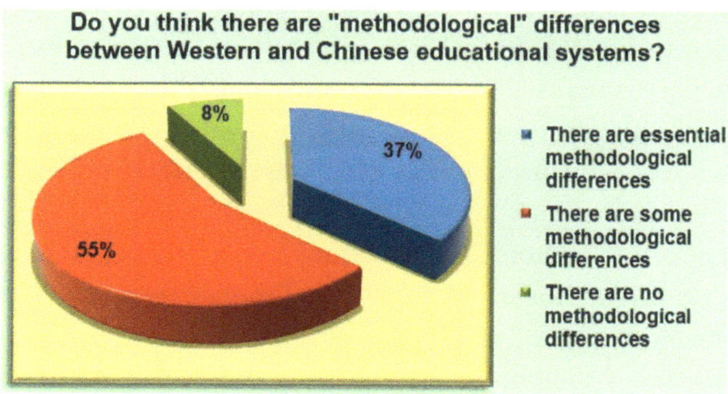

Figure 9.5 Methodological differences between Western and Chinese educational systems.

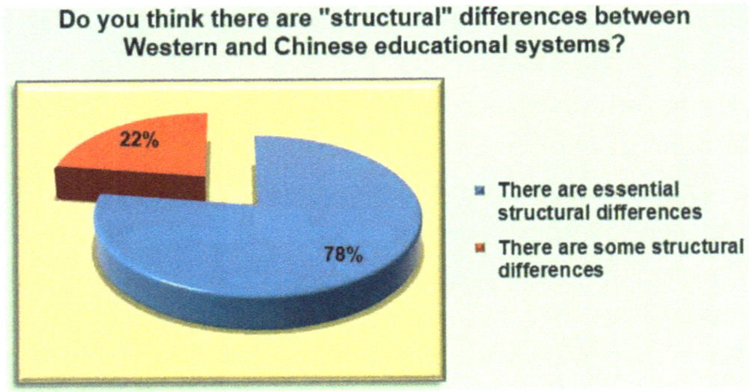

Figure 9.6 Structural differences between Western and Chinese educational systems.

Rather, they are an indication of differences in communication patterns inherent to each system. Communication is thereby seen as a mirror of structural system differences. Western centers are characterized with direct, frequent and nonhierarchical communication. Conversely, in the Chinese system characterized with a high volume of students, communication is obscure, top-down and hierarchical—happening through the middlemen (teaching assistants) who serve as negotiators between parents, children and teachers. Respondents acknowledge the advantages of a hierarchical Chinese family setup that instills flexibility because it enables the children to switch between different contexts, a skill acquired from having to communicate differently with people of different seniority. Simultaneously, they see the advantage of the Western schooling environment, where they spend a substantial amount of their time. Because the Western school setup is independent from the hierarchical, societal, and family webs, it enables them to experience new forms of communication not otherwise available in the traditional family or in the public schools.

As shown in Fig. 9.7, for 59.2% of the respondents, in-person communication, (i.e., personal selling) was the only marketing tactics used in the process of school selection. The remaining 40.8%, who used advertising (26.5%) and social media (14.3%), used these channels only in combination with personal selling.

We suggest that a choice of marketing tactics is an expression of paradoxical value orientations. Although paradox management is inherent to this consumer group, they seek personalized guidance through this process and this influences the choice of marketing tactics. Because the nature of communication with Western service providers is used as a benchmark of differences between the two systems, communication has a strategic role

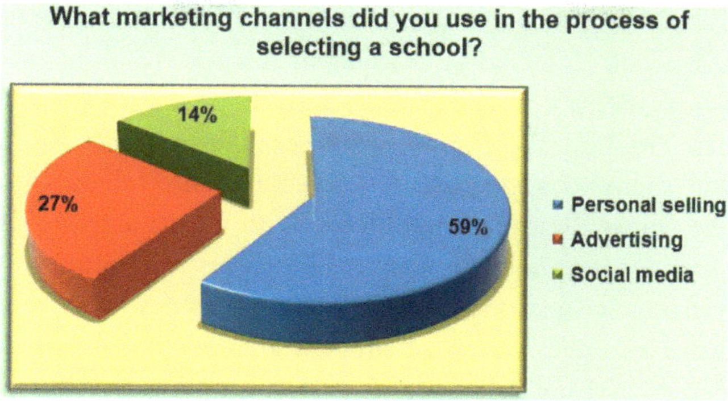

Figure 9.7 Marketing channels used in the process of selecting a school.

in the client management process. Communications based on the ability to understand the paradoxical nature of values serves as a source of competitive advantage.

Beyond exerting influence on marketing tactics, paradoxical value orientations call for a change in organizational structure, role allocation and class scheduling. Our ethnographic case revealed that client communication functions are built into every organizational role, rather than having fully dedicated marketing roles. This implies bridging the traditional divide between faculty and administrative staff. Because faculty need to perform marketing roles, scheduling becomes increasingly complex—considering that in-person time with clients and prospects needs to be built in between the classes on an ongoing basis.

9.5.1 Contradictory Values

In this section, we demonstrate the presence of contradictory value pairs. We focus on three out of eight pairs of paradoxical values used as the conceptual framework for our research: Traditional creeds vs Modern approaches; Aversion to law vs Respect for legal practices; and *Guanxi* vs Professionalism.

Paradox management process related to "Traditional creeds vs Modern approaches" is particularly apparent in services with high credence characteristics. These services promote many of the apparently "irrational" reactions toward uncertainty (Kahneman, Slovic, & Tversky, 1982). This was clearly demonstrated in the example of education. In line with the Confucian tradition, the majority of Chinese parents believe that every child could excel academically if they studied hard: almost everyone is capable of improving through education and only the most intelligent and the most stupid do not change (*Confucian Analects*, 1893, 17, p. 3). While parents wish to identify unique talents and design a personalized learning path for their children, the pressure to succeed in multiple academic areas is prompting them to augment the Chinese public education with private tutoring across all academic subjects. With China actively stepping on the global scene, a new societal ideal encompasses the notion of "bringing up global citizens with strong Chinese roots." This desire is prompting the parents toward a large amount of supplementary classes in Western educational centers in English language, in addition to tutoring in Chinese. The range of options between traditional creeds and modern approaches results in a process of endless tradeoffs between a belief that each child can succeed in multiple academic areas owing to hard work, and a desire to identify their unique talents and strengths. This is reflected in the following statement by one of the respondents: "We may not attribute success to supplementary Western education but we are very likely to blame ourselves for not doing so if the children don't succeed academically and in life."

The education system in China is hierarchical and defined by test performance (Huang & Gove, 2012). While the majority of respondents acknowledge that a university degree matters, most believe that passing the *gaokao* (高考), the college entry exam, is no longer a prerequisite for academic and professional success. Yet, equally, a belief in the efficiency and the ultimate authority of the strict Chinese testing system remains a strong driver of behavior. In the Western centers, however, they are introduced to new, personalized approaches to learning. New learning methods hold a promise of installing new skills otherwise missing in the Chinese public system. In order to determine the effectiveness of new programs the parents still often revert to familiar indicators derived from the Chinese traditional education. As indicated by one respondent: "Our Chinese system does not divide the children according to IQ, but instead into 'children that obey' and 'children that don't'. But this (Western) is a different system. Pushing them harder does not work since they are not working to pass a test, and then another test. Yet still, we need to know how many new words they learned at any point or how many pages they need to cover for each homework."

"Aversion to law vs Respect for legal practices" presents one of the most challenging aspects of service adaptation in China for TEs. The "rule of man" profoundly affects interactions in China, and relational ethics as a management tool prevails over the "rule of law." Interpersonal relationships are the ultimate point of reference for problem solving, rather than contracts. Contracts merely serve as a starting point for relationship building; when there is a conflict, a humanistic approach wins over the legalistic one.

Our observations indicated that management of service contracts presents a major hurdle for cash-strapped TEs. The cash flow predictions in a retained service business are based on an estimated flow of service fees, such as regular tuition fees in the education segment, which should be relatively easy to predict, due to nature of education as a service. Despite this, relationship development between clients and the service providers often results in renegotiation of the service terms, and this greatly increases the complexity of client management process. In practice, this implies that substantial concessions and discounts are expected as a prerequisite for client retention. Moreover, it has a strong impact on client acquisition in service domains where word-of-mouth has a prominent role, such as our ethnographic case where 69.4% of the respondents used friend referrals as the sole method for selecting the school; similarly, 65.3% would not select a school that has not been recommended to them by their peer groups. This tendency to mitigate the two opposing values requires a fair amount of flexibility to ensure the financial health of the business on one side, whilst ensuring client retention on the other. In particular, one of the biggest challenges for TEs is billing for services (i.e., professional time) provided as part of relationship building outside of the service scope as such. Although clients understand the terms of service contracts, the time invested in relationship building is not seen as "professional time," and therefore can't be billed.

The rule of man is strongly related to the value pair of "*Guanxi* vs Professionalism." We established that a majority of TEs find the client ability to balance between *guanxi* (relationships) and professionalism extremely challenging. The main challenge lies in their lack of ability to understand the contexts in which *guanxi* is favored over professionalism (and vice versa). The interplay between these two values has a particularly strong impact on service dynamics and affects all aspects of client management. The tendency to revert from professionalism to *guanxi* and back exerts a strong influence across all stages of client management, including both acquisition and retention, in B2B as well as B2C domains. Although clients expect service quality and thereby seek to select (and stay with) the service providers based on their track record and their ability to deliver, they simultaneously revert to *guanxi*-based interactions throughout the service process. This is also one of the main reasons why Chinese service clients require a substantial amount of in-person time which is hard to bill.

9.5.2 Dialectical Approach to Communication With the Chinese Service Clients

Our research suggests that communication with the Chinese service clients is at the core of the aforementioned challenges and it suggests the benefits of paradox theory to interpret the nature of communication in China. Academic research on Chinese communication has, thus far, focused primarily on understanding the impact of traditional Confucian cultural values. While their influence remains powerful and exerts strong influence on communication between Chinese and Westerners, the paradox inherent in the Chinese culture and communication has rarely been researched (Fang & Faure, 2011). Dialectical prism for cultural analysis reveals that communication in China reflects the co-existence of two opposite but complementary forces of *Yin and Yang* (Chen, 2008, 2009; Fang & Faure, 2011). As such, communication is an evolving, nonlinear process (Chen & Starosta, 2003). At the core of this process is the notion of "harmony" as a symbol that provides the Chinese people with cognitive and affective orientations (Chen, 2011). Harmony is interpreted as a process rather than a destination, and it is achieved through the endless dialectical interaction of the opposing forces of *Yin and Yang*. Harmony, however is also the main goal of communication and a measure of communication competence (Chen, 2011; Chen & An, 2009).

Our ethnographic case has shown that communication is an indicator of differences between the Chinese and the Western educational systems for the Chinese clients. As such, it also presents one of the main benchmarks for gauging the service value. While the clients expect results in terms of their children's performance, they have very limited points of reference to gauge the value of credence service, in particular because the new mode of education is not geared toward testing.

We suggest that research of communication with the Chinese service clients from the standpoint of paradox theory and dialectical logic presents an interesting area for further research. A better understanding of contexts in which one of the contradictory values wins over the other would help decrease complexities in client management. In the service segments identified by the TAS framework, it is safe to assume that many service consumers have limited points of reference from their prior experience, therefore, are likely to use communication as an important benchmark of service quality. Communications based on the understanding of contradictory values and the contexts in which they arise could become a source of competitive advantage.

9.6 CONCLUSIONS

The current transformation of China from production to a consumer-and-service society is unparalleled in its history. This change of context necessitates a paradigm shift for devising successful internationalization strategies. Considering that startups in the emerging industry segments face different challenges than established companies in mature segments, our research has enabled us to shed light on issues that otherwise may not be pertinent, or apparent, to large multinationals in China. Our findings suggest that a growing number of successful entrepreneurs in China follow the TAS framework. This approach to internationalization allows the TEs to become a part of the transformation process China is currently experiencing and assume a proactive role in this process. Adaptation stage of Western services in China presents a particular challenge for TEs, however it simultaneously offers most opportunities for innovation and for achieving competitive advantage over large multinationals.

This chapter contributes to transnational entrepreneurship research in a number of ways: It suggests a new internationalization model to meet the emerging needs of TEs operating in the Chinese services industry, taking into consideration contextual and specific cultural factors affecting service adaptation. TAS framework is specifically tailored toward entrepreneurship, rather than being a customized framework designed for large multinationals.

Our research demonstrated that "eight pairs of paradoxical values" framework could be applied in the service segment in China toward gaining a better understanding of cultural factors that drive service adaptation. A dynamic startup environment provided a good opportunity to apply this framework as an alternative to prevalent binary approaches to cultural analysis. To our knowledge, no other empirical studies applying this framework have been conducted in China to date. Application of this framework has helped identify new factors of success for TEs in the Chinese services market. These findings suggest that understanding the nature of contexts in which one of the opposing values prevails relative to the other decreases the complexity of service management. We reveal the elements that could be used as a source of TEs competitive advantage over large multinationals, such as communication.

Fang (2011, p. 46) suggested that although Chinese management research has attracted increasing interest in the recent years, in many cases, however, China has been used as a "venue for collecting empirical data to blindly please 'established' Western models, without seeing China as an important source of inspiration for theory building and theory rebuilding". This chapter contributes to the body of research that acknowledges the value of applying ingenious Chinese frameworks to understand China's rising role in the international business domain. Future research using this dialectical approach is encouraged in other markets, considering that all cultures have the same potential and, despite the different expressions of their dynamics, similar paradoxical propensities.

REFERENCES

Briley, A. D., & Aaker, J. L. (2006). When does culture matter? Effects of personal knowledge on the correction of culture-based judgments. *Journal of Marketing Research*, *43*, 395–408.

Bunnell, T. (2014). *The changing landscape of international schooling: Implications for theory and practice*. Abingdon: Routledge.

Chaney, L. H., & Martin, J. S. (2010). *Intercultural business communication*. New Jersey: Prentice Hall.

Chen, G. M. (2008). Bian (change): A perpetual discourse of I Ching. *Intercultural Communication Studies*, *17*(4), 7–16.

Chen, G. M. (2009). Beyond the dichotomy of communication studies. *Journal of Asian Communication*, *19*(4), 398–411.

Chen, G. M. (2011). An introduction to key concepts in understanding the Chinese: Harmony as the foundation of Chinese communication. *China Media Research*, *7*(4), 1–12.

Chen, G. M., & An, R. (2009). A Chinese model of intercultural leadership competence. In D. K. Deardorff (Ed.), *The SAGE handbook of intercultural competence* (pp. 196–208). Thousand Oaks, CA: Sage.

Chen, G. M., & Starosta, W. J. (2003). Asian approaches to human communication: A dialogue. *Intercultural Communication Studies*, *12*(4), 1–15.

Child, J., & Linda, Hsieh (2014). Decision mode, information and network attachment in the internationalization of SMEs: A configurational and contingency analysis. *Journal of World Business*, *49*(4), 598–610.

Chu, G., Hsu, M., & Li, S. (2008). *Perceptions of integrated marketing communications among advertising agencies executives in China*. <http://www.racombooks.com/ijimc/index.php?option=com_content&view=article&id=19:perceptions-of-integrated-marketing-communications-among-advertising-agencies-executives-in-china-&catid=2:fall-2009&Itemid=9>. Accessed 25.12. 15.

Confucian Analects. (1893). Translated by James Legge, Oxford: Clarendon Press.

Connelly, B. L. (2010). Transnational entrepreneurs, worldchanging entrepreneurs, and ambassadors: A typology of the new breed of expatriates. *International Entrepreneurship and Management Journal*, *6*(1), 39–53.

Drori, I., Honig, B., & Ginsberg, A. (2006). *Transnational entrepreneurship: Toward a unifying theoretical framework* (Vol. 1). Atlanta, GA: Academy of Management, Best Papers Proceedings.Q1–Q6.

Drori, I., Honig, B., & Wright, M. (2009). Transnational entrepreneurship: An emergent field of study. *Entrepreneurship Theory and Practice*, *33*(5), 1001–1022.

Dunning, J. H. (1977). Trade, location of economic activity and the MNE: A search for an eclectic approach. In B. Ohlin, P. O. Hesselborn, & P. M. Wijkman (Eds.), *The international allocation of economic activity* (pp. 395–418). London and Basingstoke: Macmillan.

European Bank for Reconstruction and Development. (2014). *Transition report 2014, Innovation in transition*. <http://2014.tr-ebrd.com>. Accessed 28.12. 15.

Fang, T. (2003). A critique of Hofstede's fifth national culture dimension. *International Journal of Cross Cultural Management*, *3*(3), 347–368.

Fang, T. (2011). Yin Yang: A new perspective on culture. *Management and Organization Review*, *8*(1), 25–50.

Fang, T. (2014). Understanding Chinese culture and communication: The Yin Yang approach. In B. Gehrke & M. C. Claes (Eds.), *Global leadership practices* (pp. 171–187). London: Palgrave Macmillan.

Fang, T., & Faure, G. O. (2011). Chinese communication characteristics: A Yin Yang perspective. *International Journal of Intercultural Relations*, *35*, 320–333.

Faure, G. O., & Fang, T. (2008). Changing Chinese values: Keeping up with paradoxes. *International Business Review*, *17*(2), 194–207.

Forbes. (2014). *Alibaba claims title for largest Global IPO ever with extra share sales*. <http://www.forbes.com/sites/ryanmac/2014/09/22/alibaba-claims-title-for-largest-global-ipo-ever-with-extra-share-sales/>. Accessed 05.01. 16.

Fu, P. P., Kennedy, J., Tata, J., Yukl, G., Bond, M. H., Peng, T., et al. (2004). The impact of societal cultural values and individual social beliefs on the perceived effectiveness of managerial influence strategies a Meso approach. *Journal of International Business Studies*, *35*(4), 284–305.

Fung, Y. -L. (1966). *A short history of Chinese philosophy*. New York, NY: The Free Press.

Global Entrepreneurship Monitor Report. (2010). <http://www.babson.edu/Academics/centers/blank-center/global-research/gem/Documents/GEM%202013%20Global%20Report.pdf>. Accessed 05.01.16.

Hanson, G., Mataloni, R., & Slaughter, M. (2001). *Expansion strategies of the U.S. multinational firms*. NBER Working Paper No. 8433. Cambridge, MA: National Bureau of Economic Research. <http://www.nber.org/papers/w8433.pdf>. Accessed 07.01.16.

Hayden, M., & Thompson, J. (2011). *Teachers for the international school of the future. Schooling internationally: Globalisation, internationalisation and the future for international schools*. London: Routledge.83–100.

Heine, S. J., Lehman, D. R., Kaipeng, P., & Greenholtz, J. (2002). What's wrong with cross-cultural comparisons of subjective likert scales? The reference-group problem. *Journal of Personality and Social Psychology*, *82*(6), 903–918.

Hendryx, S. (1986). The Chinese trade: Making the deal work. *Harvard Business Review*, *July–August*, 78–84.

Hofstede, G. H. (1980). *Culture's consequences: International differences in work-related values*. Beverly Hills, CA: Sage.

Hong, Y., & Mallorie, L. M. (2004). A dynamic constructivist approach to culture: Lessons learned from personality psychology. *Journal of Research in Personality*, *38*, 59–67.

Huang, G., & Gove, M. (2012). Confucianism and Chinese families: Values and practices in education. *International Journal of Humanities and Social Science*, *2*(3).

ICEF Monitor. (2014). *New data on international schools suggests continued strong growth*. <http://monitor.icef.com/2014/03/new-data-on-international-schools-suggests-continued-strong-growth-2/>. Accessed 10.11.15.

ICEF Monitor. (2015). *Number of Chinese outbound students up by 11% in 2014*. <http://monitor.icef.com/2015/03/number-of-chinese-outbound-students-up-by-11-in-2014/>. Accessed 10.12.15.

IFC, International Finance Corporation, World Bank Group. (2012). *Study on the potential of sustainable energy financing for small and medium enterprises in China*. <http://www.ifc.org/wps/wcm/connect/39ecf5004ff94de2acc8ff23ff966f85/China+SME+Report+for+web.pdf?MOD=AJPERES>. Accessed 26.11.15.

International School Consultancy Group. (2014). In World Education news and reports (2014). *The Booming International Schools Sector*. <http://wenr.wes.org/2014/07/the-booming-international-schools-sector/>. Accessed 12.12.15.

Jacobs, L., Gao, G. P., & Herbig, P. (1995). Confucian roots in China: A force for today's business. *Management Decision*, *33*(10), 29–34.

Kahneman, D., Slovic, P., & Tversky, A. (1982). *Judgment under uncertainty: Heuristics and biases*. Cambridge: Cambridge University Press.

KPMG. (2015). *China outlook*. <http://www.kpmg.com/ES/es/Internacionalizacion-KPMG/Documents/China-Outlook-2015.pdf>. Accessed 12.15.15.

McKinsey and Company. (2014). *A pocket guide to doing business in China*. <http://www.mckinsey.com/insights/strategy/a_pocket_guide_to_doing_business_in_china>. Accessed 10.12.15.

McSweeney, B. (2002). Hofstede's model of national cultural differences and their consequences: A triumph of faith—A failure of analysis. *Human Relations*, *55*(1), 89–118.

Mooij, M., & Hofstede, G. (2010). The Hofstede model applications to global branding and advertising strategy and research. *International Journal of Advertising*, *29*, 85–110.

Morgan Stanley. (2011). *China education services. Buying leaders in a defensive*. <http://www.morganstanleychina.com/conferences/apsummit2011/research/47ChinaEducationBuyingLeaders.pdf>. Accessed 15.12.15.

Navaretti, G. B., & Venables, A. J. (2004). *Multinational firms in the world economy*. Princeton, NJ: Princeton University Press.

O'Driscoll, A. (2008). Exploring paradox in marketing. *Journal of Business and Industrial Marketing*, *23*(2), 95–104.

Särndal, C., Swensson, B., & Wretman, J. (2003). *Stratified sampling: Model assisted survey sampling*. New York, NY: Springer.

Terjesen, S., & Elam, A. (2009). Transnational entrepreneurs' venture internationalization strategies: A practice theory approach. *Entrepreneurship Theory and Practice*, *33*(5), 1093–1120.

Tung, R. L., & Verbeke, A. (2010). Beyond Hofstede and GLOBE: Improving the quality of cross-cultural research. *Journal of International Business Studies*, *41*(8), 1259–1274.

Ybema, S. (1996). A duck-billed platypus in the theory and analysis of organizations: Combinations of consensus and dissensus. In W. Koot, I. Sabelis, & S. Ybema (Eds.), *Contradictions in context: Puzzling over paradoxes in contemporary organizations* (pp. 39–61). Amsterdam: VU University Press.

Yeung, H. W. (2002). Entrepreneurship in international business: An institutional perspective. *Asia Pacific Journal of Management*, *19*, 29–61.

Zhang, J., Beatty, S. E., & Walsh, G. (2008). Review and future directions of cross-cultural consumer services research. *Journal of Business Research*, *61*, 211–224.

CHAPTER 10

China versus India: Emerging Giants in the World Economy

Nirjhar Nigam
ICN Business School, Metz, France

The key issue is the shift of the centre of gravity from the West to the East, the rise of China and India.

Klaus Martin Schwab (German Economist)

10.1 INTRODUCTION

The dawn of the 21st century witnessed a spectacular uprising of China and India as global market leaders. The effects of this phenomenon reverberated across the entire global economy and brought about a shift in the products markets, patterns of buying and selling, investment strategies, as well as natural resources and the environment (Winters & Yusuf, 2007). India and China have become epicenters of world economy due to their unprecedented economic growth, spanning across three decades. China has consistently registered high growth rates since 1980, whereas India has ranked amongst the top 10 fastest growing nations between 1980–1990 and 1990–2000 (Izurieta & Singh, 2008). This unparalleled economic success is popularly attributed to, largely, the integration of these countries into the global economy (Ahluwalia, 2002; Chow, 2007; Mahtaney, 2007; Nolan, 2004; Rodrik & Subramanian, 2005). Without a doubt, both India and China are economies which hold great promise of becoming titans in the global economic panorama.

China became the leading manufacturing factory for the World while India has positioned itself as a major outsourcing and Information Technology hub for multinationals. Their emergence on the global economic stage has become the subject of discussion in developed nations, amongst policy makers and academics, within international media, and the general public.

China and India, as economies, are carved out of strong fundamentals and are pillared upon a plethora of well-established corporate

The China Business Model. DOI: http://dx.doi.org/10.1016/B978-0-08-100750-1.00010-3

giants within the global corporate landscape. According to the Global Competitiveness Report (2015–2016) covering 140 countries, India is ranked at 55th position while China holds the 28th position. These two countries have achieved high rankings in key parameters like Market Size (3rd rank for India and 1st for China), Innovation (42nd rank for India and 31st rank for China), and sound financial market development (53rd rank for India and 54th rank for China), despite the fact that corruption and efficiency of legal system remain a cause of concern for both the countries.

The Indian economic view, fueled by a plethora of steady reforms since 1991, has started reflecting strong growth patterns and integration into the global economy. A noteworthy example is the financial sector reforms—prompting a complete overhaul in the Indian Banking Sector and enabling an easy market-entry for private entities and foreign banks. Today, the National Stock Exchange (NSE) is the 12th largest stock exchange in the world per number of transactions, while Bombay Stock Exchange (BSE) is ranked 11th by market capitalization. China's role in the global economy, however, is much greater than India's. Since 1978, China's expansion has arguably already been the largest growth spurt ever experienced by the world economy. There are two main stock exchanges in mainland China: the Shanghai Stock Exchange (SHSE) and the Shenzhen Stock Exchange (SZSE). Shanghai Stock Exchange (SHSE) holds the fifth position as measured by market capitalization whereas Shenzhen Stock Exchange (SZSE) is ranked eighth, worldwide.

With unprecedented growth rates, rising foreign direct investment (FDI), and enormous population growth, people are curious to know where these nations are headed to. Will China and India emerge as superpowers and dominate the world economy? How are they currently positioned in terms of global economic growth? What is their predicted growth chart? Can India and China leverage their enormous demographic dividends? How has this impacted the rest of the world? Our objective is to seek answers to such questions in this chapter.

In this chapter, we provide a comparative study between China and India, relevant to their current global economic standing and future prospects regarding demographics, economic growth, investment climate, global competitiveness, ease of doing business, and environmental performance. We provide current statistics and future projections for each country related to its demographic and economic growth. We provide the ranking of both countries pertaining to their global competitiveness, ease of doing business, and environmental performance. For this purpose, we rely primarily on secondary data sources from credible International organizations such as: United Nations, World Bank Data, International Monetary Fund, the World Factbook of Central Intelligence Agency, World Economic Forum, United Nations Conference on Trade and Development (UNCTAD), and Yale Center for Environmental Law & Policy (YCELP) and national sources such as: Reserve Bank of India (RBI) and National Bureau of Statistics of China.

Our study can help familiarize people with the investment and business nuances prevalent in India and China, and develop basic foundations required for investing in these countries or initiating business opportunity. It can also help the policy makers and academics review the prevailing conditions and develop reforms in order to carve out better future for these countries, their people, and for the global economy.

10.2 DEMOGRAPHICS[1]

As of 2015, China has the highest population—with over 1.4 billion inhabitants, while India is ranked second with an estimated figure of 1.3 billion people. Together, this amounts to 37% of the total world population. Recent projections indicate that India's population is likely to surpass China's population by 2022, with its recorded population growth rate of 1.22% and fertility rate of 2.48 children per woman. On the contrary, China's population growth rate was 0.45% and fertility rate was 1.6 children per woman. It is also estimated that India's population will grow to 1.5 billion by 2030 and 1.7 billion by 2050. In contrast, China's population is expected to remain fairly constant until 2030 and decrease slightly thereafter. Fig. 10.1 shows these population trends and forecasts for both countries.

Further, China's "One Child Policy," implemented in 1979, has caused a continuous decline in the ratio of employable population (15–64 years) to the total population. As a result, China's employable population will start declining sharply between 2020 and 2030, as shown in the Fig. 10.2. It is expected that India will surpass China, in working age population by the year 2030, while India continues to witness an upsurge in employable

[1]The statistics related to population come from United Nations Department of Economic and Social Affairs (2015) http://esa.un.org/unpd/wpp/Publications/Files/WPP2015_Volume-II-Demographic-Profiles.pdf.

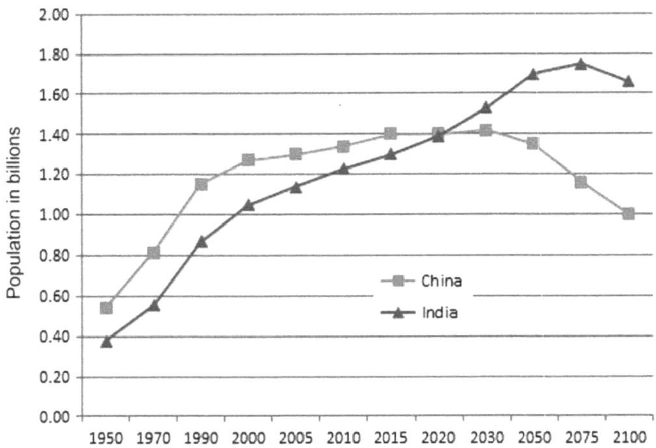

Figure 10.1 Population trend and forecast for India and China (1950–2100). *United Nations, Department of Economic and Social Affairs, Population Division. (2015). World population prospects: The 2015 revision. New York: United Nations.*

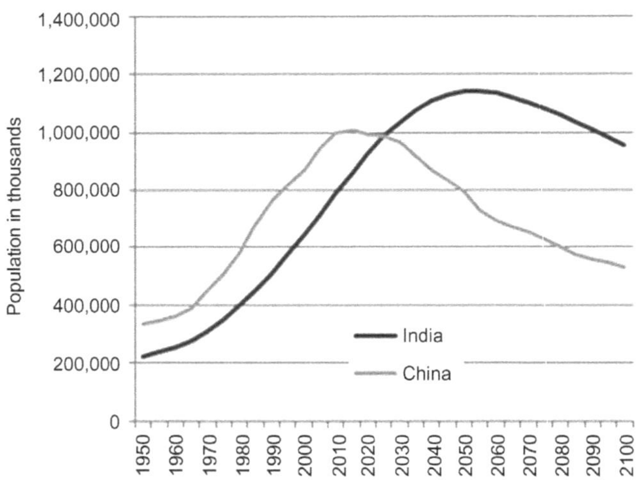

Figure 10.2 Comparison of working age (15–64) population for India and China 1950–2100. *United Nations, Department of Economic and Social Affairs, Population Division. (2015). World population prospects: The 2015 revision. New York: United Nations.*

workforce owing to higher population growth and higher fertility rate. According to United Nations projections, advanced economies' working age population will also shrink by almost 5% by 2050. Thus, India could leverage its demographic dividends and accelerate its economic growth. India has to bear in mind, however, that a large population can serve as an effective labor force and foster economic development only if properly educated, trained, and provided a healthy environment in which to flourish. Otherwise it can prove detrimental to the country's economic growth. It currently remains to be seen whether India can benefit from its large working age population or not, and to what extent.

10.3 WHICH COUNTRY WILL BENEFIT FROM ITS LARGE EMPLOYABLE POPULATION?

Chinese economy previously grew at an unprecedented growth rate, leveraging its demographic dividend, but this trend can soon change owing to China's one child policy and, for the first time in decades, its working population saw a decline in 2012. Furthermore, World Bank reports indicate that China might witness a further decrease of more than 10% in its working age population by 2040, despite relaxation measures of its one child policy. This could equate to a net loss of 90 million workers and can have significant negative impact on its economic growth and generate a slowdown. On the other hand, India is poised to benefit from its growing and young workforce in the coming years as economists agree that having a large and growing workforce at a time when many other large economies are dealing with ageing populations brings about a demographic dividend. In 2015, the mean age in India was recorded to be 27.3 years as compared to 36.8 years in China. The United Nations study of global population trends, predicts entry of 150 million Indians to the global workforce by 2030. Thus, in future India can greatly benefit from its young population if properly educated and trained.

Social elements such as health, education, and technical skills also play a vital role in shaping a country's young population and directing them toward economic progress. These become even more important for densely populated countries like India and China. Let us see this with the help of data.

According to the Global Competitiveness Reports (2014–2015, 2015–2016) which ranks 144 and 140 countries, respectively on higher education and technical skills, India climbed up from 98th position to 84th, while China moved up from 56th rank to 44th rank. In 2015, India ranked 90th and China ranked 68th in the health and primary education category (see Table 10.1). It is clear that China is leading when it comes to social infrastructure relevant to health and education. Although India has shown some signs of improvement in 2015–16, it is still far behind China on such a scale.

Table 10.1 Performance of India and China in social infrastructure

Parameters	India			China		
	Rank in 2015	Rank in 2014	Change in rank	Rank in 2015	Rank in 2014	Change in rank
Health and primary education	84	98	+14	44	56	+12
Higher education and training	90	93	+3	68	65	−3

Source: World Economic Forum. (2014–2015). *The Global Competitiveness Report 2014–2015*. Geneva: World Economic Forum; World Economic Forum. (2015–2016). *The Global Competitiveness Report 2015–2016*. Geneva: World Economic Forum. http://reports.weforum.org/global-competitiveness-report-2014-2015/economies/#economy, http://reports.weforum.org/global-competitiveness-report-2015-2016/economies/#economy.

Additionally, in 2015 the literacy rate in India was 71.2% and 96.4% in China. The lower literacy rate can also be a distinguishing factor for the slow economic growth in India. Another factor for consideration is the unemployment rate which, in 2014, was 4.1% in China compared to 7.3% in India. This reflects China's ability to create more jobs for its growing population in contrast to India's. Experts have also suggested that if India is to make progress, there needs to be a shift in its economic policies favoring a high-quality educational system easily accessible to all, and creation of enough jobs for its employable population in order to reap the benefits of demographic dividends. How India improves upon these critical factors to increase its economic growth will be interesting to observe.

10.4 WHAT ABOUT ADVANCED ECONOMIES AND REST OF THE WORLD?

Alarmingly, within the next 40 years, most of the developed countries in East Asia and Europe will have one-third of their population over 65 years of age. According to an OECD report (2015), the world is ageing at an alarming rate. This was further verified by the current statistics published by United Nations wherein 12% of the global population or 901 million people are over age 60, and this number is expected to grow at a rate of 3.26% per year. In 2015, three countries—Germany (21%), Italy (22%), and Japan (26%)—are termed as super-aged societies. In the next 5 years, Bulgaria, Finland, Greece, and Portugal are expected to join them, and in the next decade, Austria, France, Sweden, United Kingdom,

Canada, Cuba, and South Korea are also predicted to join this list. The number of people in the world aged 60 years and above is projected to reach 1.4 billion by 2030 and 2.1 billion by 2050, possibly rising to 3.2 billion by 2100. On average, nearly one-fourth of the population in every major area of the world, except Africa, will be 60 years of age or more by 2050. Furthermore, the diminishing income gap between developed- and emerging nations will decrease immigration flows and shrinkage of workforce in the Eurozone by 20% and 15% in the United States. This shrinking workforce, as a result of ageing, will slow down annual economic growth from an average of 3.6%, in the next 10 years, to ~2.4% in 2050–60. The World must deal with the problem of ageing and its diminutive effects on economic growth.

A few notable consequences to consider are: (1) increased burden on a country's social security system when more people are claiming pension benefits, and lesser people working and paying taxes, (2) increased Government spending on health care and pensions, and (3) because of the shrinkage of workforce due to ageing, employed people may have to pay higher taxes to support the balance in social infrastructure. This is a definite challenge for Governments and policy makers worldwide and needs deep consideration.

According to the World Population Prospects Report by United Nations (2015), the period of 2015–50 will witness nine countries as the main contributors of half of the world's population growth: India, Nigeria, Pakistan, Democratic Republic of the Congo, Ethiopia, United Republic of Tanzania, United States of America, Indonesia, and Uganda. These countries are ordered in this list according to their contributions to the population, from highest to lowest, India will continue enjoying a dynamic and young workforce, but, will it be able to deliver and help anchor the global economy into stability? To answer this question, we need to understand the Indian business and economic context and Sections 10.5 and 10.6 are devoted to this quest.

10.5 ECONOMIC GROWTH

In terms of global economic contributions, it is clear that India and China have established themselves as new epicenters of world growth, registering average growth rates of 8% and 10% respectively in the recent past. The aftermath of the 2008–09 global financial crisis caused fluctuations across the world economy. Despite this, these two countries continue to sustain consistent growth rates. This has attracted the attention of global investors and global institutions alike. In Section 10.6, we analyze the historical events leading to these phenomenal high growth rates.

The 1990s marked a decade of beneficial reforms for the Indian economy, with the inception of policies toward economic liberalization and globalization by the Government of India. Many regulations and restrictions were also withdrawn, making the economy more market-oriented, and private and foreign investment much easier. By 2007, India consequently developed into a trillion-dollar economy (according to exchange rate) and in 2014, India was ranked as the ninth largest economy per nominal GDP, and third largest in purchasing power parity (PPP).

Meanwhile, in China, Deng Xiaoping reformed the Chinese economy in 1978 by moving away from a centrally planned framework and incorporating capitalist structures and policies. This boosted the Chinese economy with such fervor that the resulting growth has spanned across the last 35 years. An annual growth rate of 10.12% in GDP from 1983 to 2013 has earned China the title of the world's second largest economy according to nominal GDP. China surpassed the $1 trillion mark in 1998 and secured the first rank of PPP in 2014.

Recent data, as shown in the Fig. 10.3, suggests, however, that India would overtake China in its growth rate and this trend has already commenced. India is expected to benefit from recent policy reforms and the

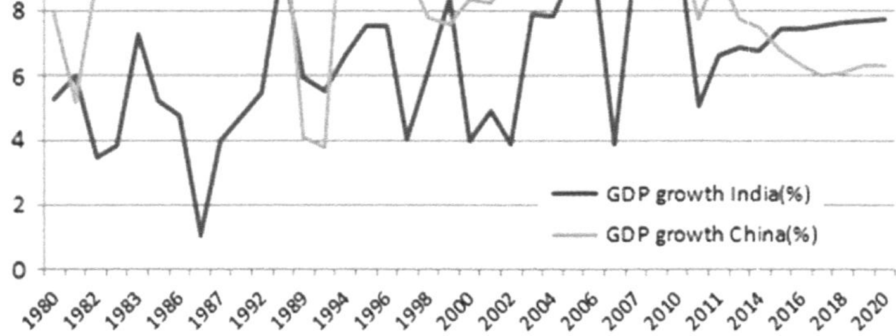

Figure 10.3 GDP growth rate India versus China, current trends and forecast. *IMF staff estimates, International Monetary Fund World Economic Outlook (April 2015). http://www.imf.org/external/pubs/ft/weo/2015/01/pdf/text.pdf.*

resulting growth in FDIs. The growth rate—7.2% in 2014, grew to 7.5% in 2015 and is expected to increase further in 2016.

On the other hand, growth rate in China dropped to 6.8% in 2016 and might drop further to 6.3% in 2016. China is undergoing an industrial slump which has worsened in recent months, even beyond the speculations of the country's leaders. Manufacturing, which was China's strength and contributed to 59% of the Chinese GDP, has taken a hit with the slowdown in European Union, Japan, and South Korea—China's largest trading partners. Unfortunately, manufacturing and construction, which were considered China's biggest growth proponents are now amongst the biggest burdens on its economy. To make matters worse, Chinese stock markets continue to be volatile, causing concern in the minds of investors.

For over two decades, both India and China have shown consistent growth in their GDP's and have been the major contributors to the World Economy. Since 2014, 25% of the total World GDP came from India and China combined. While China contributed 16.32%, India contributed 6.83% to the total World GDP. China also remains the biggest contributor, just ahead of the United States, which contributed 16.14% to the World GDP. It will be interesting to see the sector-wise composition of China and India's GDP and how their economies have shaped between 1980-2014.

Observing the changing sectorial composition of GDP for bother countries: India 1980–2014 (Fig. 10.4) and China for 1980–2014

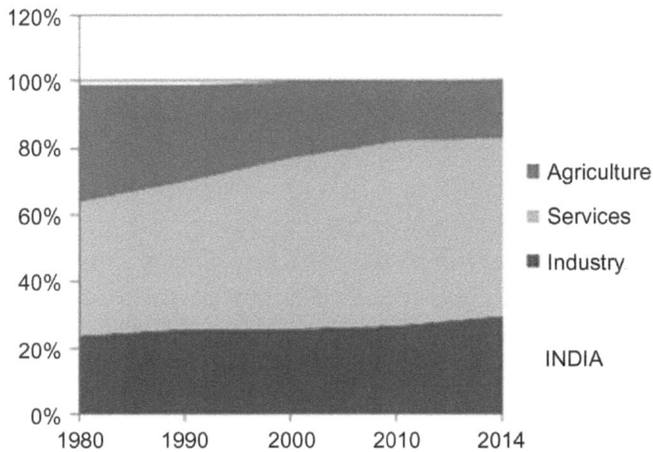

Figure 10.4 Changing sectorial composition for India (1980–2014). *Planning Commission, Government of India.*

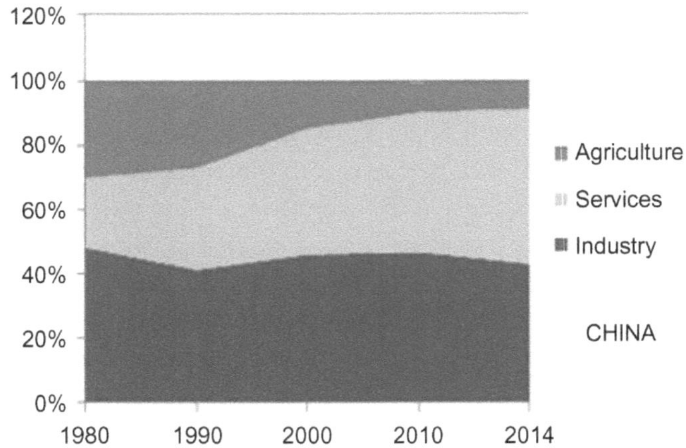

Figure 10.5 Changing sectorial composition for China (1980–2014). *National Bureau of Statistics of China.*

(Fig. 10.5), we notice that GDP of both the countries experienced a shift toward services and away from agriculture. The GDP composition of India (sector wise) in 2014 was as follows: Agriculture (17.9%), Industry (30%), and Services (53%). India's growth has been primarily lead by a boom in the services sector while the agricultural contribution toward the GDP has gradually diminished. The manufacturing sector has yet to stand up to its expectation.

This shift can be particularly observed in the Fig. 10.4. The contribution of Agriculture toward the GDP has gradually declined, despite the fact that at least 60% of the rural population is dependent on it and Indian farmers feel overburdened. Indian agriculture is still dependent on rain. If rain fails, the crops fail. Getting credit for farmers is not an easy task and because of their low literacy, they are exploited by local money lenders charging exorbitant interest rates.

There is also a big difference between the price a farmer gets for his crops and the price a consumer pays for them: The middle man, who knows that these poor farmers do not have sufficient knowledge of current market conditions, pays meager amounts to them and then sells the stock for higher prices to the consumers, thereby making a sizeable profit for himself. This process is detrimental to both the farmers and the consumer. Another issue for the agricultural sector is the lack of proper storage facilities for farmers to store their crops, and the reason for tonnes of agricultural product wastage. The issue of concern is that the Government has not been pro-active in preventing these grave situations hindering required progress in the agricultural sector in India.

According to the Economic Survey (2014–2015), India's service sector grew at the rate of 10.6%, compared to 9.1%, the year before. This established India as the second-fastest growing service sector while first place went to China. For India, the pillars on which its service sector has grown are Information Technology and Outsourcing services. Availability of a large and talented workforce specializing in cost-effective and in-demand software technologies, alongside high level English language fluency, and a demand from foreign investors, have been important attributors to the enormous growth visible in the Indian Service Sector. In addition, India specializes in providing worldwide quality services in the banking and insurance domain, data entry services and business consultancy to name a few.

As mentioned, India's growth has been primarily fueled by the explosive growth in the services sector, while the manufacturing sector has been largely under-utilized. In order to boost the Indian economy further, the Government should take a clue from China where the manufacturing sector has been nurtured and utilized in an optimum manner, leading to phenomenal revenue generation and establishing its name in the global arena.

The uprising of China from a simple, rural, and agricultural economy to a manufacturing and service sector giant has had rapid transformative effects across its infrastructure, urbanization, per capita income, and an impressive GDP growth. China's GDP in 2014 was primarily contributed by three sectors: (1) Agriculture (9%), (2) Industry (Construction and Manufacturing) (43%), and (3) Service Sector (48%). Fig. 10.5 shows the changing sectorial composition of China.

Over the years, Industry has been the solid cornerstone of the tremendous growth of China's GDP. Chinese Government gave much thought and attention to developing its industries by introducing favorable mechanisms and policies, and now China ranks second in its industrial output and is also termed the "manufacturing hub of the western world." The agricultural and service sector, however, were not given much focus and hence their growth rates were, traditionally, suboptimal. Despite this, the service sector is improving and registered its most-impressive performance in 2013, owing to China's 12th Five-Year Plan (2011–15) that forcefully addresses the development of services sector, making it the major contributor toward the country's GDP, surpassing the industry sector.

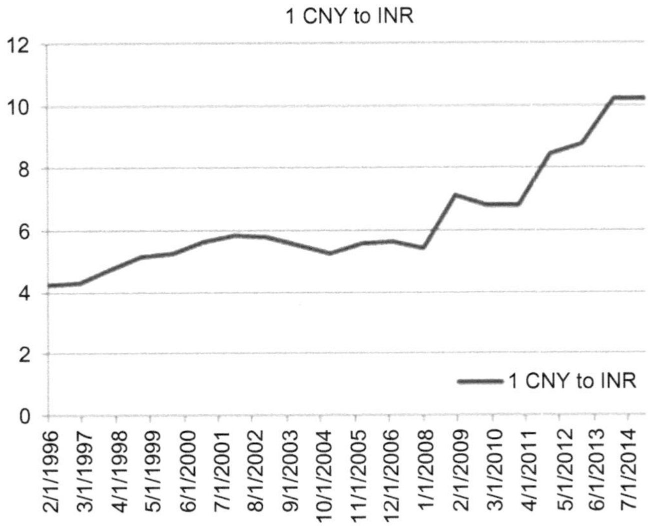

Figure 10.6 Comparison of Indian Currency (INR) with Chinese Currency (CNY) from 1996–2014. *IMF staff, International Monetary Fund World Economic Outlook (April 2015).*

The service sector currently contributes the most toward GDP, but manufacturing and industrial sectors were the major catalysts which helped China in reviving 680 million people from poverty during the record period during 1992–2011. In contrast, India has not been as efficient as China in alleviating poverty. About 22% of the Indian population remains below the poverty line, compared to just 6% in China. India could learn from China and start concentrating on the development of its manufacturing sector, creating more jobs and focusing on rural development in an attempt to alleviate poverty.

Regarding currency, China's shows a gradual appreciation in value with respect to India's, as seen in Fig. 10.6. On January 1996, 1 Chinese Yuan was equal to 4.23 Indian Rupee, which has grown to 10.18 Indian Rupee as of January 1, 2015. The last 6 years have seen a consistent appreciation of the Chinese Yuan. Despite the fact that, during the crisis period Yuan was almost frozen, the appreciation was closer to 7% per year. This pattern changed in 2015 when Chinese Central Bank diminished its currency value by 3% in an effort to boost its exports.

China has been witnessing a continuous decline in its exports and by devaluing the currency it intends to make manufactured products low-cost for other countries to buy, thus racing ahead of its competitors. If other Asian countries (mainly Japan and Korea) follow suit and devalue their currencies in a bid to get competitive edge over others, it could ignite a crisis in the Asian markets. Experts feel that the same could happen with Indian Rupee which also depreciated by 5% against the USD and shows signs of further depreciation in 2016.

10.6 INDIA AND CHINA: CURRENT POSITIONING AND FUTURE PROSPECTS

An interesting pattern emerges observing Table 10.2. Until 2010, the top 10 biggest nations in PPP were: United States, China, Japan, India, Germany, Russia, United Kingdom, France, Brazil, and Italy. Six out of 10 are developed countries. By 2014, however, emerging economies started to rise up the list. China overtakes the United States and becomes the world's largest economy by 2014 and is set to maintain its position in 2020 (as predicted by Euromonitor International, International Monetary Fund statistics). China registered a PPP growth rate of 7.1% in 2000 which increased to 13.3% by 2010. By 2020, China's global share of PPP is expected to reach 20.7%.

India overtook Japan to become the world's third-largest economy and will continue to maintain its place in future, owing to its young and growing population that will contribute immensely toward the growth of GDP.

Now, let us look at the projections for the year 2020, in terms of GDP measured by PPP, for the following three countries: (1) Russia seems poised to become the fifth largest economy, ahead of Germany. (2) Brazil looks all set to become the seventh largest economy, ahead of France and United Kingdom. Being amongst the world's major exporters of energy and natural resources, Russia and Brazil's growth chart look promising although Russia will have to work on diversifying its economy further to avoid any obstacles in its growth. (3) While Mexico would have raced ahead of Italy to become the world's 10th largest economy.

Interestingly, the list of largest economies now contains five advanced nations and five emerging nations. The balance of power seems levelled at this point of time and a pattern is visible that emerging economies are catching up with the advanced nations.

Table 10.2 Top 10 largest economies by GDP (purchasing power parity): 2010 and 2020

Rank	Country-2010	GDP (US million)	Country 2014	GDP (US million)	Country 2020	GDP (US million)
1	United States	14,808,081	China	18,088,054	China	28,124,970
2	China	9,711,244	United States	17,348,075	United States	22,644,910
3	Japan	4,267,492	India	7,411,093	India	10,225,943
4	India	3,912,911	Japan	4,767,157	Japan	6,196,979
5	Germany	2,861,117	Germany	3,748,094	Russia	4,326,987
6	Russia	2,221,755	Russia	3,576,841	Germany	3,981,033
7	United Kingdom	2,183,277	Brazil	3,275,799	Brazil	3,868,813
8	France	2,154,399	Indonesia	2,685,893	United Kingdom	3,360,442
9	Brazil	2,138,888	France	2,591,170	France	3,214,921
10	Italy	1,767,120	United Kingdom	2,569,218	Mexico	2,838,722

Source: Euromonitor International from IMF, International Financial Statistics and World Economic Outlook/UN/National Statistics (2015).

10.7 THE DIMINISHING GROWTH RATE OF ADVANCED NATIONS

The global financial crisis of 2008–09, ageing of population, shrinking of employable workforce, along with the proliferation of emerging nations measured by their contributions to the global GDP and PPP, are some of the key elements of the slowdown which advanced nations are experiencing. The United States enjoyed the status of world's largest economy for a long time, but its world GDP share according to PPP is on a decline. It was 17.1% in 2000, which dropped to 16.14% in 2014 and is forecasted to drop to 15% by 2019. Japan's economy recovered slightly in the mid-2000s after a prolonged period of slowdown, but after the global crisis of 2008–09, it plunged further, owing to its dependence on trade. Prolonged deflation and ageing population are other contributors to its continued downturn. Japan's contribution to world GDP has fallen from 4.9% in 2010 to almost 4% in 2014 and is estimated to be at the same level by 2019. The European Union (EU) also saw a decline from 18.77% in 2000 to 16.94% in 2014, and is expected to be 15% in 2019. Fig. 10.7 shows this decline of advanced economies while India and China show an upward trend. Many advanced economies face challenges of reducing public debts and government budget deficits while the emerging countries sustain their growth.

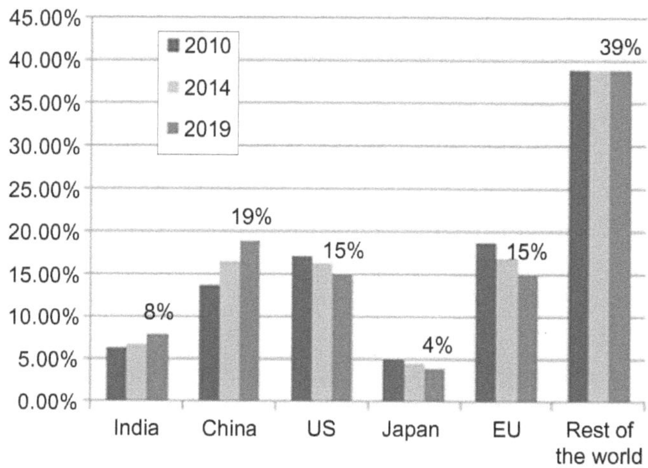

Figure 10.7 GDP share of World Total GDP (PPP) for India, China, United States, Japan, Eurozone (EU), and rest of the world. *IMF staff estimates, International Monetary Fund World Economic Outlook.*

In an earlier paragraph, we have seen a movement of worldwide power from advanced nations toward rising economies. This ascent in the significance of rising economies will impact worldwide investment flow, trade and commerce dynamics, and the environment. Substantial consumer markets, rising incomes, and huge population in developing economies will open vast opportunities for businesses worldwide, and opportunities like luxury goods will become attractive as middle classes continues to grow in spending power. In China, the number of family units with yearly extra cash above US$10,000 (in nominal terms) was 57.1 million families in 2010 and is expected to grow to 222 million families by 2020. Notwithstanding populace maturing in a few emerging nations including China, the population in developing markets is, for the most part, more youthful than in developed economies. Youthful customers are increasingly demonstrating abilities to make substantial purchases: automobiles, houses, and consumer goods, for example. Thus, foreign capital will keep flowing into developing nations. Rising nations will likely produce more investors, too, which will enhance their impact in the worldwide economy. Foreign investors will need to confront overwhelming regulations and corruption, and find measures to adapt to the local environment. For India and China, it is evident that FDI will play a crucial role in further developing these two economies. Can foreign investors and policy makers leverage their options within these two economies? An exploration of the prevalent investment and business climate in these countries will be discussed in Section 10.8.

10.8 INVESTMENT CLIMATE IN INDIA AND CHINA

China and India have favorable climates for international business. Various studies recently conducted by prestigious institutions such as Ernst and Young (2008), KPMG (2008), PricewaterhouseCoopers (2008), UNCTAD (2013–2015) have confirmed this. In particular, UNCTAD's World Investment Prospects Survey 2013–15 found out that China was the most attractive destination for FDI, while India ranked 6th in this list (as seen in Fig. 10.8).

In the same survey, 159 Transnational Corporations (TNCs) were asked to choose the top promising economies and China secured the first position by earning 46% of the total votes. United States came second, followed by India as the third most promising nation (Fig. 10.9). Notably, 6 of the top 10 promising countries are from the emerging nations' list. According to a study conducted by Zelaya and Yuce (2014) about the

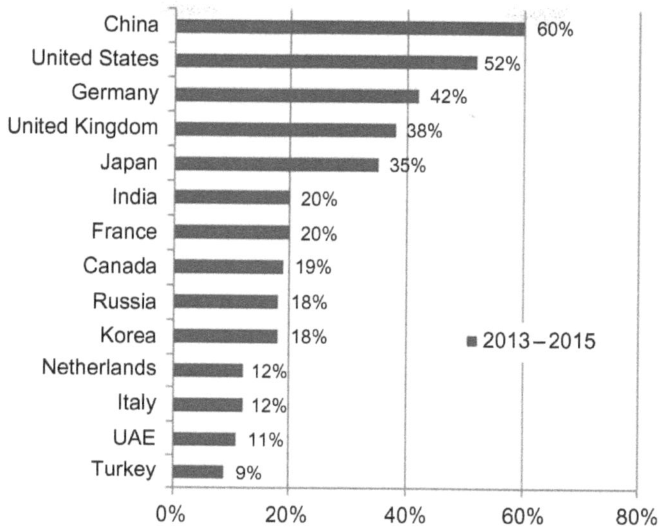

Figure 10.8 Most promising investor economies of FDI (2013–15). *UNCTAD. (2013–2015). World investment prospects survey. New York and Geneva: United Nations Conference on Trade and Development. Available from http://unctad.org/en/PublicationsLibrary/webdiaeia2013d9_en.pdf. World Investment Prospects Survey Note: Based on 64 Investment Promotion Agencies (IPA) responses.*

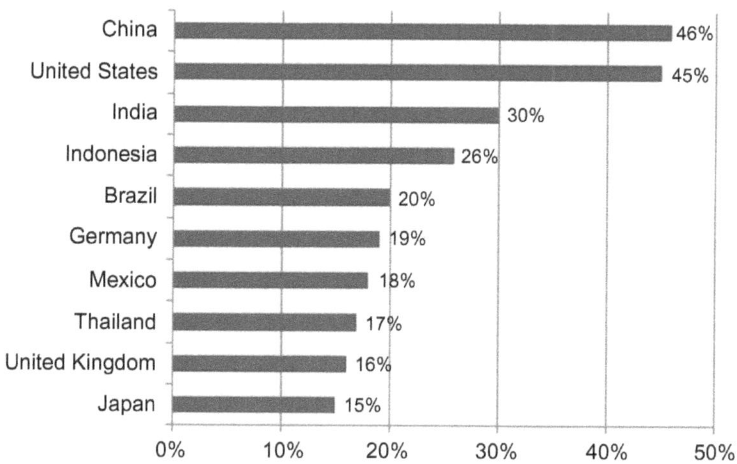

Figure 10.9 Most promising investor economies for FDI (2013–15). *UNCTAD. (2013–2015). World investment prospects survey. New York and Geneva: United Nations Conference on Trade and Development. Available from http://unctad.org/en/PublicationsLibrary/webdiaeia2013d9_en.pdf. World Investment Prospects Survey Note: Based on 159 Transnational Corporations (TNCs) responses.*

reasons behind increasing FDI of multinational companies in China and India, it was revealed that bigger market size, rapid GDP growths, low wages, easy labor availability, and flexible regulations as the main deterministic factors.

According to the survey, (and in comparison to India), China is the most promising investor economy and top prospective host economy for TNCs, consequently attracting more FDI. Let us try to investigate some reasons for this.

First, China introduced pro-FDI and flexible trade policies in 1979—much earlier than India—and received the first-mover's advantage. These policies included: low labor costs, incentivized investment schemes, and liberal policies for foreign investors. Second, China has heavily invested in building and nurturing its manufacturing sector, which has contributed significantly to its GDP and attracted many foreign investors. Third, China has a higher literacy rate than India—an appealing factor for foreign investors.

Alternatively, India incorporated its FDI plans only in the 1990s, with gradual progress made in the 2000s to remove restrictions and facilitate foreign investments. This late implementation by India and the early-adopter advantage of China is one reason between the disparities in results between them. Moreover, entry into India's manufacturing sector was more restrictive than into China's. With time, India has made efforts to remove restrictions for foreign entry into most of the industries and simplify associated procedures. This has increased the inflow of foreign capital in recent years.

Despite these facts, India may have an advantageous position in comparison to China regarding language and business culture. Having been under the British rule for over three centuries, India is reminiscent of a business culture, administrative procedures, and judicial system which many western countries can relate to. Furthermore, the prevalence of English language as the main language of business tilts the balance in favor of India for English-speaking nations.

Having seen the investment climate and FDI, it is necessary to understand the Banking system in India and China: how it is regulated and the financial stability it provides to the country and its global positioning.

10.9 BANKING SYSTEM IN INDIA AND CHINA

China's regulators are classified mainly by the range of activities they supervise. Banks are regulated fundamentally by the China Banking

Regulatory Commission (CBRC), securities and monetary markets by the China Securities Regulatory Commission (CSRC), and insurance by the China Insurance Regulatory Commission (CIRC). The Chinese Central Bank, also called as the People's Bank of China (PBOC), is responsible for governing and maintaining financial stability and drafting regulatory policies related to systematic risks and monetary policies. Additional duties of the PBOC covers: control of foreign exchange rate, and setting limits on deposit and lending interest rates. Both the exchange rate and the interest rate limits, however, are eventually decided by the State Council, the most elevated government body. Like all central banks it can act as a lender of last resort during financial exigencies.

On the other hand, India has a boisterous, straightforward, transparent, and stable financial market, which has progressively evolved from a profoundly controlled system to a liberalized one. RBI, which is the central bank of India, was established on April 1, 1935 and is responsible for formulating the monetary policies, regulating foreign exchange markets, and supervising credit markets. It also prescribes and controls the lending and deposit interest rates and can act as a lender of last resort to other banks in times of financial distress. The Securities and Exchange Board of India (SEBI) which was established by SEBI Act of 1992, is a regulator for securities market in India. SEBI has statutory powers to protect the interest of investors and regulate the securities market in relation to issue of security and promote the development of securities market of India.

10.9.1 Chinese Banking System

The existing banking structure of China has gradually evolved from a soviet-style mono-bank system (PBOC) to a plural banking system, since the inception of reforms in 1978. Before the reforms, PBOC was the only major bank responsible for managing deposits for state-owned enterprises (SOEs), and played the major role in mobilization of household savings. After the reforms, PBOC was granted the status of Central Bank. A series of banking sector reforms (1978–84) were adopted, wherein "big four" state-owned banks were reinstated and separated from PBOC—each designated with a function distinct from the other three. The big four state-owned banks were originally responsible for serving distinct economic sectors and to grant loans for policy objectives. With the reform of 1994, however, they were absolved of their policy lending objectives and were reinstated as commercial banks, with the capacity to enter into direct competition with one another (Wong and Wong, 2001).

Table 10.3 Financial intermediaries in China (as at end-December 2014)

Category	Assets (RMB 100 million)	% of total assets
1. Commercial banks		
a. State-owned commercial banks	710,141	41.2
b. Joint-stock commercial banks	313,801	18.2
c. City commercial banks	180,842	10.5
d. Rural commercial banks	115,273	6.7
2. Co-operative banks		
a. Urban credit co-operative	88,312	5.1
b. Rural co-operative banks	9570	0.56
3. Policy banks	156,140	9.1
4. Other institutions		
a. NBFIs	50,123	2.91
b. Postal savings	70,981	4.12
c. Foreign banks	27,921	1.62
Total (1+2+3+4)	**1,723,104**	**100**

Source: www.crbc.gov.cn, http://www.cbrc.gov.cn/chinese/files/2015/0F19960DD41D4206A246251A7225773E.pdf.

As a result of these reforms, the current Chinese banking structure now encompasses various financial institutions in the form of commercial banks, policy banks, co-operative banks, and nonbank financial institutions. By the end 2014, China's banking system comprised of 5 state-owned commercial banks (SOCBs), 12 joint-stock commercial banks (JSCBs), 133 city commercial banks, and 665 rural commercial banks. The co-operative banking system in China consisted of 1596 urban credit co-operatives and 89 rural co-operative banks. Furthermore, there are 3 policy banks along with China Development Bank and 41 foreign banks. Chinese nonbanking financial institutions encompass financial leasing companies, auto financing companies, trust and investment companies, postal saving institutions, and asset management companies. Table 10.3 provides information on the assets of the various financial intermediaries of China. The banking system in China is dominated by the SOCBs and JSCBs that comprise nearly 60% of the total assets.

JSCBs were primarily conceived for specialized financial products; today they offer a wide range of financial services. These banks are partly owned by local government, SOEs, and—in a few cases—private corporations. Since the reform of 1994, the Chinese banking system introduced three policy banks for handling the policy objectives which were previously met by SOCBs. They grant loans for infrastructure projects and work on the principle of no-profit no-loss. They do not enter into competition with other commercial banks and largely fund themselves from central bank loans and governmental deposits.

10.9.2 Indian Banking System

The Indian banking system has gradually evolved over several decades to become robust, elaborate, and financially stable. It caters to the credit needs of varied kinds of consumers and borrowers in the country. The main objective is to mobilize savings and promote economic development. The RBI is the central bank and the supreme authority for regulating the banking system. The commercial banks in India accept deposits and lend loans to retail consumers as well as corporate clients. They comprise public sector banks, private sector banks like ICICI and HDFC, and foreign banks like Barclays and HSBC. State Bank of India is the largest commercial bank, according to assets. The co-operative banks in India play an important role of providing rural credit and are built on the principle of co-operation and mutual help. Furthermore, there are development banks like IDBI, IFCI which provide long term loans for the development of the industrial sector. Lastly, there are nonbanking financial companies (NBFCs) that consist of asset finance companies, investment companies, loan companies, and infrastructure finance company.

The Indian banking system consists of scheduled commercial banks (public sector banks, private sector banks), foreign banks, co-operative banks comprising of urban co-operative banks and rural co-operative credit institutions, and NBFCs. According to RBI, in 2013–14 there were 27 public sector banks, 23 private sector banks (old+ new), 45 foreign banks, 90 co-operative banks, and 428 NBFCs. Table 10.4 provides the structure of Financial Intermediaries in India. It is observed that the Indian banking system is dominated by the scheduled commercial banks which constitute nearly 73% of the total assets.

In both countries, commercial banks play a dominant role—especially the state owned public sector banks. As such, the relative significance of commercial banks in both the countries is similar. Foreign banking share is more significant in India than in China, while the share of co-operative banks is more in China, compared to India. Lastly, NBFCs have more share in total assets in India than in China. Both China and India have an elaborate banking system comprising of commercial banks, co-operative banks, foreign banks and NBFCs.

Table 10.4 Financial intermediaries in India (2012–2013)

Category	Assets (INR 100 million)	% of total assets
1. Scheduled commercial banks		
a. Public sector banks	62,318,798	65
b. Private sector banks		
i. Old private sector banks	4,044,366	4
ii. New private sector banks	13,649,183	14
c. Foreign banks	4,917,430	5
2. Co-operative banks	262,000	0.3
3. Nonbanking financial companies	11,177,000	12
Total (1+2+3)	**1,723,104**	**100**

Source: Reserve Bank of India.
Note: Information on development banks not readily available.

10.10 FINANCIAL STABILITY INDICATORS FOR INDIA AND CHINA

Having discussed their banking systems, we now delve into understanding the financial stability for these two countries. First, we present a comparative analysis of selected financial stability indicators for both India and China and then provide global positioning for these countries.

10.10.1 Nonperforming Loans (NPLs) India and China

The International Monetary Fund (IMF) compilation guide on Financial Soundness Indicators (IMF, 2014) recommends reporting loans as nonperforming when "(i) payments of principal and interest are past due by three months (90 days) or more, or (ii) interest payments equal to three months (90 days) interest or more have been capitalized (reinvested into the principal amount), refinanced, or rolled over (that is, payment has been delayed by agreement). In addition, NPLs should also include those loans with payments less than 90 days past due that are recognized as nonperforming under national supervisory guidance." Although IMF provides guidelines on nonperforming loans (NPLs), various countries have their own slightly different implementations of it.

In the Fig. 10.10, we provide information on NPLs for India and China: Indian banks outperformed China's Bank between the period 2001 and 2007. However, after 2007, China has had very low levels of NPLs compared with Indian banks. China has reduced its NPLs from 29% in 2001 to 1% in 2015 whereas India has reduced its NPLs from nearly 11% in 2001 to 4% in 2015. Although China fared better in 2015 on asset

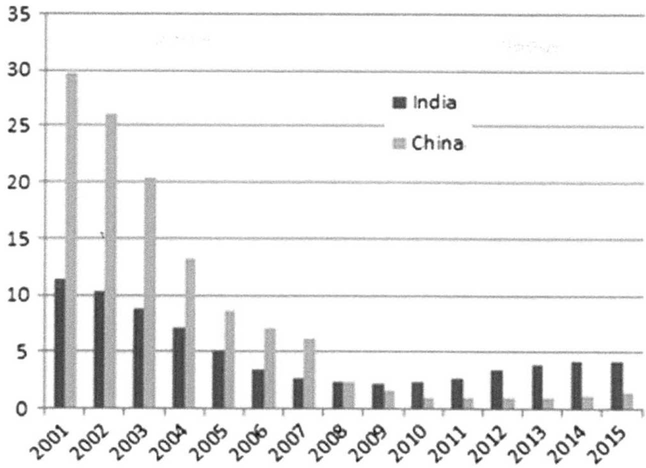

Figure 10.10 Evolution of nonperforming loans India and China (2001–15). *International Monetary Fund, Financial Soundness Indicators http://data.imf.org/regular.aspx?key=60949720.*

quality against India, both countries have shown improvements in asset quality over a period of 15 years. During the 2000s, extremely high levels of NPL's were being registered on account of small, SOEs. Chinese banks in 2000s often worked under the instructions of government and granted loans under credit programmes for small SOEs. In the mid-2000s, the Chinese government began to acknowledge the relevance of a robust banking system and started undertaking measures[2] to reduce the large volumes of NPLs. So far, it appears that Government efforts have paid off and NPLs have dropped to as low as 1%. Indian banks showed better asset quality than China's bank but recently asset quality has deteriorated, largely attributable to bad loans from the infrastructure and steel sectors.

10.10.2 Capital Adequacy Ratio (CAR) India and China

According to IMF, Capital Adequacy Ratio (CAR) is calculated using total regulatory capital as the numerator, and risk-weighted assets as the denominator. It ascertains the capital adequacy of banks and inhibits them from taking excess of debt beyond a certain level. This level of CAR is decided generally by the central banks that regulate the banking system. It is also

[2] For detailed measures refer to page 15: http://www.brookings.edu/~/media/research/files/papers/2013/07/01-chinese-financial-system-elliott-yan/chinese-financial-system-elliott-yan.pdf.

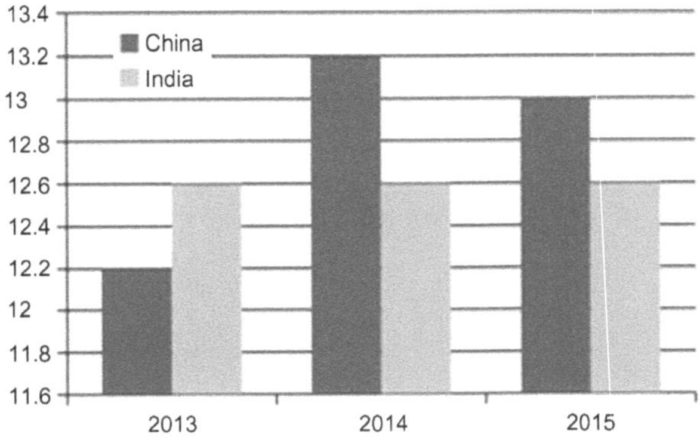

Figure 10.11 Capital adequacy ratio for India and China (2013–15). *International Monetary Fund, Financial Soundness Indicators http://data.imf.org/regular.aspx?key=*60949720.

known as CRAR: Capital to Risk-weighted Assets Ratio. As per Basel III norms, a CAR of 8% should be maintained by banking institutions to withstand any shocks on their balance sheets. India and China both maintain higher levels than this. Indian public sector banks should maintain a CAR of 12% as per the guidelines of RBI, while Indian scheduled commercial banks in the private sector should maintain a CAR of 9%. The CBRC released a consultation draft of new measures on capital management for banks on August 15, 2011. In principle, other commercial banks should satisfy the following conditions by the end of 2016: (1) Core Tier 1 Capital Adequacy Ratio: not less than 7.5%; (2) Tier 1 Capital Adequacy Ratio: not less than 8.5%; (3) Capital Adequacy Ratio: not less than 10.5%. With approval of the CBRC, banks can meet the standards by the end of 2018. Rural co-operative banks and rural banks should satisfy the following conditions by the end of 2018: (1) Core Tier 1 Capital Adequacy Ratio: not less than 7.5%; (2) Tier 1 Capital Adequacy Ratio: not less than 8.5%; (3) Capital Adequacy Ratio: not less than 10.5%. Fig. 10.11 provides the statistics on CAR for India and China. Both India and China have satisfactory levels of CARs. As of 2015, Chinese bank have CAR of 13% whereas Indian banks have CAR of 12.6% which is sufficiently higher than the required regulatory levels.

10.10.3 Comparison of Lending and Deposit Rates in India and China

In the Fig. 10.12, we provide a comparison of lending and deposits rates for banks in India and China. The difference between lending rate and deposit rate, also called net margin, is higher on average for India. In

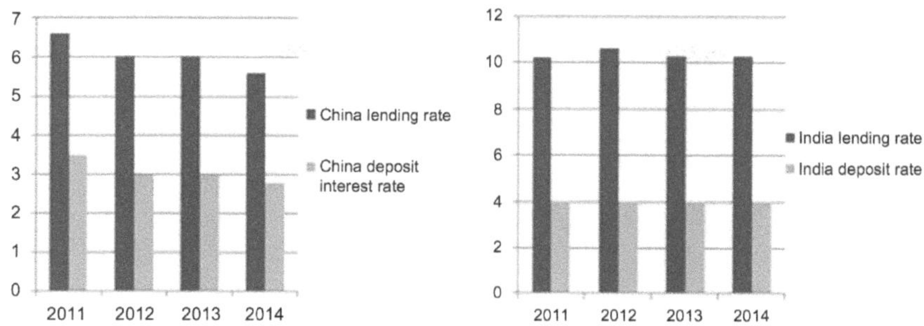

Figure 10.12 Lending and deposit interest rate in India and China (2011–14). *World Bank Database and Reserve Bank of India http://data/worldbank.org/indicator/FR.INR.DPST/countries, https://www.rbi.org.in/scripts/BS_ViewMasCirculardetails.aspx?id=9059.*

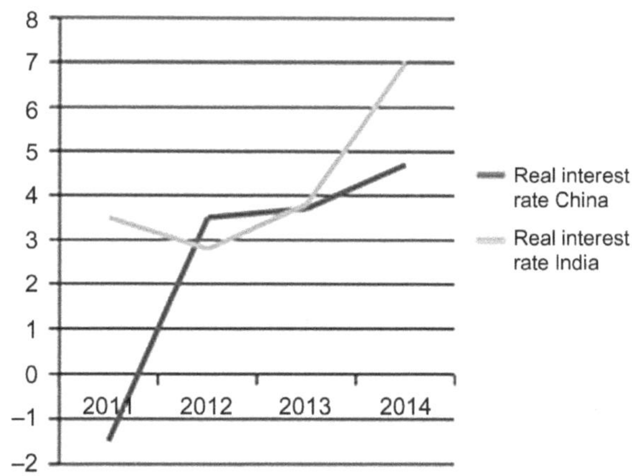

Figure 10.13 Real Interest rate comparison India and China. *World Bank Database and Reserve Bank of India http://data/worldbank.org/indicator/FR.INR.RINR/countries.*

China, banks are allowed to set their own deposit and lending rate, but only within the limits set by PBOC. RBI established changes in 2011, which authorized the bank to decide the interest rate they wanted to pay on their savings bank accounts (based on amount and duration of deposit). This could vary from one bank to another and also depend on the bank's profitability and liquidity. Despite variable rate of interests which banks decide according to their own policies, RBI rules direct the banks to provide at least 4% of interest. In our study we take 4% as the rate of interest as it would cover most of the cases.

Fig. 10.13 provides the real interest rates for India and China. The real interest rates are lower in China, which implies that an Indian lender is earning more than Chinese lender. On the other hand, real cost of funds

Table 10.5 Return on assets comparison between selected advanced economies and emerging economies

	2007	2008	2009	2010	2011	2012	2013	2014	2015
Advanced economies									
France	...	0.1	0.3	0.6	0.4	0.3	0.5	0.3	...
Germany	0.3	−0.1	0.2	0.4	0.5	0.4	0.4	0.4	...
Greece	1.0	0.9	0.4	0.0	−9.5	−1.8	...	−3.5	−39.1
Italy	0.8	0.3	0.3	0.3	−0.9	0.1	−0.8	−0.2	0.2
Japan	0.5	0.3	−0.2	0.2	0.3	0.3	0.4	0.3	0.3
Portugal	1.2	0.3	0.4	0.5	−0.3	−0.3	−0.5	−1.5	0.5
Spain	1.1	0.8	0.6	0.5	0.1	−1.4	0.4	0.5	0.6
United Kingdom	0.4	−0.1	0.0	0.3	0.3	0.3	0.2	0.8	...
United States	1.2	−0.1	0.2	0.9	1.2	1.4	0.4	0.3	0.4
Emerging economies									
Russia	3.0	2.1	0.7	2.0	2.5	2.4	1.9	0.9	...
China	0.9	1.0	0.9	1.1	1.3	1.3	1.3	1.2	0.6
India	0.9	1.0	1.0	1.0	0.9	1.0	0.8	0.8	0.8
Brazil	3.5	2.1	1.7	1.9	1.7	1.4	1.4	1.4	1.5

Source: International Monetary Fund, financial Soundness Indicators http://data.imf.org/regular.aspx?key=60949720.
Note: ..., data not available.

for the borrower is lower in China than in India, which makes borrowing costs feasible for businesses in China. In 2011, China shows negative real interest rate, which means that inflation was higher than the nominal interest rate.

10.11 GLOBAL POSITIONING

10.11.1 Return on Assets

Return on assets is often used as an indicator to understand the profitability of the banking system. Here we provide information (refer Table 10.5) on India and China's banking system along with major advanced economies and some emerging market countries. While most of the advanced economies plunge to negative returns on assets, or show very low return on assets, emerging economies maintained a positive return on assets from 2007 to 2015, despite the global financial crisis. Although China's return on assets has dropped to 0.6% in 2015 from 1.2%, both India and China maintain a stable return on assets ratio.

10.12 NONPERFORMING LOANS (NPLS)

In Fig. 10.14, we provide an average of NPLs to gross loans for a 15-year period, for selected advanced economies and emerging economies. In the advanced economies, we can observe that Greece and Italy have high-and rising levels of NPLs. For these two nations, the bulk of NPLs comes from the period between 2011 and 2015, when both countries recorded high NPL ratios. Since the onset of the global financial crisis, NPLs for Greece increased eight times from 4.6% in 2007 to 34% in 2015, and for Italy, they tripled to 18% (2015) of total loans, from just 5.8% in 2007. In the emerging economies, we have China followed by Russia and India equal levels. China saw high rising levels of NPLs in the year 2001–05 and even in years prior. One of the major challenges in China's transition from a planned to market economy is reforming the banking sector. Earlier, the banks traditionally enjoyed the status of being the primary money-lenders to SOEs. This practice was often based upon political, instead of economic rationales, and had taken deep roots into the Chinese economy. By late 1990s, almost 40% of Chinese bank loans could not be repaid (Naughton, 2007). During the mid-2000s, Chinese government was actively involved in reducing NPL's ratio and restructuring the banking sector. Consequently, by 2015, the ratio had reduced to 1.5. On the

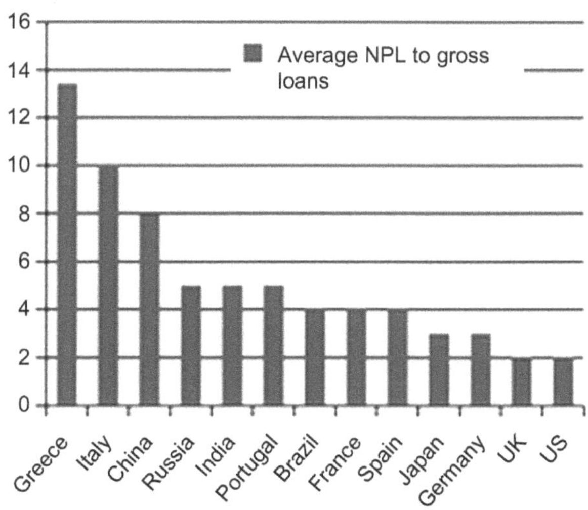

Figure 10.14 The share of bank nonperforming loans to total gross loans in selected advanced economies and emerging economies (% average of 2001–15). *World Bank Database http://data.worldbank.org/indicator/FB.AST.NPER.ZS/countries.*

contrary, in 2015, the following advanced countries were struggling with high NPL to total gross loan ratio: Greece (34 NPL ratio), Italy (18 NPL ratio), Portugal (12.3 NPL ratio) and Russia (7.4 NPL ratio) and Spain (7 NPL ratio).

The financial sector reforms in India and China were introduced at approximately the same time and resulted in significant improvement, especially in the asset quality of banking systems. Remarkably, the Chinese banking system has emerged significantly larger in size, than that of India. In 2014, China had four banks listed amongst the top five Global banks as measured by asset size. Whereas, India does not even have 1 bank listed in top 50 Global banks. This clearly reveals that China's banking industry is much larger as compared to India. For economic growth, and for providing ambient investment climate, both countries need to continue improving their banking systems and offer a viable and profitable experience to consumers and businesses.

As previously mentioned, India and China have begun to attract FDI in recent years, and have become top prospective host and most promising investor economies. In order to sustain and keep up with investor confidence, they need to find creative ways to improve their global competitiveness and business environment, which is analyzed in the Section 10.13.

10.13 GLOBAL COMPETITIVENESS[3]

Global competitiveness is an important determinant for attracting and sustaining investment inflow and profitable business activity. Its constituent pillars are: fair and transparent processes for policy formations, regulations, and implementations, combined with an autonomous judicial system. Any weakness in these can adversely affect the level of global competitiveness, impact investor sentiment, and harm business opportunities. A ranking of 140 countries is done by the Global Competitiveness Report, based on 12 pillars: (1) institutions, (2) infrastructure, (3) macroeconomic environment, (4) health and primary education, (5) higher education and training, (6) goods market efficiency, (7) labor efficiency market, (8) financial market development, (9) technological readiness, (10) market size, (11) business sophistication, and (12) innovation. In Table 10.6, the Global Competitiveness ranking for India and China for 2014 and 2015 is highlighted.

[3]The *Global Competitiveness Report* (GCR) is a yearly report published by the World Economic Forum since 2004.

In 2015, India ranked 55th out of 140 countries whereas China ranked 28th. This regular higher-ranking of China compared to India in global competitiveness pillars, reveals that China is providing better investment opportunities than India.

India moved up 16 spots in 2015 after struggling from almost 5 years of decline in ranking. This improved ranking is primarily attributed to the pro-business decisions and policies implemented by the Government, and has also strengthened the business community's faith in the government. On the other hand, China maintained its last year's rank of 28th and in the past 6 years has been able to sustain a stable performance. Overall, China trumps India in the Global Competitiveness ranking.

In analysis, the biggest obstacle for foreign companies in India is corruption and efficiency of the judiciary. The Institutions indicator, in Table 10.6 tries to measure the independence of judiciary and level of corruption in public and private contracting. In this respect, India has a ranking of 60 where as China ranks 51st. While India has seen a significant improvement by moving up by 10 spots, China has, on the other hand fallen back by 4.

Table 10.6 Ranking for India and China in Global Competitiveness Report (2015–16)

Parameters	**India**			**China**		
	Rank 2015	**Rank 2014**	**Change**	**Rank 2015**	**Rank 2014**	**Change**
Institutions	60	70	+10	51	47	−4
Infrastructure	81	70	+6	39	46	+7
Macroeconomics environment	91	101	+10	8	10	+2
Health and primary education	84	98	+14	44	46	+2
Higher education and training	90	93	+3	68	65	−3
Good market efficiency	91	95	+4	58	56	−2
Labor market efficiency	103	112	+9	37	37	0
Financial market development	53	51	−2	54	54	0
Technological readiness	120	121	+1	74	83	+9
Market size	3	3	0	1	2	+1
Business sophistication	52	57	+5	38	43	+5
Innovation	42	49	+7	31	32	+1
Overall rank	55	71	+16	28	28	0

Source: World Economic Forum. (2014–2015). *The global competitiveness report 2014–2015.* Geneva: World Economic Forum; World Economic Forum. (2015–2016). *The global competitiveness report 2015–2016.* Geneva: World Economic Forum. Authors Analysis http://reports.weforum.org/global-competitivenes-report-2014-2015/economies/#economy, http://reports.weforum.org/global-competitivenes-report-2014-2016/economies/#economy.

Infrastructure in China outperforms India by a huge margin. China's ranking in 2015 is 39th as compared to India which is ranked 81st. This pillar is based on quality of transport, electricity, and telephony infrastructure. For India, there are no easy measures to improving its infrastructure challenges and, according to experts, over $200 billion per year is necessary for handling this situation. An advantage to India, however, is its high savings rate which can be utilized for this purpose. Increased inflow of foreign capital also seems to be another helpful option.

Regarding macroeconomic stability, China again supersedes India by a large percentage. India holds the 91st position while China is at the 8th position. The importance of macroeconomic stability is crucial for sustained growth because such instabilities have the potential to disrupt an entire economy, as was observed during the financial crisis of 2008–09: massive fluctuations in global markets, instability of currency, job losses, and loss of investor confidence. What is worrisome for India is that macroeconomic stability is a decisive factor for attracting foreign investors. India's performance in the efficiency enhancer's index (higher education, goods market, labor market) is also not as good as China's. With respect to financial market development, however, India is at 53rd position and China is at 54th place. Out of nine pillars this is the only pillar where India is at the forefront.

In India, although positive improvements to some of the basic drivers of global competitiveness can be seen (institutions, infrastructure, and macroeconomic environment), much work needs to be done in other areas, like technological readiness—ranked 120th. According to 2014 Internet usage statistics, only one out of five Indians has access to internet, and regarding cell phone connectivity, just two in five Indians have a basic cell phone. In contrast, half of China's population has Internet and cell phone connectivity.

China has maintained its ranking, but in order to ensure it can sustain its growth and maintain its ranking long term, it must formulate a self-sustaining model of growth through innovation and domestic consumption—relying less on external trade and investment. Although China ranks better than India, in Global Competitiveness, both need to improve their efforts in order to sustain, and cater to, the demands of market dynamics and investor sentiments in the wake of increasing scrutiny by regulators and media. It will be interesting to see the performance of India and China with respect to the ease of doing business in these countries.

10.14 DOING BUSINESS AND ENVIRONMENT CHALLENGES

To calculate the "Doing Business Rankings," World Bank takes into account 11 parameters that impact businesses across their entire lifecycle: (1) Ease of doing business, (2) Starting a business, (3) Dealing with construction permits, (4) Getting electricity, (5) Registering property, (6) Getting credit, (7) Protecting minority investors, (8) Paying taxes, (9) Trading across borders, (10) Enforcing contracts, and (11) Resolving Insolvency (refer to the Table 10.7).

India is seen as one of the fastest-growing economies in the world, but it still lags behind its other BRIC counterparts: China, Russia, and Brazil. As of June 2015, India is ranked 130th among 189 countries. Since last year, India has moved up 12 places which is remarkable progress owing to its large economy.

Over the years, India has introduced various reforms to facilitate business. There are now no minimum capital requirements and no need to obtain a certificate to begin business operations. The number of days required to setup a business have decreased from 127 in 2004 to just 29 in 2015: a significant increase in efficiency. To further improve its tax system, India incorporated an online system for Value Added Tax registration and replaced the physical stamp previously required, with an online version. The establishment of debt recovery tribunals helped accelerate the process of debt recovery cases and lowered the cost of credit. NPLs also decreased by 28% and lowered interest rates on larger loans. These are

Table 10.7 Doing business ranking for BRIC and Singapore (June 2015)

	Brazil	Russia	India	China	Singapore
Ease of doing business rank	116	51	130	84	1
Starting business	174	41	155	136	10
Dealing with construction permits	169	119	183	176	1
Getting electricity	22	29	70	92	6
Registering property	130	8	138	43	17
Getting credit	97	42	42	79	19
Protecting minority investors	29	66	8	134	1
Paying taxes	178	47	157	132	5
Trading across borders	145	170	133	96	41
Enforcing contracts	45	5	178	7	1
Resolving insolvency	62	51	136	55	27

Source: Doing Business Report, World Bank Group, June 2015 http://www.doingbusiness.org/rankings.

good indicators of the way things are changing in India and if this pace is maintained, India could benefit greatly from the reforms.

In the World Bank's 2015 "Ease of Doing Business" report, China was ranked 84th amongst 189 countries. It is ahead of India and Brazil in its ranking, but still behind Russia. Although China has introduced many reforms to open its doors for foreign investors, a few broad sectors of the economy still remain either restricted or prohibited to FDI. There are bureaucratic challenges interwoven within the Chinese business landscape that are impediments to further progress. As an example, long waiting periods for obtaining construction permits and a difficult tax-paying system makes starting, and running, businesses a cumbersome task. Many foreign companies conducting business in China have raised concerns about the increasing cost of labor, lack of qualified labor force, weak investor protection rights, lack of transparency, insufficient intellectual property rights, weak enforcement and lack of regulatory interpretation, competition with Chinese companies, internet censorship, forced transfer of technology, and challenges in obtaining administrative licenses and approvals.

Table 10.7 reveals that both China and India must implement further reforms to improve their rankings in the "Ease of Doing Business" where Singapore is the benchmark and, as of 2015, the best country to start a business in—having held its position for 10 consecutive years.

Both countries still have serious problems related to starting a business: dealing with construction permits, paying taxes, cross-border trading, contract enforcement, and insolvency procedures—all of which thwarts its development. China and India both have the ability to keep growing, but in order to sustain their immense growth rate they need to provide a transparent, flexible, easy, liberalized, and harmonious business environment. Both countries should work toward improving these parameters and improve its ranking and business environment.

10.15 ENVIRONMENTAL PERFORMANCE

The Environment Performance Index (EPI) ranks countries based on their performance in two important categories: (1) protection of human health from environment hazards and (2) protection of ecological systems.

According to the 2014 EPI, India is ranked 155th amongst 178 countries in its efforts to address environmental challenges. On the same parameter, China ranks 118th (with Brazil 77th and Russia 73rd). India has scored lowest on water sanitation, biodiversity, and habitat, along with climate energy indicators compared to other BRIC nations in the list. In particular, India needs to work in the area of protection of human health from environmental hazards. Alarmingly, for some major cities, China and India's air quality are among the worst in the world, far exceeding the World Health Organization thresholds. According to Air Quality Index,[4] if a city is in the scale of 201–300, it is "heavily polluted" and its inhabitants are at severe risk of health issues. Currently, in major cities like Delhi, Mumbai, Beijing, and Shanghai, the air quality index level fluctuates between 300 and 500+ levels on daily basis—implying severe, irreversible health hazards for their populations.

The staggering level of air pollution in major Chinese cities like Beijing and Shanghai has triggered Government efforts to tackle it. Since January 1, 2014, 15,000 of the largest SOEs are now required to disclose real time data on air and water pollution. Historically, SOE's have been the greatest pollution offenders and some the least transparent with disclosures. These efforts have come in the wake of announcements of "air pollution control and responsibility" contracts, to hold provincial leaders liable for meeting strict reduction targets. It still remains to be seen, however, whether the efforts and measures implemented by China are effective or not. We hope that these efforts are able to bring change to the millions of citizens living in China who are at high risk of developing air related problems and other health issues.

On the other hand, India is yet to formulate strict policies to control its environmental hazards (air quality, water pollution, biodiversity and habitat, and energy challenges). Table 10.8 shows positive- and negative trends for both nations. Unfortunately, there are very few indicators that show a positive 10-year trend, while the remaining are either negative or exhibit no change. Undoubtedly, India and China will continue their economic and population growth spurts, but their greatest challenge will be the control and prevention of environmental hazards, and utilization of resources in an ecologically safe and friendly manner. How they cope with these challenges, while sustaining growth will be interesting to see and policy makers from both nations must give serious thought to this impending obstacle to bigger growth and contributions to the global economy, without being at risk of repercussions of their reckless actions in the years to come.

[4] Government agencies use air quality index (AQI) to communicate the level of air pollution to the people and warn them about the health hazards.

Table 10.8 Environmental performance index for BRICS countries

Parameters	Brazil	Russia	South Africa	India		China	
	Rank 2014	Rank 2014	Rank 2014	Rank 2014	10-Year trend	Rank 2014	10-Year trend
Health impacts	95	64	130	127	Positive	80	Positive
Air quality	29	49	48	174	Negative	176	Negative
Water and sanitation	84	92	107	124	Positive	109	Positive
Water resources	86	62	56	87	No change	67	No change
Agriculture	70	171	66	117	Positive	166	Negative
Forests	115	57	1	57	Positive	80	No change
Fisheries	53	92	97	67	No change	89	Negative
Biodiversity and habitat	75	106	84	125	No change	76	No change
Climate energy	57	38	65	104	No change	21	No change
Overall rank	77	73	72	155		118	

Source: EPI, Environmental performance Index is a joints project between the Yale Center for Environmental Law & Policy (YCELP) and the Center for International Earth Science Information Network (CIESIN) at Columbia University, in collaboration with the World Economic Forum a support from the Samuel Family Foundation and the McCall MacBain Foundation. http://www.epi.yale.edu/about.

10.16 CONCLUSION

In this chapter, we have made an effort to familiarize the readers with recent statistics and information related to India and China with respect to: demographics, economic growth, investment climate, global competitiveness, ease of doing business, and environment performance indicators. We evaluate the progress of these countries with respect to each other and also their future positioning with respect to developed nations and BRIC countries.

Undoubtedly, both China and India are emerging leaders of world economy. However, their challenges are: to continue to sustain rapid and profitable economic growth, and to solve challenges related to demographics, quality of education, public health, infrastructure, policies, and frameworks, in order to make the process of doing business easier.

FDI will continue to be an important determinant in the economic growth of these nations and the level of efficiency with which the policy makers and Governments address impending obstacles and deficiencies in their current systems, will determine the levels of success these nations can achieve. It is not feasible to say conclusively, at this point, which nation will supersede the other, but one thing is certain: both India and China have tremendous potential and will become economic powerhouses and contribute significantly to the global economy in the years to come.

REFERENCES

Ahluwalia, M. S. (2002). Economic reforms in India since 1991: Has gradualism worked? *Journal of Economic Perspectives, 16*(3), 67–88.

Chow, G. C. (2007). *China's economic transformation* (2nd ed.). Oxford: Blackwell.

Economic Survey, (2014–2015). *Economic survey-volume I.* Union Budget. Government of India.

Ernst & Young. (2008). *European attractiveness survey 2008.* Available from <http://ec.europa.eu/internal_market/services/docs/services-dir/studies/2008_european_attactiveness_survey_en.pdf>.

International Monetary Fund (IMF), (2014). *Compilation Guide on Financial Soundness Indicators.* Washington: International Monetary Fund.

Izurieta, A., & Singh, A. (2008). *Does fast growth in India and China harm U.S. workers?: Insights from simulation.* Centre for Business Research. Working Paper No. 378. Available from <http://econpapers.repec.org/paper/cbrcbrwps/wp378.htm>.

KPMG. (2008). *Global corporate capital flows 2008/9 to 2013/14.* A study of the investment intentions of companies in 15 countries around the world, KPMG. Available from <http://www.maths-fi.com/KPMG_Global_Corporate_Capital_Flows_June_2008.pdf>.

Mahtaney, P. (2007). *India, China and globalisation: The emerging superpowers and the future of economic development.* Basingstoke: Palgrave Macmillan.

Naughton, B. (2007). *The Chinese Economy: Transitions and Growth.* MIT Press.

Nolan, P. (2004). *Transforming China: Globalisation, transition and development.* London: Wimbledon Publishing Company.

OECD, (2015). *Aging and employment policies.* Poland: OECD Economic Department.

PricewaterhouseCoopers. (2008). *11th annual global CEO survey.* PricewaterhouseCoopers. Available from <https://www.pwc.com/gx/en/ceo-survey/pdf/pwc_11th_annual_global_ceo_survey_e.pdf>.

Rodrik, D., & Subramanium, A. (2005). From "Hindu Growth" to productivity surge: The mystery of the Indian growth transition. *IMF Staff Papers, 52*(2) Available from <https://www.imf.org/External/Pubs/FT/staffp/2005/02/pdf/rodrik1.pdf>.

UNCTAD, (2013–2015). *World investment prospects survey.* New York and Geneva: United Nations Conference on Trade and Development. Available from <http://unctad.org/en/PublicationsLibrary/webdiaeia2013d9_en.pdf>.

Winters, A., & Yusuf, S. (2007). Introduction. In A. Winters & S. Yusuf (Eds.), *Dancing with the giants: China, India and the global economy.* Washington, DC: World Bank Publications.

Wong, R. Y. C., & Wong, S. M. L. (2001). Competition in China's Domestic Banking Industry. *Cato Journal, 21*(1) (Spring/Summer 2001).

World Economic Forum, (2014–2015). *The Global Competitiveness Report 2014–2015.* Geneva: World Economic Forum.

World Economic Forum, (2015–2016). *The Global Competitiveness Report 2015–2016.* Geneva: World Economic Forum.

World Population Prospects, 2015. World population prospects the 2015 revision. Department of Economic and Social Affairs, Population Division. United Nations, New York, 2015.

Zelaya, M., & Yuce, A. (2014). Foreign direct investment decisions into China and India. *Asian Economic and Financial Review, 4*(3), 300–316.

CHAPTER 11

Conclusion: Implications and What Can We Learn?

Chris Rowley[1,2,3,4] and Elisabeth Paulet[5]
[1]Professor Emeritus, Cass Business School, City, University of London, London, United Kingdom
[2]Professorial Fellow, Institute of Hallyu Convergence Research, Korea University, Seoul, Korea
[3]Adjunct Professor, Griffith Business School and Griffith Asia Institute, Griffith University, Brisbane, QLD, Australia
[4]Visiting Fellow, Institute of Asia and Pacific Studies, Nottingham University, Nottingham, United Kingdom
[5]ICN Business School, CEREFIGE, Pole Lorrain de Gestion, Nancy, France

11.1 INTRODUCTION

China has suffered from an economic model that is too dependent on exports and low-priced and commodified products. This economic policy, of course, led to rapid development in production volumes but since it was based on an over-abundance of inputs (labor and capital), this also went hand in hand with some wastage—relatively low yields, high pollution costs and the inefficiencies of a model based on an ability to produce at speed, to the detriment of natural resources, security or maintenance. All of which is coming under increased questioning and is more commonly reported in the Western media (*inter alia*, Wildau & Weinland, 2016).

The varied contributions in our book have underlined the foundations on which China has based its business development and expansion. The Chinese Cultural Revolution of the 1960s shook the faith of families and enterprises who had originally seen socialism as an alternative model for economic growth, and one that promised economic expansion, equality and social justice. The new institutional and economic situation saw the growth of Chinese business and an economy that relied on policies that supported an export- and investment-driven model of development. This model proved to be effective, even as the 2008 Global Financial Crisis hit. Beginning in 2009, China was able to rapidly jumpstart a slowing economy with a massive state-led stimulus schedule that relied heavily on state banks extending credit for real estate and infrastructure projects and encouraged gross domestic product (GDP) growth.

The China business model has now come under increasing strain as the economy slows annually (Wildau, 2015; Wildau, 2016; Wildau & Weinland, 2016). One result is the swathes of unfinished and unoccupied

The China Business Model. DOI: http://dx.doi.org/10.1016/B978-0-08-100750-1.00011-5

buildings—even whole cities—as well as job lay-offs. The slowdown will also require further reexamination of the model. This will involve many aspects (see Rowley & Cooke, 2010; Warner & Rowley, 2011, 2014), including those we focused on in our book. Aspects such as the change and rebalancing between sets of actors and factors: exports and imports, manufacturing and services, and state-owned enterprises (SOEs), multinational companies (MNCs) and small- and medium-sized enterprises (SMEs), but also culture, *guanxi*, corporate social responsibility (CSR), and finance.

11.2 OVERVIEW OF CONTENT CONCLUSIONS

We present an overview of the conclusions of each of the trio of parts and each of the nine chapters in our book. Part I provided the reader with some basic concepts necessary to help better understand the Chinese business model. Chapter 2, *Guanxi* Culture, discussed *guanxi* and Chinese management. It concluded that *guanxi* was based on mutual interests including utilitarian and emotional aspects. Applied to the business environment it helps induce collaborative behaviors among companies implying mutual trust, information sharing, resource acquirement, cost saving, negotiation, etc. This could lead to improved performance in terms of finance, marketing, and supply chains as well. For Western people wanting to invest in China, or intend to do business with Chinese partners, *guanxi* practice with key personnel is an inevitable process. Chapter 3, Interpreting China's Model for Business: Roles of Corruption, Favoritism, Reliability, and Responsibility, covered the conditions of China's transition from a communist-style command economy to a market economy. It concluded that Chinese management remained vertically structured, with the domination of SOEs. It also detailed the dimensions that influenced the business model: corruption, favoritism (with emphasis on *guanxi*), reliability (meaning loyalty to the regime), and responsibility: separated into CSR and philanthropy. In the same line of argument, Chapter 4, The Evolution of Corporate Social Responsibility and Corporate Sustainability Practices in China, compared the differing process of CSR development with Europe and the United States, taking into account history, economics, and the development of corporations. It concluded that the reporting of CSR practices in China was an important issue for the authorities and that CSR to promote competitive business environments, social cohesion, and fostering collective responsibility for the betterment of society through business practices, was also critical.

Part II of our book concentrated on the business practices of Chinese firms. Chapter 5, The Equity Gap Amongst Technology-Based Small Firms: Challenges for Government-Backed Venture Capital in China, covered private and public venture capital for technology-based SMEs. It concluded that there was a need to improve competitiveness through enhanced technological and commercial knowledge to overcome the funding gap for start-ups, high risk and high growth technology SMEs, especially at the early stage of venture development. Crowd funding was used to narrow the finance gap, and this financial innovation expressed the orientation of government toward venture capital funds operating in a more sustainable entrepreneurial system, as stressed in our preceding Part I. Chapter 6, Assessing the Impact of the New Medical Reform on China's Pharmaceutical Supply Chain: The Case of Essential Medicines Distribution in Yuping, Luochuan, and Minhang Regions, focused on supply chain management in the medical sector. It concluded that besides the reforms, high distribution costs for medicines in rural regions still contributed to geographic disparity. This remained a problem in a country where the rural regions account for approximately 70% of the total population. Chapter 7, Exploring MEH (Manager-Employee-Heterophily) in US-owned and Managed Plants in Taiwan, explored manager-employee-heterophily—ethnic differences between people. It concluded workplace stress arose from divergent values in management style between ethnically different local employees and foreign managers.

Part III of this book discussed the financial aspects of Chinese business. Chapter 8, Monitoring Maturation in Financial Intermediation, discusses whether government organizations and banking institutions play an intermediate role in financing contracting for SME. This chapter emphasizes the importance of peer-to-peer online lending. In the same line of argument, Chapter 9, Internationalization Strategy and Service Adaptation in China: Perspective of Transnational Entrepreneurship, covered monitoring in financial intermediation. It concluded that delegated monitoring influenced both governance and responsibility upon a financial intermediary. Debates exist concerning the relevance of government organizations playing an intermediate role in financial contracting. In that context, the major improvement for Chinese financial intermediation would be to establish more resilient financial governance. Chapter 10, China and India: Emerging Leaders in World Economy, presented the process of internationalization strategies. Using the Transfer-Adapt-Scale framework, it suggested that a new internationalization model could emerge to meet the needs of transnational enterprises operating in Chinese industry. In that sense, this chapter contributed to a better understanding of China's rising role in the international business domain.

The totality of these chapters is of assistance to investigate China business model. It allows us to examine it holistically and elucidate its strengths and weaknesses.

11.3 GENERAL STRENGTHS AND WEAKNESSES OF THE CHINA MODEL

Since 2012, China's GDP growth has slowed. China posted its worst growth (6.8%) for a quarter of a century in January 2016. Indeed, India is set to overtake to China's growth rate by reaching 7.8% in 2015–16. Consequently, China has entered a second phase of economic transition in order to restore a new trend toward better opportunity of expansion. What has been a source of major strength for China (the priority given to exports and investments) now needs to be readjusted toward increased domestic consumption and value-added outputs. This is the reason why the 12th Five-Year Plan for 2011–15 sought to steer the Chinese political economy away from a pure focus on growth toward a more-balanced economic development model. Special weight rests on boosting consumption and incomes whilst expanding public welfare services and environmental protection (National People's Congress of the PRC, 2011). Rebalancing China's political economy is crucial, for socio-economic development, for global economic growth, and general stability (Clover, 2015).

With this new orientation, China could be ready to pursue its expansion by limiting its weaknesses. One difficulty to be solved is the unequal regional development of the country. Massive social and geographical inequality persists: a gulf between the country's developed and underdeveloped regions, in spite of the progress achieved over the last few years in GDP growth and development policies undertaken by the authorities to support the country's Central and Western areas. In 2009 some 50% of GDP was achieved in the coastal areas, as was discussed in Part I of our book.

A second problem is to how to define a more sustainable business model, one which can influence its managerial process. China's economy has been facilitated by a combination of factors: a vast domestic market for goods and services, a large supply of natural resources, and a large, motivated workforce. Innovation and entrepreneurship has been encouraged and facilitated in a stable business environment, due to a stable political system and consistent government policies, as well as a sizeable inflow of

Western technology and capital, and a currency exchange rate that allowed products to be exported at "dumping" prices. Today, China includes more sustainable criteria in their managerial methods in moving toward a more stable, expansionary trend, also discussed in Part I of our book.

A component of this transformation is the need to focus on the labor market and employee relations. This will be more important in the era of declining availability of workers due to demographic trends and skills shortages. They will need to be treated less as "disposable" resources, and as more as valuable assets. The model will need to incorporate the human resource (HR) factors and HR management (HRM), which in turn will encourage these increased value-added and upskilling, etc.

A third difficulty concerns the investment and financial issues in Chinese development. Since the 2008 Global Financial Crisis, the act of Western central banks pumping cheap money into the financial system was seen by many as having the dual purposes of kick-starting Western economies while pressing China to revalue its currency. Strict capital controls initially enabled the Chinese authorities to resist currency pressures. Yet, the dramatic rises in commodity prices resulting from loose Western monetary policies eventually caused rampant inflation in China. China was forced to raise interest rates and appreciate its currency to bring inflation under control. The Western central banks had been granted their wish of a revalued Chinese currency. This influenced investment policy and credit distribution, as was discussed in Part II of our book.

While the SOEs have the facilities to finance their investment projects, private firms face greater financial constraints. Substantial variations exist in financial access among private firms, with SMEs facing more constraints, whereas the more established firms have access equal to their SOE counterparts. The most pressing financial restriction facing private firms is their limited ability to secure long-term funds toward investing for growth, as was discussed in Part II of our book. This explains why a liberalized capital market is seen as a means to help improve financing policy for firms, subsequently inducing more profitability. Furthermore, integration into global capital markets demands that the renminbi is moved toward a more-freely floating exchange rate, being used as an international trade settlement currency.

A fourth difficulty pertains to the banking sector. As a whole, the financial sector has suffered from an increase in "shadow credit." A huge amount of liquidity has gone to infrastructure and real estate, creating a bubble, particularly for real estate. Chinese banks are also under-performing to a higher risk from their off-balance sheets and their nonperforming loans. In the aftermath of a crash, were Chinese banks to face severe financial problems, the chances are that GDP growth will be much slower than it is now and for a prolonged period of time. Moreover, micro- and SMEs are usually scattered in location, with frequent and urgent demand for loans, but lacking collateral. This explains why China has become the largest P2P lending market in the world. These issues were discussed in Part III of our book to give insights into the financial system and its impact on the productive issues.

11.4 IMPLICATIONS AND LESSONS

Based on the preceding conclusions and arguments, what are the implications and lessons for the Chinese business model? Could we design a scenario for next decade regarding the opportunities of China in the globalized environment? In a World Economic Forum report (2006), various scenarios were constructed for China in 2025. All of them agreed that GDP will decrease—in comparison to the best decades, varying from 6% (pessimistic view) to 9% (most optimistic situation).

SMEs could become more important (Cunningham & Rowley, 2010, 2011). They, however, have similar difficulties in finding funds to finance their productive projects, as in most other country. Banks, because of a permanent systemic risk, will need to improve their risk management and their profitability to maintain their position in a liberalized financial world.

The second element on which China could improve its position concerned transparency of data and "rules of the game," as mentioned by Bernanke and Olson (March 8, 2016, Blog Bernanke). As shown in Table 11.1, China has improved its position with regards to global transparency. Since the slowdown, however, researchers have expressed doubts as to the "smoothness" of economic data, which could partly explain the actual position of the country. In particular, China's National Bureau of Statistics provides little information about its sources or statistical framework, preventing the possibility of checking data for validity (Wildau, 2015). If announcements concerning business results are over-evaluated, it provokes skepticism internationally (Zhao, 2012; Zuiderwijk, Gaseó, Parycek, & Janssen, 2014).

As far as the "rules of the game" are concerned, China has committed to some transparency improvement on real economic aspects

Table 11.1 Transparency index in selected countries

	Global Rank		CPI Score	
	2015	2014	2015	2014
Singapore	8	7	85	84
Australia	13	11	79	80
Hong Kong	18	17	75	74
Japan	18	15	75	76
Taiwan	30	35	62	61
South Korea	37	43	56	55
Malaysia	54	50	50	52
India	76	85	38	38
Thailand	76	85	38	38
China	83	100	37	36
Indonesia	88	107	36	34
Philippines	95	85	35	38
Vietnam	112	119	31	31
Myanmar	147	156	22	21

Source: http://www.transparency.org/cpi2015.

(Koch-Weser, 2013). Among several examples, we can stress the US-China Business Council in its 2015 Regulatory Transparency Scorecard, which underlined the Chinese government's agreement to public comment periods of at least 30 days on draft laws, administrative regulations, departmental rules, and regulations. This trend toward greater clarity constitutes an improvement, but does not necessarily mean the rules are fairer. Regardless, it represents a step for better integration into the global scene.

11.5 COULD CHINESE BUSINESS PRACTICES BE AN OBSTACLE FOR FUTURE OPPORTUNITIES?

Having discussed the major outlines of macro-economic development, the specificities of the Chinese business practices are now discussed and the differing, typical Western and traditional Eastern and Chinese practices are summarized in Tables 11.2 and 11.3.

Table 11.2 Differences in Western and Eastern business approaches to business management[a]

	Western	Eastern
Time horizon	Short term; how	Long term; future
Strategy	Leading to allocation of resources today	Leading to positioning firm for the future
Management philosophy	Management by objectives	Management by shared mindset
Decision making	Fast to decide Longer to sell and implement	Slow to decide Quick to implement
Accountability	Personalized Focused on "I"	Shared Focused on "we"
Work	Linear Focused on task at hand	Cyclical Focused on context in which work is done
Career orientation	Generalist	Specialist
Rewards	High gap between senior executives and lower employees Based on performance	Low gap between senior executives and lower employees Based on tenure and position
Leadership philosophy	Hands on, walking ahead of people "Leadership is done from in front. Never ask others to do what you, if challenged, would not be willing to do yourself." Xenophon	Hands off, walking behind people "In order to guide people, the leader must put himself behind them. Thus when he is ahead they feel no hurt." Lao Tzu
Philosophical schools	Christianity	Buddhism, Confucianism, Hinduism, Integral Yoga, Islam, Taoism, Zen, Han Fei

Source: Adapted from Rowley, C., & Ulrich, D. (2012). Lessons learned and insights derived from leadership in Asia. Asia Pacific Business Review, *18*(4), 675–681.
[a]Some of the differences of East vs West can be found in: http://www.1000ventures.com/business_guide/crosscuttings/cultures_east-west-phylosophy.html referenced on July 15, 2010; http://www.thefreelibrary.com/East+versus+West+Philosophy,+Cultural+Values+and+Mindset+-+by+Hemant...-a01073951527 referenced on July 15, 2010. Hofstede (2001), Hofstede, Hofstede, and Minkoy (2010), Ouchi (1983).

Table 11.2 presents an extensive list of criteria to explain the differences between Western and Eastern business (Rowley & Ulrich, 2012), while Table 11.3 concentrates more on business practices. Variations existing between them help to understand the philosophy and values on which strategies are based to conduct companies.

Table 11.3 Western versus traditional Chinese business practices

Business practices	Western model	Chinese model
Main purpose	Maximizing shareholder value	Privileging family interest
Financing sources	Public sales of assets and banking loans	Family and friends P2P lending
Management	Professional management based on recruitment focusing on competencies	Senior managers from the families to which company belongs
Time horizon	Short term to satisfy shareholder value	Long term

Time and relationships among partners are the main factors of the two tables justifying the differences in business practices. Consequently, Table 11.3 illustrates the main arguments of our book and leads us to question the *guanxi* model to reevaluate if it cannot be at the origin of the problems encountered by Chinese management (Rowley & Warner, 2011, 2014; Wang & Rowley, 2016). In particular, could such Chinese business practices be an obstacle for future opportunities? Foreign firms are concerned with compliance policies that may prevent them from realizing a satisfying profit. The development of a business network illustrated by the *guanxi* model could be at the origin of what for some are "corrupt" practices. How? Most MNCs founded their strategies on returns and short time horizons. On the other hand, Chinese firms privilege a nonlinear business paradigm, in which the government plays a core role. The time horizon on which profit is measured is much longer. So *guanxi* is often accused of encouraging bribery or corruption because it favors Chinese family, social systems, and traditional hierarchical values, which seems in contradiction to Western business practices. This incorrect understanding of the *guanxi* model explains the accusation of corruption in business practices from Western challengers, who, of course all too often act in capricious and unethical ways.

In fact, the coexistence and interpenetration of the *guanxi* model, and Western business practices could renew and reinforce Chinese management. For example, MNC or TEs could create their own corporate *guanxi* mechanisms. One solution could be to transform their competitive approach into a more collaborative framework where all interested parties achieve shared objectives.

11.6 CONCLUSION

We have outlined the diverse elements in the development of the Chinese business model. Taking into account all of these factors we have covered, could China transform its business model to maintain it competitive advantage in the future? From the macro-economic point of view, as discussed throughout our book, China should recalibrate its strategy by integrating both internal and external factors. To preserve its position, China will need to reconsider its currency, especially if it intends to play an international monetary role. Globally, we conclude that the best strategy could be to protect its original Asiatic model and to adapt it to the new international constraints, whilst adopting more-transparent behaviors.

The future will also require the explicit and coherent recognition of issues in the labor market and employee relations. This will include the need to move up value chains and shift from competing by "perspiration" to inspiration' (in Krugman's terms). This requires employee upskilling, and investment in skills and training. These will be underpinned and partly driven by stark labor market changes, stemming from demographics and trends. There will simply be fewer workers. The over-arching ethos of the recent Chinese economic success will need to be reconsidered. From the managerial point of view, China could benefit from their own business practices by maintaining their primary characteristics, and by integrating a Western framework to adopt more transparent and sustainable strategies.

With regards to business practices, research has been produced to explore the corrosive aspects of *guanxi* (Su, Sirgy, & Littlefield, 2003). Some justify this management tool due to the immature legal and economic institutions in China (Su & Littlefield, 2001, 2003). Some note that Eastern and Western business practices are likely to become more similar (Davies, Leung, Luk, & Wong, 1995), although a long and consistent stream of literature and research also shows this may not be the case and differences will continue (Rowley, 1998; Rowley & Benson, 2002, 2004), as will types of capitalism itself (Rowley & Yukongdi, 2016).

Western companies may tend to adopt more *guanxi*-type practices by relying on their management in personal relationships of trust and reputation. Alternatively, Eastern countries intend to improve their legal and institutional rules and regulation. Therefore, far from being delegated to a negative interpretation of business practices, *guanxi* could help to better understand how private and public domains could interact in management purpose. It could permit researchers and practitioners to analyze personal relationships and rational instrumentality within companies. In that sense, one could defend the idea that Western and Eastern management practices could benefit from each other in order to a more ethical business model that better enables local, transnational, and foreign entrepreneurs in improving both the economic and social performance of their companies.

REFERENCES

Clover, C. (2015). Delivering the Jack Ma Economy. *Financial Times, 15 September*, p. 11.

Cunningham, X. L., & Rowley, C. (2010). The changing face of SME management in China. In C. Rowley & F. L. Cooke (Eds.), *The changing face of management in China*. London: Routledge.

Cunningham, X. L., & Rowley, C. (2011). SMEs in China: A literature review, HRM and Suggestions for Further Research. In M. Warner & C. Rowley (Eds.), *Chinese management in the "harmonious society": Managers, markets and the globalised economy* (pp. 47–56). London: Routledge.

Davies, H., Leung, T. K. P., Luk, S. T. K., & Wong, Y. -H. (1995). The benefits of '*guanxi*': The value of relationships in developing the Chinese market. *Industrial Marketing Management, 24*(3), 207–214.

Hofstede, G. (2001). *Culture's consequences: Comparing values, behaviors, institutions, and organizations across nations* (2nd ed.). Los Angeles: Sage Publications.

Hofstede, G., Hofstede, J., & Minkoy, M. (2010). *Cultures and Organizations: Software for the mind* (3rd ed.). New York, NY: McGraw Hill.

Koch-Weser, I. N. (2013). The reliability of China's economic data: An analysis of national output. *US-China Economic and Security Review Commission Staff Research Project*.

National People's Congress of RPC (2011). Full coverage of 2011 NPC&CPPCC sessions available at: www.npc.gov.cn/englishnpc.

Ouchi, W. G. (1983). *Theory Z*. Boston, MA: Addison Wesley.

Rowley, C. (1998). *HRM in the Asia Pacific region: Convergence questioned*. London: Frank Cass.

Rowley, C., & Benson, J. (2002). Convergence and divergence in Asian HRM. *California Management Review, 44*(2), 90–109.

Rowley, C., & Benson, J. (2004). *The management of HR in the Asia Pacific region: Convergence reconsidered*. London: Frank Cass.

Rowley, C., & Cooke, F. L. (Eds.). (2010). *The changing face of management in China*. London: Routledge.

Rowley, C., & Ulrich, D. (2012). Lessons learned and insights derived from leadership in Asia. *Asia Pacific Business Review, 18*(4), 675–681.

Rowley, C., & Yukongdi, V. (2016). Business networks & varities of capitalism in Thailand: Adding the context of history, political structures and social & cultural values. In J. Nolan, C. Rowley, & M. Warner (Eds.), *Asian business networks in East Asia* (pp. 1–32). Oxford: Elsevier.

Su, C., & Littlefield, J. E. (2001). Entering guanxi: A business ethical dilemma in mainland China? *Journal of Business Ethics, 33*(3), 199–210.

Su, C., Sirgy, M. J., & Littlefield, J. E. (2003). Is guanxi orientation bad, ethically speaking? A study of Chinese enterprises. *Journal of Business Ethics, 44*(4), 303–312.

Wang, B., & Rowley, C. (2016). Business networks and the emergence of guanxi capitalism in China: The role of the invisible hand. In J. Nolan, C. Rowley, & M. Warner (Eds.), *Business networks in East Asian capitalisms*. Oxford: Elsevier.

Warner, M., & Rowley, C. (Eds.). (2011). *Chinese management in the "harmonious society": Managers, markets and the globalised economy*. London: Routledge.

Warner, M., & Rowley, C. (Eds.). (2014). *Demystifying Chinese management: Issues and challenges*. London: Routledge.
Wildau, G. (2015). Making the numbers add up. *Financial Times, 29 September*, 11.
Wildau, G. (2016). The zombie economy. *Financial Times, 1 March*, 11.
Wildau, G., & Weinland, D. (2016). Rapid climb in China's debt raises concerns over economy. *Financial Times, 25 April*, 7.
World Economic Forum. (2006). *China and the world: Scenarios to 2025*. September, 76 pp.
Zhao, S. (2012). China's mixed transparency record. *China Business Review, July–September*.
Zuiderwijk, A., Gaseó, M., Parycek, P., & Janssen, M. (2014). Special issue on transparency and open data policies: Guest editors' introduction. *Journal of Theoretical and Applied Electronic Commerce Research, 9*(3), I–IX.

INDEX

Note: Page numbers followed by "*f*" and "*t*" refer to figures and tables, respectively.

H

I

X

Y